ALSO BY ANDREW LEVY

The First Emancipator

*The Culture and Commerce of
the American Short Story*

A BRAIN WIDER THAN THE SKY

A Migraine Diary

ANDREW LEVY

Simon & Schuster
NEW YORK   LONDON   TORONTO   SYDNEY

Simon & Schuster
1230 Avenue of the Americas
New York, NY 10020

First Simon & Schuster hardcover edition May 2009

SIMON & SCHUSTER and colophon are registered trademarks of
Simon & Schuster, Inc.

For information about special discounts for bulk purchases,
please contact Simon & Schuster Special Sales at
1-866-506-1949 or business@simonandschuster.com.

The Simon & Schuster Speakers Bureau can bring authors to your live event.
For more information or to book an event contact the Simon & Schuster Speakers
Bureau at 1-866-248-3049 or visit our website at www.simonspeakers.com.

Designed by Kyoko Watanabe

Manufactured in the United States of America

10   9   8   7   6   5   4   3   2   1

Library of Congress Cataloging-in-Publication Data
Levy, Andrew.
A brain wider than the sky : a migraine diary / Andrew Levy.
p. cm.
Includes bibliographical references.
1. Migraine—Popular works. I. Title.

RC392.L48 2009
616.8'4912—dc22   2009009484

ISBN-13: 978-1-4165-7250-3
ISBN-10:   1-4165-7250-3
ISBN-13: 978-1-4165-8810-8 (ebook)

To Siobhán and Aedan

Contents

PART THREE

Author's Note

Everything in this book is true, as best as I can remember, except for some ambient name and date and place changes. Everything historical, cultural, or medical is researched and cited. And I believe in the advice I provide here. But I'm not a "prototype" migraine patient any more than anyone else, and my experiences are not meant to compete with professional diagnosis. If I met you in the street and you told me that you had frequent headaches, I'd tell you to go to a good doctor, preferably a neurologist, preferably one who is also a headache specialist. And then, if you wanted to read this book, fine.

A BRAIN
WIDER THAN
THE SKY

Introduction:
A Man with Patches
on His Head

> If a man, with patches on his head, is asked, what is the matter? He will answer, "I had a headache the day before yesterday."
>
> —CHARLES DARWIN,
> *Voyage of the Beagle*

September: there is no line between the migraine and worrying about the migraine as one lies awake at five in the morning. There is no difference between the first pinpricks of aura and the first gray rays of dawn, either, since one looks like the other, and since the latter seems to cause the former. This light sensitivity is mad. It's no real problem to have to wear sunglasses all morning, or to have to swivel the visor on the car as I turn north–south to east–west and the sun pivots crazily in the sky in response. But the way the soft, harmless grays of dawn can make my head pound is something else.

I've been jolted awake by something; I can't tell if it's worry or the early stages of a headache, but the anticipation of some future pain is so intense that sleep is now impossible. And, of course, sleeplessness such as this is an invitation to the headache. This cycle cannot be stopped. It is almost, I hate to say, interesting.

Take two: I am lying in my son's tiny bed, and my son is sleeping in my king-size bed somewhere alongside my wife. I know *why* this happens: I don't want to disturb them, and I don't want them to disturb me. But I'm not completely sure *how* this happens: we switch beds semiconsciously, sometime in the rustling that precedes first light. Like any game, it makes its own logic.

I am watching the gray light slowly illuminate a bookshelf where his books and mine sit side-by-side. I am absolutely calm. The pain will come if it wants to come. I can feel the shuffling under my brow, the blood and the nerves meditating, a little rush, a little constriction. It almost feels as if they're considering whether to *make a commitment*. I am absolutely calm. I can do an inventory of my body and my mind, feel the breath through my nose and mouth, feel the tingle down my arms, feel the slight tension where my ankles cross.

A few minutes pass, it seems. The shuffling underneath my brow continues, and the sky continues to lighten—or, perhaps, my aura continues to enhance. But my confidence grows. I now admit to myself that my earlier calm was a kind of shock. I was so terrified that a headache was about to begin that I shut down. Maybe this is the nature of calm. But now I feel a kind of minor elation.

Then the first throb comes. Describe it: I do not like the word *stab,* because stabbing implies a process, an insertion. I really believe that if you could slow it down, you would find that it starts from a small center, and expands and contracts, like a balloon suddenly inflated and deflated. But some days

I feel otherwise, and am amazed by how much it feels like it starts outside the head somewhere, in open space.

Describe it better: *balloon* could not be a worse simile. It starts from a point somewhere and pulsates, enlarges. By the third or fourth throb, a new pain appears, something after the throbs, like the afterimage on a television, a glow that grows fainter, until the next pulsation renews it. There's a density now, a consistency. I get up, and while the rest of my body feels normal, my head feels as if it is shedding pieces as it rises, like the trail of a comet. It is hard to say if this hurts or not.

By the time I reach the kitchen, I've got one goal: subdue the headache before Siobhán, my wife, and Aedan, our four-year-old, wake up. I don't want them to have to deal with this, with my complaint, my staggering, my inertness. And I don't want to have to deal with them, either, with their noise, their shuffling, their clacking of plates in the kitchen.

I've got three options I've been exploring: steam, tea, ice pack. Ten minutes of steam—that won't get to the big block of pain, but it goes after the afterimages. Tea, as hot as it can get, can be pretty astounding: sometimes the headache lifts twenty minutes after. It's better than Vicodin, which leaves a haze and doesn't really work that well. It's better than Imitrex, which my GP has told me to stop taking for a while: it's a tough little drug, but will actually give you migraines if you take too many (which you will do if you get too many migraines, of course). And the ice pack: the deep freeze, combined with absolute motionlessness, can create a deadened territory over the left eye and across the left temple, where it's difficult to distinguish between the stinging of the cold and the frosted and subdued pulsations.

After trial, I've learned to go ice first, then tea, then steam, in sequence from around 5:30 A.M. to 8 A.M. On this morning,

I'm lying on the sofa in the family room, three pillows triangled around my face, the ice pack with its three ridges pressed against my left temple, when Aedan walks in. I can hear the shoosh-shoosh of his too-long pajama bottoms sweeping the floor as he walks, the footfall of his steps, brisker than brisk even when he's sleepy. I can imagine his posture, that slight cantilevering, his head always getting someplace before his feet, his clear blue eyes, possibly, the brightest thing in the room.

And here is the very best and the very worst. From an early age, Aedan has understood that he had to negotiate with the headache, as if it were a third party. Once, when he was two, I was watching him alone when a bad headache struck, and I was double struck by the guilt of not being able to take care of him. I lay on the floor of his nursery, my head pressed against the carpet, hoping this would not be a time he needed me to be alert or active. And he discovered me that way, and wrapped his arms and legs around my head the way an octopus might embrace a rock on the ocean floor, all firmness and feral grace, catching the pressure points on my temple pretty well, not perfect, but pretty well.

We lay like that for a few minutes, maybe longer, maybe not quite as long, and it was amazing. It transcended the simple fact of what it was, telling me (and, maybe, telling him, too) that there are empathies that go beyond what we *should* know. A year or two later, when I stumbled across the name of Saint Aed, a sixth-century Irish bishop who cured headaches with miracles, I mused over the wonderful accident that my son's unusually spelled Celtic first name was its diminutive echo. For now, though, between the throbs—this was not a throbbing migraine anymore but a steady one—I received through him the story of that headache the way you might hear a really powerful song through static on your car radio. It was not a story of awful loneliness, pain doubled with guilt. It was a love story.

Then he got up to go watch TV atop a pillowy bed in an adjoining room, not too loud, not too soft, and I opened my eyes and stared at a couple of his toy trains that met my vision, and wondered at how gracious their greens and blues were. A couple of years have passed since this afternoon, and Aedan is no longer two, and no longer gentle: my head is an interesting place, but to be pounded, struck, to act as a resting place for his hands when I carry him on my shoulders. Now, when I'm having a headache, he hops on my head and my back as if to attack the interloper, an act that should cause excruciating pain, but never does (migraines hate light, but not light-footed children).

He is like Ahab, I think, and my head is the whale. In the complex physiological and emotional calculus of the headache, I'd count it as the best of fortunes for him not to see me like this. But he does, and instead this dawn moment for us—which is becoming more and more routine, unfortunately—has become loaded with meaning.

He approaches me warily, trying, I think, to isolate my head, my face, amid the pillows. He is looking for the ice pack, too, or maybe for a warm greeting, a smile. He is on reconnaissance. And this is what I think he decides: if he sees the ice pack, he will cry out, "*Not again*," with all the exasperation one might expect from a four-year-old who realizes that he will be expected to lay low for yet another hour or two. If he doesn't see the ice pack, but I don't offer him a greeting, or only a lukewarm greeting, he will leap on my shoulders, pound on my head, a real favor somehow, a metaphysical delight even, because he reminds me with those oddly painless blows that there exists some disconnect between the head as a place in the physical world and the head as a place in the feeling world, the thought world.

And there are other mornings where he sees something, or feels something, that I can't identify or even estimate. He sidles up to me, shifts the pillows carefully, places our faces side-by-side, rubs his clean cheek against my stubbled one, and says, "You're silly. A silly billy."

I think about this dimly. He's right. To a four-year-old, *silly* is a utility word and covers a range of unusual and sometimes off-putting behavior. And *billy*—that's also utility, some bit of Irish kid's slang that he got from Siobhán. But there's something else, too, something haunting me a bit, something buried in genetics, in the sleeping history of family.

You might be one, too, pal, I say, both hoping and not hoping it's true.

Then a pause, and then the walls—you know, the ones that are always closing in—

In my twenties, when I got migraines, they were almost vacations. There was a little tingling, an aura—a neurological disruption of normal sense, usually vision—and just enough discomfort to justify the name. In my thirties, they were headbangers, once a month, like tiny anniversaries, rare enough to almost justify the feeling of clarity they brought afterward in the late afternoons. Then, one August week when I was forty-three, the headaches started coming almost daily, almost always in the mornings, for four months, humorless events as shapeless and as regular as dawn itself.

I set up a wall of drugs to stop them, and life-changing precautions to soften them when the drugs failed. Then I tired of the wall of drugs and the life-changing precautions, as many people do. Instead, I signed a fitful treaty with migraine: a more modest menu of drugs, a smaller life, but one I can savor, and migraines that still come, come like the seasons, and remind me who really rules the roost.

A Brain Wider Than the Sky is devoted to the subject of this strange and extraordinary syndrome that afflicts more than one out of every ten Americans, more than one out of every five families. In part, it is my headache diary—the journal that many specialists recommend their patients compose—the story of migraine's relatively serene presence in my life for two decades, then its hostile takeover of my life at forty-three, and then that fitful treaty we signed.

Headache diaries are supposed to detect patterns, to teach self-awareness, to make treatment easier—and that's what mine did. In part, though, this book is a headache diary with a difference. It is also a larger story, of migraine sufferers from centuries past and from the present day, of migraines treated with ancient remedies or with the newest experimental drugs. It is the story of the head itself, of the special metaphysical crisis induced by the migraine, and the special metaphysical comfort inspired by its retreat. And it is a story of family, of work, of friendship—of how, sometimes, we share pain as if it was love, and sometimes, as if it was hate.

There are many books about migraine currently available, mostly providing diet, lifestyle, and drug advice intended to help migraineurs cure their headaches. I wrote this book to provide advice, too, but for a different reason. In recent times, we have tended to treat migraine as a private affair between a migraineur and a migraineur's head in a dark room, or, in public, as something to hide. Older cultures, other cultures, however, had a different idea: they treated and still treat migraine as a public event, as Darwin discovered, cures often worn on the affected temple. The story of how migraines affect marriage, parenthood, friendship, and job, of how they change one's status as a citizen of the world of spirit and of history, is an important one—especially given how the divide itself between sufferer and nonsufferer is one of the primary reasons people have migraines. The pain is innocent. It can't help itself. But that divide—more than the pain—is the real villain here.

I gathered my story from different sources, from diary entries I wrote in the aftermath of migraines (and, occasionally, during), from recollections of migraines past, from research I conducted to help me get through weeks when migraines came daily and from research I conducted during weeks when I had a free head. In many places, I have preserved, as much as I can, the feel and flow of sentences I wrote during less disabling periods of migraines, or shortly after. I wanted something different, something that might simulate the feel, the curves, the sweep of the migraining mind. There is a kind of martial arts that requires its practitioners to mimic the attacks of the enemy in order to defeat that enemy. Maybe there is a kind of writing like that, too.

Likewise, I felt that the cultural history of migraine—its trace in literature, in art, in music, and its implication for religion—was important. I read the how-to books, the ones that recommend new diets, new drugs, new lifestyles. But I wanted to learn about migraine because I felt that learning about migraine would be its own kind of cure—the "reading cure." I explored the history of migraine because the learning made me feel better. It transformed my migraines from something that kept me apart from the rest of humankind to something that made me feel like part of the ancient circle.

I don't want to say that migraines made me happy. That's fatuous. But I am prepared to say that I found something inside myself that I would not have otherwise found. At the university where I work, the books I love most to teach are those composed by authors struggling with the unsolvable, caught in the thorns of the unreachable. Writing this book, I couldn't help but think about those authors and about their characters. Ahab wanted to crack open Moby Dick's head, sure, for revenge for his lost leg. But he also wanted to crack open that great, impassive skull because he believed that there he would find what mysteries lay underneath the surface of everyday life. Melville wrote *Moby Dick* about a search (no, search*es*) for meaning and comfort inaugurated by a season of pain: for Ishmael, the narrator, "the damp, drizzly November in my soul" with which the book opens; for Ahab, the weeks alone in his cabin after Moby Dick takes his leg. You come out of a true November of the soul crushed, or renewed, rededicated—but at what angle to reality, what angle to wisdom?

For myself, I felt inspired by a striving for contact—for real head-pounding contact with some, for contact with others through language, for a dialogue with the writers, musicians, artists, and scientists who have understood that creating words and images for describing the very private world of pain is an endeavor at which we have failed. In trying to describe mine, though, I experienced a very particular species of joy that has transformed its source, the vicious, discombobulating migraine itself, into an eerily wise, slightly deranged mentor. My head still hurts; and I still don't know exactly why, or exactly how to describe it. But I *tried*. And that, as the poet said, makes all the difference.

With aura or without, with pain or without, daily, weekly, monthly, once in a lifetime, the migraine is a simple thing. It is a nerve-storm, as the nineteenth-century physician Edward Liveing called it, as convulsive and as electric as any other storm, nerve cells and blood vessels all shook up (Elvis had migraines, too), because your eyes took in too much light all of a sudden, because of a tall cup of coffee (caffeine stops some migraines but makes others), menstruation, a chocolate bar (maybe), a glass of red wine or a glass of white, cigarette smoke, air travel, that storm front coming down from Denver, the leaves falling off the big oak in your front yard, that extra hour of sleep you got last night, the hour of sleep you lost, too much heat, too little water, too much stress or too little, that other head-ache, the painkiller you took to stop the last migraine, the last migraine itself, your Eastern European grandmother's errant genes, nothing at all.

Migraine is 50 percent more prevalent than depression, twice as prevalent as osteoarthritis, three times as prevalent as diabetes, fifteen times as prevalent as rheumatoid arthritis. It affects three times more women than men, more whites than blacks, more blacks than Asian-Americans, more working class than upper class. It's a shape shifter: the pain can relocate, change its form, from one era of your life to the next. About half of the people who have it still don't know they have it. About 20 or 30 percent who have it get auras—although some modern doctors think it's more than that. And the list of pos-sible migraine treatments almost outstrips the list of potential migraine triggers, and is every bit as complicated.

Migraines cannot kill you—although in some cases they might help. They cannot really hurt you in any lasting way. Sometimes they even just go away on their own.

And sometimes they don't.

Joan Didion, in her wonderful essay "In Bed," wrote that a time comes during a migraine attack when you stop fighting the pain, and you "lie down and let it happen"—you can't stop it or lessen it, so you make peace with it. I have tried this. What separates a migraine headache from other chronic illnesses, I believe, is that a migraine constitutes a metaphysical crisis. At first, it is simply impossible to believe that this headache is coming from within your head, which is why it is so easy to call a migraine headache an "attack." You almost believe, rather, that you can push it back, back outside your head to its starting point, out beyond the pillow, to those pinpricks of aura in the gray out there somewhere, the red digits of the clock, the pile of dirty laundry, the cat that won't stop mewing for her breakfast. Then you gradually accept the pain as your own. You acknowledge your oneness, and the throbs develop a kind of autonomy. They careen and float around an empty mind, settle, drift, still throbbing, but without stress. Didion was right, you think. The Buddha was right, you think.

And then a throb hits you on the left side of the head so hard that your head bobs to the right. You look for the referee counting you down to ten. There's no way that came from inside your head, you think. That's no metaphysical crisis. God just punched you in the side of the face.

ONE

The pain in your head, o man, may come into my head.

—SAINT AED

Ancient History

And screened in shades from Day's detested Glare,
She sighs for ever on her pensive Bed,
Pain at her Side, and *Megrim* at her Head.
— ALEXANDER POPE,
Rape of the Lock

1

Alexander Pope had style. He was small (four and a half feet tall), his spine was curved (tuberculosis as a child), but he commanded the English language with such supreme self-confidence that his physical limits became signs of strength, even sensuality. For me, though, what marks Pope as wondrous were his headaches. Pope had fierce headaches that he could best relieve by placing his head directly above a hot cup of coffee and surrounding his brain with the caffeinated steam. He kept a serving woman awake many nights bringing him these brews. And he was so well regarded by certain English royalty that they permitted him extraordinary breaches of social etiquette, despite how disrespectful his eccentric requests for relief must have appeared. One lord allowed him to sit behind a screen at social occasions. The Prince of Wales, famously, let him nap through a formal dinner, even as the Prince talked.

There is no question that Pope's headaches were the real thing. And yet, this treatment, this palliative, is so dreamy that it might be said to be every migraine sufferer's fantasy: an empire on tiptoe, at least symbolically, while the woman or man with the headache is still permitted a privileged seat at the table. Even better: the inference that underlies the scenario, that Pope's command of the language and his hypersensitive nervous system are indivisible, that the headaches and the genius are one. Better still: the deeper inference that the pain (and the physical shortcomings, as well) are like electricity to the otherwise docile brain, catalyzing something more than just inspiration. A kind of iron will that coaxes big thoughts from small ones, that makes the woman or man with the pain make something of the one or two clear hours each day before the headaches renew themselves.

As I lie in bed, the blinds down, the cold pack on my left temple (count its ridges, one, two, three, against that soft spot on my head), these thoughts do not exactly comfort me. Really, they just take me from one throb to the next, each throb, like orgasm, suddenly, charismatically, distilling all thought to a tiny pinpoint on the horizon.

The first time I ever had a migraine headache: I have parts of an answer. I can tell you about the times when I was a kid, maybe five, maybe ten, maybe a little older, when I lay awake at night watching the lights play against the enclosed lids of my eyes: something a little fluorescent, pleasant and unworldly. Shimmering, bouncing stars. But already at five, I'm thinking the words aren't cutting it. I don't know the word *metaphor* yet, but I've got a strong intuition that there's something about those lights that I'm just not going to be able to explain. That I remember clearly.

And I can tell you about the time in my early twenties, twenty-two, maybe twenty-three, a sun-drenched afternoon in my decrepit West Philadelphia apartment, when my vision started to waver and then darken, a curtain drawn from left to right, electric and jagged on the edge, and me, too dumb to think stroke, too experienced at emotional repression, to be perfectly honest, to even get a good terror going over the prospect that I was going blind.

I was just sitting at home, reading, and the reading daze became a slightly more intense daze, almost imperceptibly. As my eyesight began to disappear, I remember, I rose, I paced, wondering what I should do, but I moved slowly. By the time I eventually reached the telephone to call for help, the aura had stopped halfway across my field of vision. I said to myself: fuck it, I can see with one eye. And then the darkness faded as it came, and I didn't even have to worry about that.

Instead, though, I'd rather tell you about my older brother's first migraine headache. I'm almost tempted to tell you about it as if it were my own. It's a satisfying, neat story: most people remember their first time, and the truth is that I don't. He was eighteen years old, riding on the PATH train, the line that every weekday evening gathers up New York commuters and disperses them into New Jersey. In the tunnel between Ninth Street and Hoboken, underneath the Hudson River, hanging a strap, as they say, he feels a pain so sudden and so stunning in his head that he thinks this is the existential pain, a stroke, the end. He turns ashen, cloaked in sweat, his face so altered and slack that several of the helpful commuting New Yorkers ask him if he is all right, if he needs a doctor. But that's all they do: no one offers him a seat.

This is a classic first migraine story: the pain that is so fierce that you can only explain it by guessing that you are dying. But it's the twist at the end that makes it a migraine story: the crowd sympathizes, but only so far. You are not Alexander Pope. This is how men and women talk about their neurological dysfunctions when there's no doctors around. The face animates, the voice races, at these exact two points in the story: the description of the odd pain, the unexpected seizure, the sudden panic and fear of death; and the description of when and how the crowd demonstrates its indifference. You fall in the shower (a true story, this, told me by a colleague with grand mal seizures); the paramedics come and ask you who the president is; they laugh at you when you say Jimmy Carter, not Bill Clinton; and then, to be sure, they tear apart your medicine cabinet, looking for the illicit drug you must have taken to put you that far out to sea.

It's a reasonable guess on their part, but as you sit there, the unrinsed shampoo caked on your scalp, a wildness still in your eyes (you can feel this from the inside), you feel entirely alone. But you're not; incredibly, quite the opposite. Neurological disorders are as old as recorded history, an elemental part of the lives of hundreds of millions over thousands of years. And migraines, among neurological disorders, have the distinction of being the most popular, as common as any cold and far harder to shake.

2

Animals don't get migraines. That is, they *probably* don't get migraines. A nineteenth-century English veterinarian named Blaine believed he saw it in horses: "The animal, if in exercise, stops short, shakes the head, looks irresolute and wandering."

More recently, naturalists have seen some isolated instances among primates: an ape in the Toronto Zoo who shields her eyes from light; an orangutan in Borneo found "clutching her head and groaning, only to make a complete recovery after eating some flowers from a nearby bush." The observing scientist here, later suffering from headache, tasted the same plant, and "within 15 min," he noted, "my headache was gone."

Essentially, though, migraine, if not headache itself, is a human property, as much as reason, and has left its mark on civilizations since the beginning of recorded time. Five thousand years ago, for instance, the ancient Sumarians had *sag-gig*: it translates to "sick-head." Their legend of "Enki and Ninhursag" describes a paradise where

> The sick-eyed says not "I am sick eyed"
> The sick-headed says not, "I am sick-headed."

Babylonian and Assyrian incantations about headache were vivid. A pain in the temple was called *mukīl rēš lemutti,* or "holder of the head of evil." It was blamed on the "hand" of a ghost. They also had *di'u*—a marauding headache that may or may not have presaged typhus. "Head disease charges about the steppe, blowing like the wind," scribes etched onto tablets in the Royal Library at Nineveh around 700 B.C.:

> It flashes like stars of the sky, it runs like water at night . . .
> Headache, whose course, like a thick fog, no one knows,
> Whose full sign, whose means of restraint no one knows!

Treatment included sculpting a surrogate head out of reeds and breaking it over the skull of the headache victim, in this way transferring the pain to the effigy.

The ancient Egyptians had a name for a migrainy one-sided headache, *ges tep,* and many treatments: a hot shower, for instance, with a cloth wrapped around the temples. The *Papyrus Ebers,* a medical text dating to 1550 B.C., recommended a clay crocodile strapped to the head, or several different mortars, "Hide-of-the-Hippopotamus," "Crocodile-earth," or "Ass's Fat," "smear(ed)" on the head "for four days."

By the time of Hippocrates, around 460 B.C., migraine, if not yet by that name, was well established. Hippocrates himself described, in a beautiful staccato, a patient who "seemed to see something shining before him like a light, usually in part of the right eye; at the end of a moment, a violent pain." Aretaeus of Cappadocia, practicing medicine in the decades after the death of Christ, called migraine "Heterocrania" and authored a passionate case study of its sufferers: "For they flee the light; the darkness soothes their disease . . . the patients, moreover, are weary of life, and wish to die."

A century later, Claudius Galen, ancient Rome's most famous physician, isolated a profound one-sided headache he blamed on an imbalance of humors like black bile and blood. He called it "hemicrania," which over two millennia became *migrana* in Latin, and then *migraine.* It's a French word that we routinely mispronounce (it should be spoken "me-grain"), and it means "half a head"—a misnomer, as doctors have noted for a century, since migraines often affect more than half the head, or less.

The Ancients took their headaches seriously. Their gods delivered headaches: "Antaura arose from the sea," one third-century song, addressing a wind goddess, offered, "Antaura, where do you bring the hemikrania?" And their gods got headaches, too—important headaches. In the legendary Greek myth, Zeus, god of gods, got a headache so intense that he begged Prometheus for relief. Prometheus split open Zeus's head with an ax, from which was born Athena, the goddess of war *and* wisdom. Horus, the Egyptians' complex falcon deity, complained of *ges tep* so profound that he implored Isis, "Give me your head in exchange for my head." Instead, she treated headache with a mixture of coriander, opium, wormwood, juniper, and honey, a recipe not very different from ones sometimes employed by Victorian headache sufferers.

From the time of the Ancients to the time of the Enlightenment, migraines received a vast amount of attention from physicians in many different cultures. The Greek Paulus Aegineta, for instance, writing around A.D. 600, theorized that migraines were "liable to be increased by noises, cries, a brilliant light, drinking of wine, and strong-smelling things which fill the head." Rest and simple diet were frequently prescribed: Moses Maimonides, the twelfth-century Hebrew philosopher, suggested "bread or toast in undiluted wine" in some cases, a bath "in comfortably-warm sweet water" in others. The Talmud considered social matters and wisely prohibited nonsufferers from visiting or talking to a migraining man or woman.

Other treatments were more fantastic. Galen, among others, recommended that a stingray, what he called an "electric torpedo fish," "while still alive," be placed on the temple of the man in pain. Herbal remedies were used everywhere in the world. Avicenna, in his tenth-century *Canons of Medicine,* recommended cashews and African ginger. Indians in the Americas experimented with tobacco and beaver testes. Seventeenth-century Europeans tried roses and geraniums.

Prayer and reflection were also regarded as effective treatments. Plato recommended sublime introspection: the headaching protagonist of *Charmides* will be given a "drug for the head," he is promised, if he can first prove that he is "sound-minded," the irony, of course, being that the exam for "sound-mindedness"—a predictably Socratic dialogue—*is* the cure. Early Syrian Christians implored "Mar Nestorius, holy priest," to "bind" the headache: "Holy, holy, holy is God, I bind you, spirit of migraine."

Medieval Irish Catholics had Aed mac Bricc, that sixth-century bishop who cured headache with miracles. Legend told: he struck his head upon a stone as he launched from his mother's womb; the rainwater that collected in the dent in the "bullaun stone" ever after was sanctified and cured headaches. Over time, he, too, became sanctified: "Cool(s) the noxious fluxes that flow heated in my head," pleads an amazing hymn to him found among the manuscripts of the Reichenau Monastery. Stationed in a hermitage on a tall seaside cliff in County Donegal, Saint Aed listened to the plaints of headachy pilgrims and recommended self-reliance: "You will gain great merit," he would tell them, "if you bear it patiently." If, however, the patient responded that "the pain is beyond my forces," Saint Aed martyred himself to the cure: "The pain in your head, o man," he promised, "may come into my head."

By the tenth century, though, Saint Aed needed help. One Byzantine document from that time introduces us to "migraine" arising "from the seas, stamping and roaring," only to encounter "the Lord Jesus Christ," asking, "Where are you bringing *headache, hemikrania*?" The "headache" answers: "to take a seat in the head of the servant of our Lord, named—." Jesus instructs it instead to take a trip to "the wild mountains, and settle in a bull's head." The prayer was popular: it was still used five hundred years later in Greece, with a new focus on the double meaning of "Calvary" as "headpan-stow." That Christ was crucified on a hill covered with skulls gave him dispensation to save not just souls, but heads as well.

And anywhere that prayer, diet, magic, and medicine failed, there was surgery, an intimidating practice called *trepanning*. Here's Aretaeus of Cappadocia describing it step-by-step to other surgeons, if "light" diet had failed, and before one resorted to the toxic *hellebore* plant: Take a little blood from the "straight vein on the forehead," then shave the head, then cup "without drawing blood." Then "scarify unsparingly"—cut and cut and cut—then "excise a portion of the arteries," the ones "discovered by their pulsations."

Then some purgative, ointment, an injection up both nostrils, rinse the mouth "back to the tonsils." Then a light supper with wine. Then, next day: bleed the nostrils, and then, "whether the pain remain," burn the head "with heated cauteries," "superficially" or "to the bone." Then, third day, the nice day: "linen cloth wetted" with wine and rose oil on the scars.

There were variations across cultures and classes. Sometimes one deep incision would do. Sometimes perforating the bone was the prescription. Abulcasis, the celebrated medieval Islamic surgeon, advised carving a little hole in the temple and placing garlic into it. Probably, just the threat of trepanning cured headaches, or seemed to. But archaeologists have had no problem finding skulls that say otherwise.

3

We like to mock old science, old religion, not at all worried what men and women two millennia from now will think of us. At best, we are willing to respect those impulses from the past that most resemble us, and celebrate those thinkers as prophetic. But, if anything, migraine inspires the opposite reflection: there is something in its history and its symptoms that makes one think, instead, about how little the human body or the cures that work upon it have really changed.

Wagner and Nietzsche, for instance, whose heads turned dull when the *Föhn* wind swept through southeastern Europe, might have recognized the link between migraine and sudden weather changes in those songs and chants that personified headache as a wind goddess, as rising from the sea, as "blowing like the wind." The Sumarians recognized the link between being "sick-eyed" and "sick-headed," named formally by the International Headache Society in 2004 as "migraine with aura." Rest, simple diet, and privacy: Moses Maimonides and the Talmud, their advice still holds.

The Egyptians, similarly, recognized what every modern migraineur who has ever clamped pillow to temple, or icepack to forehead, also recognizes: that applying pressure to the tender point seems to help, whether or not a clay crocodile is the means. Pressure applied to the scalp, in fact, has been a near-universal practice through history. Pliny recommended that the headache sufferer tie a used noose around his head; when Shakespeare's Othello complains of a "pain upon my forehead," Desdemona offers to "bind it hard," assuring him that "within this hour it will be well."

From a migrainy perspective, however, some of the most alien ancient practices are also the most relevant. Galen, with his "still alive" electric torpedo fish, was plainly thinking about electric therapy—a good intuition, given that migraine is catalyzed by surges and depressions in the body's electric current. Plato, of course, was thinking that migraine was inspired by something more than physical: "Just as one must not attempt to doctor eyes without head or head without body," he writes in *Charmides,* "so also not body without soul." As such, he was two thousand years ahead of Freud (another migraineur, and an extraordinary one) and the mass of twentieth-century psychiatrists who have sought migraine's origins in the mind, and not the brain.

The Greeks who penned the story of Zeus and Athena understood that headache might be a source of wisdom, a conceit that lies at the heart of any debate about whether migraine, if not pain itself, is a transcendent or devastating event. And the Egyptians understood what any modern Christian readily recognizes: that a religion, and the world that religion defines, is utterly changed when a deity feels pain.

And then there is trepanning, about which, it would seem, no defense can be made. But no one should be surprised at its appeal or its endurance: it is one of the few headache treatments to be practiced before Christ and after Darwin. Trepanning understands migraine as a violent event and responds with violence. It is the right external drama, proportionate to the drama inside, the one only the migraineur can feel. And the Ancients always got the external drama right, which is why they treated headache like a public, even sacred, event.

That a doctor might cut a hole in the patient's head, or, maybe, saw a little jagged opening, and let out—what? smoke, bilious humors (liquid or vapor), fetid brain tissue, some unnamable soul sickness—it feels as fitting as applying pressure, or applying cold, or inhaling the steam from a cup of coffee. And any single one of these treatments, in turn, feels more fitting than the detachment of a modern pill regimen. The migraining head wants to be cut open; it longs to be cut open.

There is a splendid print, in fact, from the fourteenth century, of a trepanning doctor and patient: both stand upright, fully clothed, the doctor squinting as he chisels a little ridge across the forehead of a patient apparently untroubled by this intervention.

It is definitely outpatient work. That patient might as well be practicing his golf swing while the doctor saws away.

Ice and steam and pressure; less food and more sleep. Stay away from the saber-tooth cat: he's loud, and he'll eat you. Being human is simple, if not easy.

Enlightenment, Part 1

The influences from these three sources have been turned and twisted until they can exist side by side in the minds of the people. It is not uncommon to see a woman with a migraine headache first bind her brow with the leaf of a wild arum lily, as did her Indian predecessors; then consult a *curandera* to have the causative hex lifted, as did her Spanish ancestors in the Dark Ages; and finally go to a modern quack in the next village to have herself injected, because "injections are good."

—DAVID WERNER,
"Healing in the Sierra Madre"

1

My early migraines, I suppose, would be diagnosed as "typical aura without headache"—another International Headache Society classification, Hippocrates' "brilliant flash of light" without the "violent pain." Clearly the migraine of choice, for obvious reasons. And yet, not soul stirring: like watching fireworks without sound.

What I didn't know then was that migraines can change

over the course of a lifetime. They make one think of kaleido-scopes (Sir David Brewster, inventor of the kaleidoscope, wrote several papers on migraines). It is not only because auras so frequently resemble the geometric light dances found within kaleidoscopes. It is because migraines change, from one de-cade to the next, like kaleidoscopic patterns, an array of dif-ferent elements that shift into different patterns every time the Large Hand gives its toy a turn or two. The aura shifts away, or shifts into a different shape. The pain, which was there all along but repressed within the pattern, shifts and twirls into a new place.

And then the Large Hand, satisfied, puts down its toy until next time.

In my early thirties, I still got auras: a curtain drawing itself across my field of vision—wildly drawn, bowing out in the middle, its right fringe on fire, too, the curtain itself turning from translucent to gray, from an unstable twinkling to a calmer shimmer, as it moved left to right. This had been happening for ten years, though, and I had adjusted. So what if the left side of the airplane grew dimmer, the flight attendant moving down the aisle handing cups of coffee and tea to people, then just outstretched hands, and then into nothingness? So what if I had to lecture to a class as the fiery curtain drew, dulled, and faded, had to focus on an audience as if half of them weren't disappearing and then reappearing? That's the beauty of the headache-free migraine.

But now, too, I began to get headaches—really, headache events. A blowy morning in October, for instance: one of those days when summer and fall seem to converge, humidity in the air but leaves falling, a thunderstorm about a day away, some-where in Colorado, maybe (I used to love these days). A feeling of unease, like something small is wrong somewhere, like I'd left the toaster oven on. And then, around noon, for maybe half an hour, maybe an hour, a feeling of increasing desolation that spreads from a pinpoint of woe in the brain stem somewhere to something totally systemic, like when that cup of hot chocolate on a cold winter day warms through your body—only this the inverse. Then, something like flop sweat, a clamminess that also feels like it's coming from somewhere deeper than the surface, a metaphysical unease.

Then an aura, a new type of aura. It takes a while—ten minutes, maybe twenty—and feels like a kind of organized disorientation. All those motes of gray that routinely form a film across the screen of one's vision dance a little faster and then start to dance together until they become something more than background. In the next step, I become aware of the film across vision itself—I am never sure if the disorientation that comes at this point is a product of this realization, or a chemical reaction simultaneous with the onset of the aura, or a third thing entirely, the despair that comes with the recognition that another migraine is coming.

As the aura continues, the film gets, well, filmier: the motes of gray cohere into fields of blurred or wavy vision, not all the way across the ocular field, and with inviting bands of light around their edges. My vision is blurry as if my eyes were filmed with tears, but only partially, and as if the tears were slightly, radiantly, radioactive. In the last wave of the aura, which I only rarely experience—or recognize, or recall, I'm not sure which—the bands of light and the blurred gray fields themselves cohere into something that generally occupies the left side of my vision, that seems to rise if I look up, that quivers and is almost beautiful.

Then this shimmering weirdness disappears—I want to say, it *crashes*. Then there's a pause, a few minutes, a half hour. Eye of the hurricane. And then, a headache, only not, the way a bed frame is not the bed, the frame of the pain, but not the inside: one frame around the temple, for instance, that hole in the skull on the left side, a second frame around the eye socket. (I'm never getting used to these reminders of my anatomy, of my skeleton-ness, there's just too much foreboding in them, of the day ahead when I'm nothing but skeleton. I'm seriously considering cremation just to outsmart the headaches, but suspect I'm playing where I shouldn't be playing with thoughts like that.)

And then, a headache. But can I really call it a headache? The words are running dry now. I can say that I "flee the light," as Aretaeus wrote two thousand years ago. And sound, too. And I can report nausea, sometimes vomiting, sometimes not. But it's not so much headache as possession, my head an occupied territory, and my normal self, a disenfranchised native populace, driven underground.

Late afternoon. A wordless stillness, if I'm lucky. If not, that's another story. There is the pain, the throb (I wish there was a better word for this), the tremulousness in the belly, and that's about it. I'm very attuned to time: not the clock, I'm not clock-watching, but I'm locked into some more elemental cycle, something that starts with sunrise and ends with sunset and was probably second nature to those who held *di'u* in awe.

This goes on for a while.

Then a plateau, then the mildest of recessionals, and then a discernible turning point: for me, it's a cold sweat that coats me head to toe evenly and tenderly and quickly, an existential wash. I don't know at that moment that the attack is over, since the attack has coalesced into a series of feints and retreats, and this merely feels inside the head like another retreat. There is no relief at this moment—the relief will come, standing upright, in latest afternoon or at early dusk (my migraines almost always ending at this time of day), with some consciousness of clarity, a brain wipe, so to speak, nothing really worth remembering or worrying about, just an abundant sense of thankfulness that the attack has receded. A few distant electrical wires sizzling in puddles at the edge of the flood, perhaps, dogs sniffing in curiosity at the sparks and at the imitation of life provided by the jittery cables, but I'm over here, standing on my rooftop as the waters recede, as the front steps and the lawn reappear.

2

The scientists of the Enlightenment watched migraines with intense curiosity and recorded them with exacting precision. Thomas Willis, a seventeenth-century Englishman now recognized as the "father" of neurology, composed gorgeously detailed and sympathetic case studies, and tinkered with paradigms of nerve and brain and blood that had lingered for a millennium and a half. In *De Anima Brutorum (Concerning the Souls of Brutes),* published in 1672, he continued to endorse Galen's influential argument that an imbalance in humors inspired severe headache. But his human body was a more nuanced place, its anatomy a fleshy machine diagrammed with a new fluency. And "Headach" was among its chief ailments, a beast that might visit you in many different ways. It might come to you through the nerves, via "Nervous Fibres" that transmitted pain all over the place. Or it might come to you through blood that would "water()" parts of the brain when in equilibrium, and "pour() upon" them in cataclysmic moments of stress.

He recognized that migraine might be hereditary, that the pain usually had a prelude, that it could be triggered by hunger, or emotional upheaval, or "the drinking of wine," or "lying in the sun," or nothing: "accidental," he called them, "or chronic and habitual." His case studies were mostly women, ranging from "a venerable Matron" to a "beautiful and young Woman, indued with a slender habit of body," and "hot Blood" (for Willis, a medical classification). And he regarded them with courtly, detached affection. Of Anne, Countess of Conway, for instance, he observed that she had suffered from headache for "above twenty years," and then added that the migraine, "having pitched its tents near the confines of the Brain . . . had not taken it: for the sick Lady . . . found the chief faculties of her soul sound enough."

By the eighteenth century, other physicians, inspired by Willis, began to leave behind Galenic concepts about humors and headache. Their portrait of migraine and the body deepened, expanded, in large part because many of them also suffered from migraines (a surprising number of them, such as Brewster, the inventor of the kaleidoscope, were also astronomers, who seemed to recognize a bond between the stars they saw through their telescopes and the starrish things they saw during aura). John Fordyce, in *De Hemicrania* (1758), isolated the depression that often precedes the headache. Samuel Tissot, the influential French physician, sought out emotional catalysts for migraine and also argued for a link between stomach and head disorders. The Scot Robert Whyte, in 1765, attempted to "wipe off" the "reproach" that had been attached to "nervous" disorders like headache. He recognized the role of menstruation in their onset, and advanced Willis's idea that a "sympathy" network within the human body moved pain from one place to another, governed by "the laws of union between the soul and body."

Remarkable portraits of individual migraineurs emerged. Often, physicians told their own stories: Charles LePois, in *Hemicrania,* provided a vivid depiction of the chaotic ends of his migraines and the "welcome stupor" that followed. Sir Wheatstone noted a visual "effect like the motion of a luminous liquid," followed by a "luminous mist," followed by a "fainting sensation." John Fothergill noted "a singular kind of glimmering in the sight; objects swiftly changing their apparent position, surrounded with luminous angles." Then "giddiness comes on, head-ach, and sickness."

Other physicians circulated stories about celebrated thinkers who suffered from migrainy neurological problems, if not migraines themselves, and implied a connection between the illness and intense intellectual production. There was the case of Carl Linnaeus, for instance, the great botanist, who hallucinated that he saw himself outside of himself—"He opened the door rapidly intending to enter, but pulled up at once saying, 'Oh! I'm there already'"—and relieved his headaches with brisk exercise.

And there was Pascal, the seventeenth-century French mathematician and philosopher who "would imagine that a cavity or precipice was yawning on his left-hand side" and "reassure himself" by moving "a piece of furniture to that side." Modern observers like Macdonald Critchley have compared this hallucination to case studies who left "an inordinately broad margin on the right half of the page" when they wrote, or drew their auras onto paper whenever they could, "like compulsive doodles."

By the nineteenth century, migraine sustained a rich medical debate. Different names abounded: most called it "megrim" or "meagrim," but "hemicrania" persisted, as did "cephalalgia" and "cephalea" (ancient names for acute and chronic headaches, respectively), as did "sun-pain," "sick-headache," "sick-giddiness" (migraine without headache), and "blind-headache" (migraine with aura). Lewis Carroll, among others, called his "bilious headache"; Thomas Jefferson, "periodical head ach." And as different names thrived, so, too, did different forms of migraine. A physician named Mollendorf named the "red migraine," which featured facial flushing, and was juxtaposed to the more common "white migraine": "While the face is pale," Sir Samuel Wilks wrote in 1872, "the larger vessels are throbbing, the head is hot and the remedies which instinct suggests are cold and pressure to the part."

Some physicians refined their lists of triggers. Fothergill, for instance, blamed "melted butter, fat meats, and spices, especially common black pepper"; Fordyce implicated chocolate. While scientists could create a fuller portrait of some aspects of migraine, however, they were stuck on other matters. They could not explain aura, for instance, at least not very well. And they could not come up with a cure or a treatment that advanced significantly from what Isis cooked up. They devised various drug cures, all fairly brutal: the "blue pill," a mercury tablet; compounds featuring ammonia, steel.

Mostly, though, cures depended upon who you were or where you lived. If you had the money, you might choose bed, or "'Italy,' or 'Switzerland,' or 'walking the moors,'" as George M. Gould wrote in an early edition of the *Journal of the American Medical Association*. If, like Pope, you had servants, you might have them "apply cloths dipped in water as hot as it can be wrung out, and change them every three minutes," as Mrs. E. F. Haskell recommended in 1861 in her *Housekeeper's Encyclopedia*. You might even dab a little peppermint or lavender on that cloth: it served no medicinal purpose, but smelled nice. If you were the servant, however, you were not as lucky: one Southern slaveholder claimed that "whenever a slave complained of a headache," he "would run his penknife into the tip of his nose and the headache would be relieved."

Opiates were prescribed without ambivalence; they were often the only thing a doctor could prescribe. Mary Boykin Chesnut, the famed Civil War diarist, took both morphine and opium, and Ulysses S. Grant, Civil War general and future U.S. president, almost certainly did the same. Laxatives—rhubarb, calomel—were popular, and cannabis helped with the nausea. Champagne, or hot air up the nostrils, represented two different prescriptions with the same effervescent goal.

Trepanning still remained a steady practice, as did the administration of pressure in ornate forms. In Pennsylvania, men and women with bad headaches were still taking Pliny's advice and wrapping their heads with a piece of used hangman's noose—you could try an unused noose, but it didn't work as well. In the Bahamas, locals were using two live frogs, which you wore until they died. In Brazil, Darwin, suffering from a two-day headache, was offered remedies he regarded as "ludicrously strange, but too disgusting to be mentioned."

Often, different treatments were mingled into layered regimens: a gardener during the time of the Revolution received advice to watch his diet, avoid alcohol, dress warmly, and, when feeling the onset of a headache, "apply about six leeches to his temples and behind his ears." From a contemporary perspective, this advice blends common sense with its opposite. From the perspective of 1780, however, this advice couldn't be more obvious, nonspecific—leeches were the eighteenth-century acetaminophen. What David Werner found in the Sierra Madre, in truth, has been more rule than exception: human history provides plenty of migraine cures, and, sometimes, even now, finding the ones that work feels more like a trip back in time than a trip to the pharmacy.

Victorian and Modern

"I'm very brave generally," he went on in a low voice:
"only to-day I happen to have a headache."
— Tweedledum, from Lewis Carroll's
Through the Looking Glass

1

A headache comes in the seventh hour of a transatlantic journey and stays for three days, on the right side, at a jaunty angle, almost, like something affected I brought back from Europe, like a beret. Maybe it's two headaches: there's an almost meteorological discipline to mapping these things. It's like watching a sky where two storms are competing for the horizon: there's a dull, cottony pain that almost seems to match the shape of the skull, round like it, absent where the skull is absent, and a throbbing pain, too, that comes and goes, and provides a perverse relief by making me forget the dull, cottony pain for the length of its throbs. America is hot and dusty, caught in drought and heat wave, and I have passed through five time zones and three different kinds of weather (Europe: cool, wet; the airplane, with its artificial air pressure; dry and dusty America), and it is really no use. This headache is going to stay for days. And it does. Three of them.

Steam helps: long showers, standing over the kettle, I scald myself, but the headache only scurries to a small place for a few hours, and then regroups. Retreats again at night, returns in the morning.

At this point—I'm a thirty-five-year-old man here—I didn't know that these headaches were migraine. And, like that gardener from 1780, I wouldn't have known what to do, anyway. I tried aspirin, acetaminophen—the twenty-first-century leech—but it was, as the saying goes, like bringing a knife to a gunfight.

I began to recognize triggers: long plane flights, dramatic barometric pressure changes, those thunderstorms rolling across the Great Plains toward my little house in Indiana. I first discovered that steam helped (one reason I admire Pope as much as I do). And I discovered one single food that I could eat during an attack without making the attack worse: rice. Good, dependable bowls of rice. You can put on the steamer when you feel the headache coming on, and you can leave a bowl by your bedside for hours, and it's still good.

You won't want to touch it at first, even that little wisp of ricey smell is pretty disruptive, but within two hours you'll be able to move your head far enough to move it near the bowl, and pick up the fork. Keep the room dark. You can't quite feel the fork the way you normally do—it has a vagueness in your hand, its borders and margins no longer sharp, so you won't, quite, be able to tell if you've managed to get a few grains on its tines. A spoon would be even worse, though (I've never been able to figure out why, but it is), and after a few tries, you start to eat in earnest. And the rice helps—that and a glass of water.

This happened about ten times a year. Maybe fifteen, at most. I never felt that I had entered what Susan Sontag, in *Illness as Metaphor,* called "the night-side of life," never took what she called that "more onerous citizenship" in "the kingdom of the sick." Ten times a year. Ten times a year where I took off an afternoon from work, took off from evening chores. Ten times a year where I ate a small, simple dinner in bed. Ten times a year where I lost three or four pounds in a day or two. The pain was awful and I dreaded it. But otherwise, those headache events bore no small resemblance to spa treatment. And I never expected that would change, had no fear, no sense whatsoever that this was an illness that I should tend to.

I had misread the history, obviously.

2

Edward Liveing, if we trust his portraitist, looked like the kind of man every Victorian headache sufferer would choose as a physician. His face and his nose were long and lean, his eyes brown and warm, his mouth given to a patient, easy smile about one notch higher in intensity than Mona Lisa's. His father was a doctor, and his two brothers were a doctor and a professor. From 1863 to 1866, as Grant and Lee (one, maybe both, migraineurs) fought the Civil War here in the States, Liveing was studying medicine and found himself fascinated by "megrim" and "sick-headache" patients.

In *Megrim, Sick-Headache, and Some Allied Disorders: A Contribution to the Pathology of Nerve-Storms* (1873), Liveing did more than advance the science of migraine: he created a cultural portfolio for it. Unlike Thomas Willis, whose most famous patients were women, Liveing's case studies were mostly men, and a certain breed: "A man of high intellectual attainments in the prime of an active life, perhaps a literary man, a barrister, a member of parliament." They were dignified, elite sufferers, who often found themselves "with little or no warning, completely disabled, the victim of intense bodily pain, mental prostration, and perhaps hallucination of sense or idea." After a few hours, though, perhaps a nap, they emerged right as rain, subscribers to the cult of the stiff upper lip, able to "join an evening entertainment, to get up a brief, or take part in a debate."

Liveing, like Willis, seemed to like his patients. He acknowledged that migraines were hereditary, and was the first to recognize that they could shape-shift over a lifetime. He was fascinated by what he called the "abrupt transition from intense suffering to perfect health in this malady," fascinated, too, by what the "malady" did to otherwise "intelligent" people. He caught the edge of despair, the metaphysical grief: he liked Hubert Airy's depiction of a patient who "shudder(ed) at the very name, and turn(ed) away in horror from a drawing of the ugly sight" of an aura. He savored the drama of reason lost, reason gained, the delightful contradiction in which highly articulate men and women could describe how they had lost what made them civilized, what made them free: "I can't tell you why, but it is utterly impossible for me to speak," one of his migraining patients told him. "If I were to try, I should say words quite different from those I intended or which would have no meaning."

Liveing didn't blame humors, or sympathies, but looked instead to middle- and upper-crust Industrial Revolution concepts like "mental emotion" and "excessive brain work." His patients forgot words, stumbled through sentences, wrote down the wrong numbers, because they had worked too hard and thought too much, and their brains were rebelling using the only crude language they could speak: shafts of pain, aphasic speech, stripes of light and color. By the late nineteenth century, most medical scholars, considering the different causes of headache outlined by Willis two hundred years before, had concluded that "megrim" was a vascular illness: they sensibly reasoned that, since pressure applied to the point of pain often relieved migraine, the source of the pain must lie with angry blood vessels in the vicinity of the inflamed point. But Liveing, also very sensible, concluded that vascular theories could not explain aura. He acknowledged that blood had something to do with it—"I am not at all disposed to deny that disorders of local circulations occur in the course of megrim," he noted. But he saw, too, something explosive, deep down in the neural net somewhere, far from the pain itself. "The malady is essentially one of the nervous system," he wrote, "and of which the paroxysms may be described as nerve-storms."

Writing and practicing medicine during the latter part of the nineteenth century, Liveing stood on the cusp of dramatic changes in both the science and the culture of headache. Late Victorians like him refined their anatomies, played with a crude psychoanalytical vocabulary (the word *psychoanalysis* itself on the cusp of being coined), and began to regard the possibility that "professional" physicians might reach inside the head and extract the headache-causing agent, whatever it might be. Their cures were wildly varied. Most prescribed bed rest, water, relief from intellectual exhaustion. Others preferred herbal mixes: Liveing liked henbane and belladonna. Cocoa and caffeine were both popular, as were compounds featuring potassium and a brew of nitroglycerin and alcohol known as "Gower's mixture."

Within ten years of the publication of *Nerve-storms,* however, German chemists synthesized from coal tar a set of pills and powders with names like acetanilide, antipyrine, antifebrin, pyramidon, and aspirin, and marketed them to the public in Europe and America. Intended to treat fever, these drugs instead inspired self-medicating anti-headache regimens all over the world. Within two decades, by 1907, a pharmaceutical journal estimated annual acetanilide use in America at "ten adult doses" for every "man, woman and child," and newspaper editorials complained that the new headache medicines were "almost" as addictive "as morphine and cocaine."

And within twenty years, Sigmund Freud would author a short essay called "Migraine: Established Points." Freud, who had originally treated his own migraines as a nasal problem— a theory briefly ascendant in Central Europe in the 1890s— argued instead that migraines were caused by repressed desire, specifically sexual desire: the headache itself, a symbolic "forcible defloration" that fulfilled that desire. While Freud's essay was not widely read (it was, in fact, unpublished until the 1980s), its ideas bled into writings by him that were, and that inspired many twentieth-century doctors to see buried neurotic conflicts as the root cause of migraine.

The debate over migraine transformed rapidly, the head itself, seemingly, now open for all kinds of new inspections. Doctors rushed to try the new coal-tar medicines on their migraine patients: one physician in 1885 announced that his patients reported that antipyrine "acted like magic" and was vastly superior to morphine. By the 1920s, the drug regimens newly available to migraineurs expanded again. Physicians who had been prescribing Gower's mixture began to prescribe quinine, arsenic, or most commonly phenobarbitone, citing its success in preventing migraines before they occurred. And another German chemist synthesized ergot, a hazardous plant parasite, into drug form, and researchers in Europe and America soon confirmed that it would turn many bad migraines into milder headaches, at least until it wore off.

Soon researchers provided seemingly unimpeachable evidence that migraines were caused by dilating and contracting blood vessels on the outside of the skull. At the same time, they were also providing equally unimpeachable evidence that the source of migraine lay with waves of excited and depressed nerves deep in the brain. In 1938, for instance, John Graham and Harold G. Wolff conducted what is now known as the "smoking drum" experiment. They strapped tiny little tambours to the outside of migraineurs' skulls, and found that the blood vessels there pulsated more softly, tapping the tiny little drums less vigorously, as their migraine pain receded.

Then, in 1941, Karl Lashley, a Harvard Ph.D. armed only with a pencil and his own auras (it is hard not to adore this handmade, self-inflicted neurology), timed and measured his own "scintillations" (the electric, zigzagging edge of the aura) and "negative scotoma" (the blind spot that follows) down to the millimeter, and drew them as elegant, simple lobes one can easily mistake for Joan Miro practice sketches. Two years later, also at Harvard, a Ph.D. candidate from Brazil named Aristides Leao applied mild shocks to drugged rabbits and found something he called "spreading cortical depression": a little burst of electricity across an expanse of their rabbit brains, followed by a larger wave of diminished electric current, traveling at 3 millimeters per minute, the same pace that Lashley recorded in his own brain as his eyesight scintillated and faded.

By the 1930s, in turn, psychiatric researchers evolved the idea that migraineurs shared personality traits, an eclectic but generally unsavory set of tics packaged together as "an inappropriate protective or adaptive reaction" to "tension, hostility, frustration, and fatigue." Harold G. Wolff described the migraineurs he studied as "a well dressed group," "unusually ambitious and preoccupied with achievement and success," capable of some social "savoir faire" but generally guilty of an "exaggerated sense of personal insecurity and difficulty in establishing easy social relations." They were perfectionists who "harbored strong resentments" and responded badly to criticism, usually, by getting a migraine. In fact, what marked them as migraine personalities was how a *small* stress could provoke a migraine.

Like Liveing and Willis, the psychiatrists of the mid-twentieth century saw a certain kind of man and a certain kind of woman as their model migraineurs. The men were overachievers, as successful as Liveing's patients, but latently violent. The women were the modern versions of Willis's "hot-blooded" patients. They were described as sexually unsatisfied yet neurotically sexy: in *Some Characteristics of the Migrainous Woman*, Walter C. Alvarez waxed about shared traits like "firm, well placed breasts . . . luxuriant hair . . . these women dress well and move quickly." The children were "'goody goody' or self-righteous," and "took good or even excessive care of their toys."

Individual case studies tended to focus on unhappy, violent people, with whom the researcher played like lab rats. Jule Eisenbud, in a 1937 issue of *Psychiatric Quarterly*, wrote about a man with "complete amnesia" and familial conflicts so intense that he "put Lysol in his father's whiskey." Eisenbud's experiment: hypnotize the man into thinking that he had done embarrassingly Freudian things, like accidentally burn a hole through the hem of his girlfriend's dress with a cigarette, and see if he responded with a migraine (he did, at first, but gradually began to simply feel "low and out of sorts," suspecting,

"The doctor must have done something to me . . . because I felt swell yesterday").

Other researchers were kinder, more balanced. Caro W. Lippman's migraineurs in *Certain Hallucinations Peculiar to Migraine* were completely conventional men and women, by 1950s standards: "average in business or professional achievements," Lippman noted, "or good housewives and mothers." Their only problem: they suffered from premonitory hallucinations that made them feel that their bodies were contracting and expanding, until they were "one foot high," or tall enough to "look down on the tops of others' heads."

By the 1950s and 1960s, the clinical portrait of migraine was overwhelmingly varied, its recent history filled with accidental cures, persuasive but incomplete explanations, and a kind of credibility problem. For the most part, psychiatrists held the field: "Many physicians," Robert S. Kunkel has since observed, "thought that most chronic or recurring headache conditions . . . were mainly due to psychological disorders and related to stress."

Physicians, in turn, became headache specialists, according to Leonard Lovshin of the Cleveland Clinic, "by default," because "no one else wanted to see these patients." They gave their migraine patients ergotamine tartrate, combined with caffeine tablets, which helped but produced an unwieldy dependency. Starting in the early 1960s, they also gave them a drug called methysergide, another synthesized ergot, which also helped. They gave them tricyclic antidepressants like amitriptyline and imipramine. And, in the late 1960s, they tried propranolol, a medicine for hypertension. It seemed to help, too.

For the most part, though, these drugs had not been invented to help migraine, often didn't work, and did little to explain what a migraine was, or what lay at its roots. Vascular theories, blaming throbbing blood vessels for migraine pain, were compelling but didn't explain aura. Neurological theories, implicating excited nerves, couldn't explain why pressure worked. Even psychiatric researchers did not seem to know whether those shared personality traits they saw among migraineurs were caused by the migraine, or caused the migraine. Meanwhile, new theories evolving in postwar laboratories supplied even more potential explanations for what might cause migraine: platelet destruction, serotonin problems, microscopic malfunctions like listless mitochondria, all discovered on a freshly drawn and rapidly evolving map of the central nervous system.

The bigger problem, though, may have lain with the subject itself. As historian Jan R. McTavish has observed, headache in the eighteenth and nineteenth centuries possessed a low public profile: even men and women willing to describe in letters and diaries their most personal ailments rarely mentioned their head pain. That large numbers of people were having headaches and not writing or talking about them only became clear, as was the case with the coal-tar drugs, when a treatment became available and men and women flocked to it.

In the early twentieth century, however, this changed: headaches were everywhere, in everything. By the 1920s, Americans were using *headache* as a metaphor in conversation to signify "something, such as a problem, that causes annoyance or trouble." By the end of World War II, encouraged by the availability of drug treatment and the intellectual framework supplied by Freud's adherents, they began to regard headaches themselves "as the result of an inability to deal with the 'resentments and dissatisfactions' that were a part of everyday life."

Once a word becomes a metaphor, of course, the object that the word originally defined has a problem. It is in the public eye like never before, but its presence is unstable, easy to blur and to distort. That was the twentieth-century headache. It was taken seriously, was examined from every side by modernist-era scientists the way Picasso deconstructed a chair or Joyce reconstructed human consciousness. But it was also transformed into a metaphor for the inability to cope, a second-rate illness, really, if illness at all.

Migraine, however, was a little more elusive, a little more resistant to the packaging. It may have been the auras. It may have been the degree of incapacitation. But it was *something,* this pain, this strange pain, really this constellation of pain symptoms (let's not forget numbness in the limbs, stupor, the anorexia, the depression, the weird visions, or that almost existential nausea) that seemed to have nothing to do with the body dying or even being harmed. It provided no obvious early warning sign for something else, and seemed to be primarily just pain without meaning, without discernible source. It eluded modern science as much as it eluded the Egyptians and the Irish who prayed to Saint Aed. And one has to admire the modern scientists for that, admire their humility and their recognition that here lay rich and mysterious avenues into understanding the brain and the mind, and which was which, and when was when. Uncontestable symptoms, hauntingly similar from case to case, but as different as snowflakes from case to case. No clear origin for those symptoms, again, from case to case. An understandable challenge to anyone studying migraine. Or anyone having one.

TWO

Do not undervalue the headache. While it is at its sharpest it seems a bad investment; but when relief begins, the unexpired remainder is worth $4 a minute.

—MARK TWAIN, *Following the Equator*

Tongue-Tied

English, which can express the thoughts of Hamlet and the tragedy of Lear, has no words for the shiver and the headache. It has all grown one way. The merest school-girl, when she falls in love, has Shakespeare or Keats to speak her mind for her; but let a sufferer try to describe a pain in his head and language at once runs dry.

—VIRGINIA WOOLF,
"On Being Ill"

1

I got migraines from my mother, who got them from her mother. I ask Mom about her symptoms, and she says very bad pain, across the nose and brow, and nausea, really vomiting. She asks me if I have auras, so I say yes, and ask her if she has auras, and she says it hurts too much to tell. Then she amends: no, it hurts too much to remember clearly.

But here's what she does remember: her own mother, alone in a room for hours, shades drawn, cold compress across fore-head, but no doctor, no complaining. Mom remembers being a little girl very clearly: "What was I supposed to do?" she asks.

Her strongest memory of migraines is her inability to help her own mother with hers.

And here's what else she remembers: she didn't even know what she had were migraines until I got a diagnosis for myself, and that inspired her to go see a doctor. And she didn't know what her mother had were migraines until after she got her own diagnosis.

For that matter, I never knew until last year that my brother had migraines twenty-five years ago. You would think we would have talked about it.

The language of migraine is a language of indirection and gaps. A man, a good friend, brings his own mix to your parties and makes everyone Cosmopolitans, and never tells a story about himself unless he can do an impression or two, something in the Marvin Gaye/Jay-Z range, and he just says, "Yep, I had migraines." You expect something good, a little fake percussion, but instead he just places his hands in the vicinity of his temples and then moves them outward, a gesture meant to simulate his head blowing up, and then he says, "Yep, a long time ago, and they were bad"—he's stumbling for words now—"I wanted to die." And then he changes the subject.

A domestication, maybe. Something made every day, part of the household, that doesn't belong there, like a zebra in your kitchen, a cactus in your bed. Migraines are just in the wrong place.

Another friend: garrulous, abrasive Paul. Tall, thin, mid-forties, talks too loud, leans over too closely, but still. He's had one migraine in his life, over a decade ago. He describes it as a headache that wasn't like any other headache he had ever had. He describes a craving for paralysis, for absolute motionlessness, the inability to answer questions more than monosyllabically, absolute darkness. His face freezes as he talks to you, his mouth drops, as if in total torpor, all goes blank, he even seems to get a little paler (and he's a pretty pale guy). Then his face returns to its normal animation, and he says, "Never had one since," with some slight pride in his voice.

Virginia Woolf was right: "It has all grown one way," she said, meaning, writers and artists for centuries have refined the language of love, of thought, of soul, but not of pain. But Woolf makes it sound like there was even a choice: pain, as Elaine Scarry observes in *The Body in Pain,* fights language and usually wins. It does so, in part, because it shuts down and then vandalizes brain space, inhibits and even lays waste to the parts of consciousness that think and shape and speak. But it also does so because of pain's social contract: pain is the surest thing in the world to the person feeling it, and the least sure thing to the person hearing about it, and that's a bad deal all around.

So most people clam up. But some don't. In desperation, Scarry notes, men and women yield to two metaphors to describe pain, neither one really helpful. In the first, there is a clear pain-giving agent, even when there's not: "God just punched you in the side of the face," for instance. In the second, there is a concrete image that sounds right but isn't. Here is someone describing the pain of a migraine: "the feeling of a spike being hammered into the back of your eyeball every single time your heart beats." This is powerful, but what does it really mean? The author doesn't know what spike-in-eyeball actually feels like, nor do the overwhelming number of potential readers. The miracle of such language is that we all feel the same visceral unease. But it's not the truth.

Here's another: "Hell even my own breathing is like a chainsaw to me." This is better, because it's worse: How is one's own breathing like a chainsaw? Is it as loud as a chainsaw, as rough, as painful as one slicing through? Not knowing the answer, because the sentence is a little aphasic, its meaning just to the left or the right of its words, gives the reader a far better sense of disrupted sensibility, of what it means to have a migraine.

Here's another one: "I'm the crash in between the two cymbals. Rather, my head IS the crash my ears are making. If that makes any sense." This is even better, because this author recognizes that a concrete metaphor won't work. She repairs the metaphor, she reaches, she expands the language, she gives up. It's a story in twenty-three words.

Here's another one: "someone crying but trying not to as crying makes the pain worse." This one's best, because it's absolutely true. It's a metaphor, sure. And it's not.

2

I didn't (and still don't) know how it started, and I barely remember when, or what it felt like. It was August 2006, a sodden late August in Indiana. The whole month was like this: clear, then progressively grayer and more humid for two days, maybe three, then a thunderburst, twenty minutes, no more, then clear, then the whole thing over again. Plants were bursting everywhere like we were in the tropics; trees hung low over streets and driveways like they were praying.

I woke up one morning with a sudden, severe throbbing over the left eye, a real surprise, no premonition, no aura. It rapidly settled into something oppressive, something with weight and heft that displaced whole cubic centimeters formerly occupied by my frontal lobe. It felt so heavy that I found myself ducking down and to the right.

The headache stayed until two or three in the afternoon. I remember a sofa, a pillow, a TV with the sound off, a certain tilt to things, as if I was not in my family room but in one of the villains' lairs on the old *Batman* show, the camera always tilted at around 30 degrees to suggest, I suppose, the failure of the Joker's or the Riddler's moral compasses.

Finally, I took an Imitrex, that useful migraine drug that my GP first gave me a year before. It cut through the migraine roughly, like a, like a chainsaw, a constriction in the throat, a lot of vomiting. The migraine lost its oppressiveness, started to feel like a couple of smaller migraines, like the first migraine had been cut in two, a diagonal cut from the middle of the brow upward to the left temple.

What *was* that, I thought.

The next day, I got another migraine, the left eye, the throb, the oppression. I was still ducking down and to the right, but this migraine was not occupying my brain. It was occupying air space, like a pocket of turbulence moving as I moved, and I was ducking my head to keep clear of it.

I took another Imitrex. The day after that, I got another migraine and took another Imitrex. The day after that, I got another migraine but was out of Imitrex. I called the pharmacy and they told me that the refill would cost over two hundred dollars, because my insurance company would only cover the first eight tablets in a month. I was angry at the insurance company. But I was angry at myself, too, for not realizing that I had taken eight Imitrex that month.

My doctor told me to come in right away, told me I was in a "bad patch," and handed me a photocopied sheet of paper explaining what a "rebound headache" is—the migraine you get from taking too many migraine drugs; an appointment for an MRI; a prescription for Vicodin; a bottle containing sample tablets of Topamax, an anti-epileptic drug prescribed for chronic migraines; and a blister pack of Frova, another migraine drug. I carried them out of her office in one hand, the photocopied paper crumpled around the drugs, everything a little damp.

The MRI was hilarious, as they always are, the large machine, the rattling noise, the heavy iron apron, country music coursing around the big room—a start-up MRI firm, with a big pot of coffee brewing alongside a basketful of tiny bags of Oreos and Chips Ahoy, and a smiling receptionist who cheerfully hands me a big manila envelope filled with slick snapshots of my brain. All nonurgent health care in Indianapolis, particularly in the glossy new suburbs, is insanely wholesome.

The brain was fine. I've still got the pix, wedged behind a bookshelf somewhere. But the headache didn't go away for four months. I'll never know exactly what started the hostile takeover: a shift in the humidity or my body's tolerance to some food or to the ever-present moldy oaks, a tick in the tick-tock of the clock that counts down the days to my death, a lightning strike too nearly ambient or a movie screen too bright that shorted out my circuits. The Large Hand. I can make guesses, can align my symptoms and its timing to any number of diagnoses, but the thing about a migraine is that you can always do that.

3

Maybe the language of migraine is a run-on sentence, in part because you can't ever find the right words, in part because the migraine is also a compound of too many interlocking features, as in this nineteenth-century description of an aura: "the outward spread of the cloud, its arched shape, its serrated outline, with smaller teeth at one end than at the other, its remarkable tremor, greater where the teeth are greater, its 'boiling,' its tinge of scarlet."

Maybe the language of migraine isn't really language at all. It's language just disappearing: "The printed letters ran into large angular black zigzags," Sir John Herschel, reading while migraining, wrote in 1868, "and then I knew what was coming."

Maybe the language of migraine is silence: "All words and letters covered by this strange intruder," Hubert Airy, also reading while migraining, observed, "are completely blotted out."

Maybe the language of migraine is playful, even if you're not: "My head is aching awfully," Rudyard Kipling, an ace migraineur, wrote. "And the letters are hopping about in front of my eyes."

Maybe migraine is a visual medium. Some people don't try words; they try art. In 1981, the British Migraine Association promoted a juried competition for migraine art, and the concept has been popular in many countries ever since. The therapeutic and diagnostic value of such work, as Klaus Podoll and Derek Robinson observe in *Migraine Art,* is profound: painting the illness names it, and then treats it. And, yet, while some of the paintings are quite wonderful, take them all at once—walk all the way through the virtual gallery of the National Headache Foundation, for instance—and you'll get dizzy and very, very pensive.

It's a bit like a collection of heavy metal album covers from the 1970s, always some sort of violence being done to the head, or half a head, of the portraited person: a split right down the middle of the head against a blood-red backdrop, as words like "Stop shouting!" and "What should I do!" float by the cracked-open skull. A dragon latched onto the head and back of a morose nude looking into a mirror. Another migraineur looking into the mirror, doing, evidently, her makeup (she's wearing a robe), while a feathery multicolored aura effaces the left side of her face. Then there are abstracts: a realistic portrait of light seeping through drawn translucent curtains, a lovely palette of grays and washed-out whites. These are the 2003 "Migraine Masterpieces."

At the "Art Gallery" of the American Headache Society Committee for Headache Education (ACHE), the art on display features a range of deep, almost electric blues, and that's pretty inspired. Heads in pain, people holding their heads, people with little gremlins pounding on their heads with mallets and blowing in their supine ears with trumpets, one completely dissociated head, eyes and ears awash against a backdrop of chalkboard black (my favorite), heads and bodies twisted like Dalí's clocks, heads split in two and badly stitched back together, perhaps a photograph on top and a painting below, or two photographs silkscreened with slightly different techniques matched by slightly different (but equally glum) expressions (*Underworld,* there's a fair title), heads split everywhere, cracks right down the middle, holes shot through foreheads (not as bad as it sounds), the occasional abstract *(Headache II, Thunderhead),* a quite decent wash of blues and a swipe of red right where it should be, two heads, one screaming the other screaming in a slightly different way, the tops of heads being opened up, all sorts of visual trepanning, to say the least, more heads cracked, enlarged foreheads used as the canvas for all kinds of dramas (knives through eyes, bells flying around), lots of hands reaching up toward lots of foreheads, hands in motion always upward, heads when not morose then screaming, rays of flat golden light shooting outward from a head like an anatomy class cadaver, fresh grays and reds for the muscle groups (*Loneliness, Pain, Tears*—sorry, not a good title), masks, drills through heads, lots of sharp objects through lots of heads, heads being pulled off, lots of flowing hair (what's hair got to do with it?), heads in vises.

Children's migraine art, experts say, has essential diagnostic value. Some children are lucky and have parents in the know. Oliver Sacks went to his mother to tell her about his first auras, for instance: "She was a doctor," he notes, and "a migraineur," too, and knew the score. Other children make it obvious: a two-year-old with her head burrowed into your hip to keep out the light, bursting into tears in response to sounds you barely notice. But most migraining children escape attention. One headache specialist describes asking an elementary school classroom to draw their heads: three out of twenty kids drew shafts, arrows, something sharp and undefinable, piercing the head, on its way in, on its way out. Drawings like these can be found in the pages of *Migraine Art,* or in the *Journal of Childhood Neurology.* The familiar images: a hammer hitting the head, a vise. And some less familiar: a head divided, like a checkerboard, into black and white squares. A head filled with a swirl like a two-toned lollipop. Crown of thorns. Fire. Bomb. Kid's giant head on road, a truck slightly smaller than the head bearing down. Says *truck* on the side. Smiling face, the word *softly* scrawled alongside. Something, two bodies, stick figures and oval heads twined together with something else, maybe a third body.

There's 3,902 hits on flickr.com for the search "migraine"— people wincing, or as if caught in uncomfortable sleep, or red-rimmed eyes, or, frankly, just sad-looking. Somber photos of pharmaceuticals, some efforts at kaleidoscopic forms, and a couple where the face, the head, the upper body, is trapped behind a spidery frame, or tied up with something. Processions of heads, heads lying down, shinerish eyes, heads in hands, sometimes just the hands, titles like *15/365 Fifth Migraine in Two Weeks,* just a head poking out of covers wrapped around a fetal body, lying on the floor of the bathroom, a toilet right center, and in front of the toilet, a little three-eyed black monster doll (a note says he's called "stealthy ninja pain"). It's a good picture. *Migraine Office,* quite good, a venetian blind and painting, an ordinary wall, but a shimmer and distortion, like heat distortion but vertical and diagonal as much, if not more than, vertical.

On youtube: a short film called *Migraine,* a young woman suffering from migraine, this suffering conveyed on the soundtrack by what sounds like a muffled human heartbeat. In response to a neighbor braying, "You poor thing, you must be burning up," our heroine chokes her and feels relief, which leads her, during her next attack, to stab that same neighbor to death and feel even greater relief. "It most likely goes without saying that I think this film is awesome," notes one commentator.

In comix, there's Migraine Boy, the protagonist of the eponymous cartoon *Migraine Boy.* He's low-tech, always drawn with gritted teeth, a single line representing a single eyebrow, and pain lines radiating from the top of his head like gnarled musical notes. He's easily irritated: responding to a question like "What are you doing there, 'migraine boy'?" he might say, "I'm mowing the god-damn lawn! What does it look like? It's bad enough I've got this @*!?#!@?!! headache, now I have to deal with *your* questions?!" But it's not the text that makes *Migraine Boy,* it's the subtext: it looks like it was drawn *during* a migraine, the large heads swelling atop bodies that the artist barely bothered (or could barely bother) to draw, the deader than deadpan humor, the casual mutilation of bodies, especially from the neck up.

After his head is chopped off by executioners, Migraine Boy cheerfully exclaims, "Hey my headache's gone!"

It is just so hard for anything really deep and true to leak through the mesh, though, and that's no one's fault. Many of the photographs lie: if they are self-portraits, the migraineur had the strength and the sense to pose for the shot, and if they are not self-portraits, then there is someone in the room taking the pictures instead of helping the woman on the floor. Many of the painters lie, because what they represent they represent in retrospection: you can't paint well with a migraine, and you can't really remember one, either. The films almost always show someone having a migraine—reaching for pills, stumbling along, throwing up—while the video attempts to simulate the distortion of vision associated with migraine. And that's false artistic economy, feeding right off the heart of the problem: how does one create an objective portrait of a deluded perception of an experience when the deluded perception is part of the experience?

But this, too, is really no one's fault. The fault, again, lies with the subject. Photographers, painters, other artists, even children have searched for metaphor, have tried to say something indirectly. The prone body, a reminder of the near-deathness of the migraine experience. All those blown and fragmented heads, trying to speak to the sense that migraine feels like a cataclysm. Migraine is a kind of explosion, and the paintings of such almost always try to catch that moment when the head blows, when it collapses, when it tears apart, when it is penetrated or overwhelmed, that split second, that orgasm of pain. But it's another lie: migraines go on for hours and hours, if not days and days, and there is no easy way to paint, film, photograph, or write about monotonous pain.

Do not undervalue the headache.

4
———

I start to stutter, meander. Talking to Siobhán about a babysitter, for instance, I say, *No chores extra, paying him to do.* It is not forgetfulness or a tired tongue. Someone inside me is saying that.

Or, while typing, I suddenly discover that I'm not striking (or striking hard enough) certain keys, vowels, not consonants: *i* especially, but *e* and sometimes *a*, too. So what inspires this? I stop and write in longhand this note to myself, which I don't understand to this day: *Something a little more brainy, less fingery, something I can't quite see or emphasize the way I might otherwise.* Then, when I start typing again: the vowels return, but *t* and *r* and *s* disappear.

Feelings of confusion in speech and thought during migraine have fascinated medical researchers over the last two centuries. Hermann Lebert, a nineteenth-century German physician, made a tremendous list of his own confoundings: "incoherence of ideas and difficulty in finding words"; "strange and wandering . . . mind"; "double-consciousness"; "the past and present confounded"; and (my favorite, and Aedan's, too) "feeling silly."

Liveing collected portraits of men and women who couldn't write what they intended: "Instead of the words *fifty dollars, being one half-year's rate,*" one patient complained, he wrote "the words *fifty dollars, through the salvation of Bra*—." Oliver Sacks, in *Migraine,* similarly transcribes stories from migraineurs whose worlds come undone: "He finds it very difficult, for example, to tell the time from looking at his watch. He must first gaze at one hand, then at the other."

Freud isolated the confusion he experienced before and during his migraines as perhaps the most striking element of the entire syndrome: "The mild attacks of migraine from which I still suffer, usually announce themselves hours in advance by my forgetting names, and at the height of these attacks," he told one correspondent, "it frequently happens that all proper names go out of my head."

Liveing saw mistakes like this as neutral physiological disturbances, accepting his patient's claim that "I cannot recollect any perception or business which I had to transact that could, by means of an obscure influence, have produced this phenomenon." But Freud did not: proper names, he wrote, are forgotten "when the name itself touches something unpleasant." And the wrong words pass one's lips, he claimed, for a "more remote psychic motive."

I'd like to believe Freud, but I suspect Liveing has got a point: the migraine does release a repressed self, but not the way you'd think. Mostly, it is a reminder of the anarchy that lurks just inside of us, a formlessness, or better, a form as yet indecipherable. Migraine inspires a sense of systemic incoherence, and sometimes it feels like a worldview. And because migraine cannot really do anything lastingly bad to me, this, instead, is what worries me most: I'm a pretty sharp guy, but there are times when I am, well, not too sharp. Not sharp at all, in fact. And there is something about migraine that one feels in the grip of something larger, not just the headaches, or even the aura, but a general syndrome, what neurologists call a psychopathology, an organic propensity, a fucked-up nervous system, a brain on the fritz.

Are the words slow to come? I ask myself. Then why? And when they do come, why do they seem to come from a faraway place, muffled, half silenced before they are even uttered? Do I, from time to time, slur my sentences, mumble, do I hear ringing in my ears, feel a trapdoor open in the brain stem somewhere and a little, unmistakable, melting of some kind? Everyone feels these things, of course: everyone has on days and off days. But now I think about migraine and wonder if my on days and off days are more profound than those experienced by non-migraineurs (or that their on days and off days are migrainous, too, and they just don't know it), if the whole topography of sharp and flat, major and minor, that makes up a human life is all about these miniscule chemical altercations, and is completely out of our control.

Nerve-Storm

Sick headache, real or feigned, is now firmly established in your home; and it proceeds to play its part. . . . O perfidious headache! O fascinating headache!

—HONORE DE BALZAC,
The Physiology of Marriage

1

In certain cultures, Elaine Scarry observes, professional torturers use household objects as implements of pain-giving. By taking objects that were designed to provide comfort and using them to inflict pain, the torturer "unmake(s)" the victim's world, unmakes the home, unmakes civilization itself.

Analogies between political violence and chronic pain traumas require many leaps in comparison and context. But they do share some essentials. Pain that appears when your loved ones appear, when you enter the light, when you hear noise, the routine noises of the microwave oven, the radio, the vacuum cleaner, the icemaker—this kind of pain makes you loathe civilization and becomes political, even if it has no conscious agenda. The politics of migraine is one of isolation, of the soul retreating from the made world. Robert A. Davidoff, in his textbook *Migraine,* writes about olfactory triggers that migraineurs are "literally tortured" by perfumes, soaps, detergents. One senses a little extra, untextbooklike intensity in his voice (he's got migraines, too, like many doctors), something that traces the outline of something deep and hard to say: that loved ones, friends, the incidental sensory stimuli of American culture, are what hurt.

In that sense, no one can really turn off what hurts a migraineur, and no one really wants to. The random migraineur's abject frustration with the fresh scent of Dove detergent is just a small representation of the problem, that migraineurs in midattack require the world to be emptied out. What would it mean to respect such a demand? Millions of Popes with millions of screens, an almost dazzling burden to the economy of the nation and the psychic economy of all those households. Davidoff, instead, refers to the "sensible" decision of migraineurs to withdraw upon onset, to seek a dark, quiet room. This, too, multiplied by millions, becomes a kind of spontaneous public policy. The migraining man, the migraining woman, should be not seen or heard. And they don't want to be seen or heard; they don't want to see or hear you.

2

After a month of daily migraines, hours if not days of disabling head pain, nausea, my life took on a deranged normalcy. The days became a dream landscape, with some strange symbolic fixtures present from dream to dream: a dark room, a pillow, a cold compress, or worse, an ugly ritual, the rise out of bed, followed by a half-blind walk through a world occluded at times by an unsteady (and quite beautiful) dance of gray-inflected iridescent stars. In the evening, the dream dissipated, displaced by a shocked calm that itself took on as many forms as the headache itself. Then, sleep, until the daily cycle renewed itself in the shards of dawn.

The list of foods that made me sick increased: one need only throw up a piece of chocolate four or five times before its sweetness loses its charm, but there's something vastly more sinister when one's stomach starts rejecting inoffensive staples like apples and toast. On the bad mornings, I might have to move around on all fours. On the good mornings, I would go to work and run errands, but I was intermittently dangerous: is a migraineur behind the wheel of a car as impaired as a drunk, a cell phone user, some otherwise preoccupied soul behind the same wheel, or not impaired at all? There's no Breathalyzer for migraine, no machine that can measure the intensity of your attack, but this is what you're probably thinking, as you make that turn: am I really supposed to pull over for a *headache?* For a fit of nausea? For an aura, as one migraineur told me, that turns a STOP sign into an OP sign? You think you might, you even sense the horrendous ethical problem, you know you should rethink the journey, but who's going to believe you? So you probably don't.

This is the ironic consequence of living in a culture that undervalues your headache: just as there's no privileged seat for you at the table, there's no active disapproval at those times when you actually need it.

Soon there was just this little extra madness in the air, just a flirt of something. Early, still August, and the left side of my vision clouded over like a snowstorm, more blurring than blocked, and *irritating*—I can't explain it, but it really angered me, so bad I almost wanted to punch myself. I was slowing down, too, missing my cues. Standing in the center aisle of a pharmacy, blinking into its lights, forgetting what I wanted or even how I got there. At home, Aedan peppering me with shrewd, trigger-happy questions: Why does Indianapolis have a Michigan Street and a Michigan Road? Or: How does that work, how does that work, how does that work, how does that work, pointing, in order, at an air conditioner, at a film projector, at a pizza oven, at, I don't know what, a table leg. Or: How do you make that, how do you make that, how do you make that, how do you make that, pointing at a wall, at a television, at a rug, at a favorite toy. He enjoyed the cadence; his world was wide open, waiting. But I couldn't follow: the wall, the what, the what else? I could almost see the questions in the air in front of me, zigzagging like hummingbirds, un-catchable. I felt terrifically guilty—and stripped of something really valuable.

As a husband, as a father, as someone to work alongside, I became something different, not-very-nice, edgy. I learned how limited Didion's or Davidoff's otherwise excellent advice was: you can only spend hours in bed communing with your migraine before other communal yearnings and obligations drive you from bed into some halfway house of ineptly ex-ecuted domesticity, work, and society. You run on autopilot for a while, and then you realize that not even the autopilot is functioning. And then someone tells you what's obvious. A September barbeque at a friend's house, for instance: a slow dusk, Aedan and three other kids wedged happily inside a small plastic-and-cedar clubhouse across a leafy backyard from the porch where the grown-ups sat. A perfect old suburban porch with boards missing and a large cat dozing half visible in one of the openings, a neighbor on his roof hammering down shingles (hailstorm the week before) as the sun went down, and this menu: steak, salad, gin and tonics, s'mores.

I sat in a deep Adirondack chair at the edge of the patio, while the adults swirled around the barbeque, the table, and the children. My headache was done for the day, but I still felt submerged in something viscous. I said a few things, took a gin and tonic, but didn't drink it, took a s'more, but didn't eat it, let the conversation drift in and out of my reach. Then someone said Poor Andy, and it was certainly meant well, but I heard something different. I was a ghost: people talked about me in front of me. I didn't want to imagine what I looked like. It was at that point I decided that I didn't want anyone else to know about the migraines. It wasn't a plan, it was an instinct: keep away from people unless I could act like one of them.

3
___

At home, no such luck. A schedule evolved, since the migraines were now coming like clockwork. Banned from Imitrex, I perfected my synthesis of ice, of tea, of steam. Some mornings, it worked; some, not. Aedan kept watch for the ice pack: he knew by heart that it meant a jagged end to play. And Siobhán responded with a slightly different combination of resentment and tenderness. There is a love story here, too. Let's get to it.

Honore de Balzac, in *The Physiology of Marriage* (1895), put it bluntly. "Sick headache," he wrote, wasn't just a "weapon" in the battle of the sexes. It was the "queen of maladies," the best "weapon," the "easiest of all maladies to simulate." But

Balzac wasn't sure what else he wanted to say: he called them "at once the most pleasant and the most terrible weapon which women can employ" (he never conceived that men might have them), both "fascinating" and "perfidious." He wasn't sure if they were "real or feigned." But it didn't matter. Balzac was interested in effect, not cause (not a bad way to look at migraines), and the effect was this: the headaches set agendas. They silenced men, rich or poor, powerful or powerless. They got a woman out of her social duties, let her get up and take a walk whenever she felt like it. They were, to Balzac, clearly political: "It seizes her when she likes," he wrote, "where she likes, for as long as she likes."

From inside the migraining brain, of course, Balzac seems out of his mind: no one *likes* a migraine, no one *chooses* to get one. But his point: if marriage is even partly politics, an ongoing series of negotiations over power and resources, then migraine, like any chronic disease, is a real declaration. And, as the migraineur, I am the one who declares war. I am the aggressor, even as I am the victim.

And if marriage is not politics—if marriage is a love bond, a sacred and erotic sharing—what then? What exactly are you promising when you promise to wed yourself to someone forever? The vows (and migraineurs love to talk about those vows) say that you promise to stand by through sickness let alone health, but, really, isn't there an implicit promise to get what you test drove during the courtship? If you were sickly, chronic, and got the offer, then didn't your beloved accept the sickness as part of the grand contract? If you weren't, but became sick afterward, then who breaks the bargain when the marriage breaks down: the one who implicitly promised health but became sick, or the one who resents having taken the vow to stand by?

I think we know that some of us believe the promise is all, but for others the answer is complicated by fine print. The deterioration of the body is inevitable, so the only people who are going to miss watching their loved ones get sick and die are the ones who die young (and vice versa). But the fine print is where guilt lies, where the promises splinter into smaller promises, and no one escapes that. I honored the contract, but my migraine didn't. I might as well have shown up at the house driving a pink Cadillac, one I bought by emptying out our bank account—the transformation is no less drastic, no less destructive.

The changes, at first, were subtle, almost ambient. Siobhán expecting me to be in one place, when I was in another: how often we-in-marriage compute silently to ourselves a set of probabilities about where the other person is. Those patterns, suddenly disrupted, recomputed: Hey Andy? Yeah? You in the kitchen? No. Never mind, then.

Then the misplacements turn into little absences. A family of three starts to become a family of two. Here is the scene, and there, in the background, you can see me passing through it, on my way to bed, fiercely scowling at the angry sun, like the spirit in one of those accidental photos people use to prove the paranormal. Aedan, kicking a soccer ball past Siobhán and hitting the garage door used as a makeshift goal, Siobhán not really exerting: "Mommy," Aedan says cheerfully, "you're the worst soccer goalie ever!" Siobhán, hands on hips, flicker of a smirk, flicker of her Irish accent: "Well, thank you very much." Aedan kicks again, scores again, Siobhán, punching the air stagily, through clenched teeth, because this time she was trying: "Curses!" she says, like a silent movie villain.

That little black-and-white soccer ball, the trail of iridescent gray it leaves . . .

Then a slightly larger tear. Migraine can transform a marriage—but not, as one might expect, because the headache-free spouse can't empathize, can't "feel" the pain. Migraine transforms marriages because the headache-free spouse can't understand the pain *aversion,* the hard fact that he or she is now married to one of those lab monkeys who gets a diabolical shock every time a certain button is pressed—and because there is no way for the migraining spouse, in turn, to make things right in the marriage while still avoiding all those malicious triggers.

Siobhán listened to me, absolutely, as I tried to describe to her what was going on; she held my head, stroked it abstractly, gazed up at my blank forehead as if something might be written there. She let me stay in bed, kept watch, brought me water, steamed the rice. But such grace, no matter how much I valued it, did not mean that she could see inside my brain or sacrifice her own life to the action there, which looked to her, of course, exactly like inaction. And so, at the same time, we fought new fights, too: over conversations I'd suddenly truncate, errands I'd suddenly decline to run. We fought over light switches, window blinds. I wanted them off and down, and she on and up.

It sounds like a joke, but it really isn't. There was, obviously, a disruption of physical intimacy, but not where you think. We did, oh, all the usual things: the story of migraine and human touch, migraine and eros, is exactly what you think it might be, a story of rainchecks and deferrals. But you'd be amazed how much migraines also love that stuff, how much, at the right times—those plains of relief after the headache, for instance— they can make a simple hug thrill your shoulder blades, or a kiss to the temple send a blissful shock down your carotid. Light and sound, though, are also both fantastically sensual— and that's where the damage occurred. We no longer saw, felt, heard, the same sensory world. This sounds small, but what marriage would long endure one partner who craved light and one who craved dark, one talk, the other silence?

We fought, absolutely: this was, in a very real way, not personal. No one in this marriage ever stopped analyzing anything. That was our deal—we are smart, neurotic people, and that's what we do. I married her, I think, because at some point it became clear that she would never stop being beautiful and never stop being funny. We fell in love talking, telling jokes, and even after ten years of marriage, we spend so much time together that it's easy to miss the fact that we don't know how to bore each other. But I married her for her bullshit detector, too, which is always ticking, always kept oiled and ready to hum, part of the never-be-boring karma: if I tell her she's beautiful or funny, for instance, she'll say, "I'm not," her voice getting husky, "Are you a bloody lunatic?" Nothing gets by her—no television mystery solved more than halfway through the hour, guaranteed—including this: Was this migrainy interruption in our lives something I was making, employing conveniently for my own uses? Was it a marker, a sign that I wasn't all I was cracked up to be? Was it, well, real?

Her anger was every bit as authentic as the humor, or her compassion. But it was not exactly directed at me, but around me, at some target just over my shoulder, I think, toward the migraine itself. If I told her I was having another migraine, disappearing for another afternoon: "For God's sake," she'd say. If I said I had none: "Get out of town!" she'd say jovially. She hated the missed dinners out, the friends I didn't host, and would try a rough joke as salve: a Victorian heroine, she might say, that's what you are, practically winking me into the bedroom for my daily slump. But after the missed dinner or the friends I didn't host, she'd introduce potential diagnoses for what was wrong with me, not instantly wrong or right (some would be right, in the end, and some not), but sounding like old grievances warmed up in the microwave: You work too hard (on a new book, not this one), she might say. You don't work hard enough (I was getting some release time). It was worth a shot.

But all that—that was just the warming up, the stretching exercises. One day—it took maybe three weeks, maybe a month—we each began to sense a new normal. Her solicitude began to fade, and so did the fights. Instead, a new routine emerged, especially on those days when Siobhán worked a little late and I had to look after Aedan. I could do it—this is precisely the kind of thing one decides to do no matter what. But it was a bad caricature of our lives before, when looking after Aedan in the afternoon was part of the basic economy between myself and Siobhán, and where the time spent with him was pleasant, desultory, especially in the downtime just after school. I just couldn't do the play, for instance, the elevation changes where you lower yourself to the floor to get down to kid level, to move the plastic dinosaurs and the action figures in their amiable pantomimes: this was literally nauseating. I left him to watch television more. He didn't complain, but I felt fantastically guilty—he on the floor, me on the sofa, blanket around my head, watchful, sure, but not as much a father or even a babysitter as another inert toy in Aedan's collection. Every fifteen minutes or half hour, the guilt would rouse me to play with him for five minutes, shuffle the toys around, read a book, make him a snack, go out to the driveway to ride a bike, feed the pretend animals, or play hide-and-seek dizzily in the overgrown bushes out back.

And then, even worse: Siobhán half an hour late, an hour late, and all I wanted was relief. I resented the lateness, as slight as it was, I hated the guilt about how I was treating Aedan, but none of it compared to the desire for relief, the absolute carnal, primal desire to dive into a dark, silent bed. By the time Siobhán returned, by the time I heard her at the door, I was already up, already moving to the bed, already moving past her in the hall, her startled, disappointed, hurt. She calls this phase Babysitters Passing in the Night, and remembers it better than anything (as do I).

Or: if there was one thing Siobhán really hated, it was not what you think. Siobhán's soft spot, her ritual: she loves to tell the news of her day, a headline-filled battery of staged outrage at the foolishness of others that bursts out for five or ten minutes before turning into an excited dialogue, then a calm, good-natured one. For her, it's a big part of the social contract of marriage: share my day, she says, I'll share yours. These conversations now took place in darker rooms, often on days where I did not need to rush to the bedroom (or did, but felt too guilty to do it). And I began missing my cues there, too, looking at something in the distance, even wishing she would wrap it up. My unresponsiveness was unmistakable. And when I said it was because I had a migraine, because to me it seemed she had completely forgotten, did not know what I was going through, would not possibly talk this way if she was cognizant of how my head felt, she would respond, sharply, *yes,* I know.

We fought over the fact that I didn't listen to her very well, which was absolutely true. The phrase "you don't listen to me" has become such a cliché of modern romances in middle age that it was almost startling to hear the claim employed in a situation where it possessed complete accuracy and some freshness. But it went somewhere deeper, too. After a while, it became clear that without those bursts of early evening conversation, Siobhán lost some of her balance. What she needed from me wasn't a fair split on the chores (which I obsessively tried to provide) but a partner in smoothing out all the small tensions of the everyday, the ones that mounted until you blew them away, dandelion petals, in the cool and the clear of an Indiana evening. I was messing with the physiology of our marriage, something I had never contractually promised but had evolved on its own over two thousand days and nights. And, truthfully, no one else was really helping her. No one really showed her any sympathy, or took her very seriously—it's just a headache, no one's going to die, they reasoned, it's just not tangible enough.

It's not necessarily that hard to be the spouse of a migraineur, who upon onset can just go to bed and who probably doesn't even *want* attention. But I had gone missing, and the only word I can envision to describe Siobhán's situation was *deserted*. Truthfully, though, I'm not sure where I left her. I *can* tell you what she did with her days—her work, her friends, her hobbies. I *can* recite the facts: I know that someone telling a realistic narrative and trying to provide all perspectives would want to do that. But she's been through enough already. And it would be a false move, anyway: it would make you think that we weren't growing apart. And we were. It would make you think I knew what was going on. And I didn't.

You really need to picture her in silhouette, if you want to know the truth. That's how the migraine makes you see other people, even the ones you love. You need to see her at the edge of the bed, framed by the curtains. You don't need to see, or hear, anything that even implies, or subliminally gives the impression, that we saw things eye-to-eye, that I understood her any better than she understood me, or that the arrangement was fair and square.

"It wasn't *that* bad," she'll tell me later, when we finally start the business of figuring out what it was, "and you don't need to be that melodramatic." Then she'll add: "I was so lonely," but in a farcical melodramatic voice. Then a certain fierceness in her expression, maybe something else, maybe resignation, frustration, a redness around the rims of her eyes, and I change the subject.

Nights were more animated. Siobhán is pretty sweeping in her surface disregard of the invisible sources of discomfort. To a pulled muscle in her own back, for instance, she might yelp—*ow!*—and then turn around and look down over her own shoulder blade doubtfully, as if she thought she might see the gremlin that pinched her. Once she admits the possibility of ailment, in child, adult, or nation (she's a political scientist), though, she will want to trace its source and root it out, a process that requires inspections of the house, hour-long Google searches, consultations with experts, the whole range of worry, the whole postmodern electronic exorcism that follows.

For me and Siobhán, the intimacy we lost at four in the afternoon could sometimes be regained at eight at night—but transformed. This could be weirdly wonderful sometimes. In the evenings, after my headaches passed, we would sit in our living room in shadows and try to figure out why this was happening, wondering aloud about what, in our environment, was causing my headaches, and whether it could be causing her back pain, too, and Aedan's allergies as well, some kind of unified field theory of what was wrong with all of us. Is it in the chimney, in the trees? The streaks of algae on the side of the house? The house itself, which is painted blue and feels underwater anyway?

Not only did the conversation restore some warmth to our circle, but it reminded us of the other times we worried as a team, of how one of the reasons we married was that we were such good worriers together. Her nursing Aedan at three weeks old at 4 A.M., her red hair and sharp brown eyes melting into the half-dark, the gentle conflagration of her personality washing off her as plain as the aura traces described by Tibetan monks. And me sitting with the laptop on the floor, manically typing "infant sniffles" or "infant fever red cheeks" into Google, looking for the trip wire that would send us scrambling to the emergency room, both of us feeling crazily alive and in love with each other and with Aedan in the moment we let our overprotectiveness run a little wild.

I want to tell you that I tried every drug, contacted every specialist. I owed it. As the twentieth-century sociologist Talcott Parsons wrote, there is a social contract between a sick person and a sick person's audience (of readers, of friends, of coworkers, of loved ones). The sick person "should be regarded as the victim of forces beyond his control." In exchange for this grace, however, which includes "exemption from ordinary daily obligations and expectations," the sick person has to acknowledge that "being sick is undesirable and that measures should be taken to maximize the chance to facilitate recovery." A straightforward deal. But I didn't honor it: I tried the drugs I was given, the obvious ancient cures (tea, steam, etc.), kept my follow-ups with my GP. But that's all I did.

It is hard to explain why. I might point to another part of Parsons's contract, the idea that illness is equated with deviancy, with, at least, the need to adapt, and tell you that I felt ashamed and confused. I might tell you that I was depressed, exhausted. I might tell you that I was hopeful, that I woke up every morning believing that this was the morning where those shuffling nerves and blood vessels under my brow would make a commitment to relax. I might tell you that I was looking for something else, and that my brain was probably too flooded with blood and electricity to know exactly what it was.

I obsessed on the importance of having this headache in private, on making it as invisible as I could to other people. I told myself, over and over, I can make it through this, it's going to end right now, it's going to end at sunrise tomorrow. But I also began to contemplate the possibility that this was a new permanent state. Virtually every migraine sufferer has a story of "toughing it out": precisely because a migraine cannot do anything lastingly bad to you, no bar exists to stop you from trying to complete the most mundane task, like cleaning the kitchen or changing a baby's diapers, while maddened with head pain. So I toughed it out in critical passages throughout my day. A fight with Aedan: just when I think there must be more headaches, he insists there must be more play, so we compromise, two hours at Toys 'R' Us as it tilted wildly to one side (Aedan was showered with toys during these four months, for reasons too obvious to mention). Ninety minutes in a supervisor's office trying to squint past his godawful fluorescents. Classtime: my student evaluations in this migrainy era became schizophrenic, some students finding me "brilliant," others "incoherent." There's more than one story there, no doubt.

But everything keyed around that grim period from five to eight in the morning where I tinkered with everything from the Vicodin to the bowls of rice (good for the starch, better for the steam), desperately trying to outlast the headache before wife and son awoke, and everything domestic would be tainted by my pain, and the workday would start with this colossal companion occupying my skull. I was just trying not to disappear. It became kind of a job, and a job I wasn't doing very well.

Enlightenment, Part 2

The Brain—is wider than the Sky—

—EMILY DICKINSON

1

October 6: some mornings are fine, a cool surprise, but there's always a foreboding. This is amazing weather, highs in the low nineties, fat brown leaves swirling in the pseudotropical breeze, no drugs, a little breakfast, some cereal and bread, then a noontime run with Siobhán, Aedan, and the out-of-town guests to an apple orchard, Ida Red and Golden Delicious, and a gorgeous picnic, grilled corn-on-the-cob and bratwurst (you just can't not eat around guests, they look at you like you're crazy), then the drive home, and on the drive, an odd feeling across the front of my face. It could be numbness, but it feels as if my nose and brow were made of wax and had been left out in the sun too long.

It's not a bad feeling, but certainly a strange one, and within two hours it resolves itself into a thick, throbbing pain like a band across my forehead, a little between the eyes, a little alongside the left eye socket, a little on the left temple, just a grace note there. Lots and lots of nausea. I'll weigh three-and-a-half pounds less when this one's done, and one of the out-of-town guests will wish aloud the following day that she could get migraines with weight-loss results like that.

I try a nap, which comes in beats and provides beats of relief—then up to look after Aedan for a while, and at this point (we're about 4 P.M. now, the headache starting around 2:30), it's clear that this is going nowhere. Light is not just uncomfortable, it's positively searing, the monochromatic glow of a 75-watt bulb dancing like lightning. Aedan is playing a game that involves a lot of climbing and wrestling, then Siobhán is up from her nap and I give her the report, and go to bed for what will turn out to be eighteen hours.

I dig up an old Imitrex, just past its expiration date, swallow it down, and then lie still, looking at the clock, hoping the Imitrex will start to work. Ten minutes, then twenty, then thirty, I'm telling myself that I gotta give the Imitrex forty-five minutes at least, but this is a bad one, and by the time the clock reaches an hour, I start to worry. I have to tell myself that this will end at some point.

I try to feel the pain. It's actually better to do this sometimes. It's a galloping throb that comes in runs, bu-duh, bu-duh, bu-duh, actually not too intense but so steady and so quick and, mixed with the nausea, I start to panic. Panic, I have found, is even harder to describe than pain.

I have to tell myself to take it easy. This works better than you think.

The bed is cool, the pillows soft—any light is searing, though. Siobhán brings a bowl of rice and then takes the guests out, alone, for mussels and fries. I'm not touching that rice, as plain as it may be. Then there is a long nothingness. Bu-duh, bu-duh, bu-duh. What else can I say? There's no vocabulary for monotonous pain.

By ten or eleven, the migraine lifts, it rises like leavened bread and grows light and airy, and then floats away.

2

And then there was something else. Amid the pain and the visions and the damaging transformation of my personal life came a sneaky dose of enlightenment. What a migraine induces remains a stunning testament to what Emily Dickinson meant when she wrote, "The Brain—is wider than the Sky—" In themselves, migraines seem to pull back curtains on everyday life: just before the pain, a remarkable moment of clarity; just after the pain, a feeling of relief so intense it borders on the unearthly.

What to say about the auras, for instance? What are they? Visions, hallucinations? Something in between? Once experienced, one ever after feels a certain surreality at the heart of things. One talks, drives, works, kisses, as a curtain of fire moves from left to right, as the sky turns into Guernica. Normalcy seems paper thin after one aura—after dozens, it wears right through.

Whatever it is, though, when the combination of disorientation and aura gels, it can shake open new worlds. And this "shaking open" became an essential event for me, a timed chemical process one could no more control than religious possession, its very uncontrollability part of its beauty. One November day, for instance, I was standing in the supermarket express lane, my items on the belt, and realized I had forgotten a crucial item: the American cheese, the only cheese I could eat, the only cheese Aedan, like many four-year-olds, *would* eat. So I made my excuses to the cashier, a wry middle-aged man with a droopy mustache and strange droopy eyeglasses that matched, and ran across the store to the cheese section, and then ran back to the checkout. In the background, k.d. lang's "Constant Craving" played: *Maybe a great magnet pulls all souls toward truth / Or maybe it is life itself,* she sang. Behind her, I heard the mysterious low hum of supermarkets everywhere.

The exercise was slight but sufficient to induce migraine. As I reached the checkout, I saw my food and the cashier. He smiled. But everything was soon blocked by a tall tower of iridescent light that reached to the ceiling of the store: that shimmering weirdness always seemed to love the high ceilings and lighting of American big box retail stores. I was relaxed enough to take a good look at it, which I rarely did, and it was peculiarly beautiful and unstable: small, fluid bars of colorful light stacked roughly upon each other, that little gray inflection, all backlit like stained glass and jittery like the inside of a broken kaleidoscope.

"How are you, sir?" the cashier asked.

"Good question," I answered. "How are you?" I asked. Perhaps he was having a migraine headache at exactly that moment, I wondered. It has happened. It is happening all the time.

He was fine, though, or at least, so he said. The tower of iridescence swayed. The hum behind k.d. lang disappeared. *Constant craving*, she sang, *has always been.* And then, I had a thought that came as uninvited as that aura or the pain that would soon follow: this moment as easily as any other, this world as easily as any other. And I felt something more, too, something deeper, something that fit the politics of the migraine, the way it was seeping into my subconscious and shaping my view of the world. I felt a sudden conviction that all this noise—the bright lights and the brightly colored food packages, the scrape of money in register and card in machine, the lives around me, my life, too—was as unstable and as impermanent as that strange tower. I didn't really know what the origin of that observation was, couldn't trace it to something inside me. But it took up my whole brain.

Everything stilled wonderfully. And then the tower swayed again, and then it crashed, and my normal vision was restored. And I knew, as I knew every other time it happened, that I better get home and get ready for what would come next.

3

This happens to me more than I can imagine. I have a headache, and I'm on my way to the bank to deposit a check, and as I stand at the kiosk, I look up and to the right—away from the pain—toward a shard of gray sky lolling over the fluorescent bank icon (a single letter, blue and white, all squares and triangles, endearingly like something from an aura), the brown brickwork, and suddenly, it seems imaginable to me that life is a miracle, something I can't explain, but something I shouldn't spend standing at the ATM. This is not, again—it never is—a conscious, structured thought—even my paraphrase is a sort of fiction—but the feeling of intense alienation coupled with intense pleasure that this other place exists, even in glimpses, even if it is chemicals altercating (even better that it is chemicals altercating), even the pain, all of this, is, unmistakably, part of what generates the moment.

In this case, no worse migraine follows. The headache recedes, and with it, the strange feeling. Which I keep to myself. Oliver Sacks observes a case study where a husband describes "'greater depth and speed and acuity of thought'" during his auras: "'I keep recalling things long forgotten, visions of earlier days will spring to my mind.'" His wife, however, "is less impressed with them; she remarks that during his auras her husband 'walks back and forth, talks in a repetitive manner in a sort of monotone; he seems to be in a trance.'"

It is not just hard to explain the pain of migraine. It is hard to explain the pleasures, too.

Or there is this: I've gotten so used to interference, discomfort, and outright pain inside my head, and a dimness, a bleariness if not an actual blockage, in my vision, that when nothing is going wrong—when there is clarity—I don't actually recognize it at first. But then I do, and it stuns me. It is the opposite of the disorientation that begins many migraines: a reorientation, a joy, an implicit relief as the senses clear and the world comes back into focus.

These are really *good* moments, good in a moral sense, and one can't help but be thankful to the migraines for them. They could not possibly exist without the contrast. The high, pure sounds of the mandolins, banjos, slide guitars, not just any but fine antiques, the finish kept to a high gloss, the sun glinting off them through the open door of the barn (there is nothing about sunlight reflected off the blond finish of an antique musical instrument that can tempt a migraine into onset), played in public only at special events like All-American Music Day at the Indiana State Fair, for instance, and not really played all that well. But instruments like this play so clearly that even the missed notes are somehow pure on a surprisingly cool and dry

August morning, the men in overalls and plain cotton shirts and jeans, the women in genuine calico dresses meditatively peering down on their music stands through Ben Franklin–style bifocals, all this wood and the smell of the hay and the Polish sausage and the ironsmith and his bellows and there is nothing you can't take in.

All this elation, of course, is Migraine 101: feelings of transcendence have been a recorded part of the migraine experience since the Middle Ages. Nine centuries ago, the Abbess of Bingen, Hildegard, described her spiritual visions, and twentieth-century observers have been struck by their resemblance to common migraine auras: "I saw a great star, splendid and beautiful . . . and with that star came a great multitude of shining sparks, which followed the star toward the south . . . they were all extinguished and were changed into black cinders . . . precipitated into the abyss and vanished from my sight."

Various observers have noted that auras have many characteristics that overlap with mystic experience. This isn't always visual: novelist Siri Hustvedt beautifully describes "a powerful internal sensation of being pulled upward, as if my head were rising, even though I knew my feet hadn't left the ground . . . accompanied by what can only be called awe—a feeling of transcendence." As Richard Grossinger notes, auras also often trip feelings of déjà vu and jamais vu, as well as "sometimes an intimation of being more than one person" (like Linnaeus) "or having access to separate minds." Podoll and Robinson have noted that the migraine itself, particularly its onset, produces "the idea of a presence": "I have a feeling of emptiness and being able to see into the back of my eyes," one of their cases observed. "A feeling of someone or something standing just behind my left shoulder, but when I turn around, it's still just behind me out of view."

And at the exit, too, countless observers have noted the elation afterward, the extra surge of insight that often accompanies the end of the migraine. Virginia Woolf, arising from a three-week headache, once described herself as feeling "like sand which a wave has uncovered." "I'm not sure that there isn't some religious cause at the back of them," she added: "I see my own worthlessness and failure so clearly . . . and then one gets up and everything begins again and its all covered over." Madhuleema Chaliha, in a 2003 essay, writes that "a migraine almost always goes away leaving a strange feeling of wholeness inside my mind . . . it is the most destructive poison that I know of that contains within itself the seeds of regeneration."

This is the even-handedness of migraine. On the one hand, it does inspire those feelings of powerlessness, of a confusion beyond the ordinary, that so fascinated Freud and Liveing. But on the other, it also inspires feelings of intense power and clarity so coherent one can also call it a worldview. The descriptions of aura symptoms tend toward the otherworldly, but what makes them really remarkable is their mundaneness. If one saw jagged lines in the sky, or felt ten feet tall, or saw ten hands where there should only be a more practical two, and did not know that migraine was involved, then one could only conclude that something supernatural, some rift in the real, was occurring.

But, of course, one knows better: there is no rift in the real. Instead, what it means to be *real* is reimagined. And, in many ways, that's vastly more subversive, because it invites one to contemplate migraine's implication in the long history of vision and awe. How many souls experiencing dynamic visions of blinding light, or transporting passages of joy and wonder, were actually experiencing aura symptoms? In 1995, three German and Swiss headache specialists diagnosed the "thorn in the flesh" experienced by Saint Paul as migraine, the flash of light he saw on the road to Damascus an aura, followed, like many auras, by spiritual elation—his conversion, of course— and three days where, like many migraineurs, he could neither eat nor drink. Has the history of religious vision, then, actually been a neurological history?

And does it really make a difference? What speaks better of God: that He might impose visions on normal human brains from a safe distance, or that He endowed normal human brains with the capacity to experience blinding flashes of light and hallucinatory disorientation, occasionally veiled all around with a transporting sensation of awe, of joy, of clarity?

I suspect most people will answer the former, or, at least, experience disappointment and even despair when confronted with the clinical description of the latter, precisely because it implies that there is no God, just chemical altercations. But the devil, so to speak, lies in the details: where is God, and how does God work in the world, if God works in the world at all? That God might place this capacity to feel something unworldly within the world—within the brain, coded deep in its secret places, triggered not by prayer or passages of doubt but by nitrates or aspartame or desert sun—is this really a bad thing? Contrarily, if one can produce from within deep awe and blind- ing vision, then what might that imply about the need for a God at all? Who needs Him, if we can do this stuff ourselves?

I've talked about this with other migraineurs: how the mi- graines make the clear moments that much clearer, the dark moments that much more unreachable. The migrainous sensi- bility understands life as an oscillation between utterly blocked and utterly clear perceptions of the world, because that's ex- actly how it looks from here.

Reading

Do you know what hemi crania means? A half head ache so—I've been having it for a few days and it is a lovely thing. One half of my head in a mathematical line from the top of my skull to the cleft of my jaw, throbs and hammers and sizzles and bangs and swears while the other half—calm and collected—takes notes of the agonies next door.

—RUDYARD KIPLING, 1886

1

At some point, an illness memoir, if the illness has the right shape and proportion, starts to feel more like a memoir of drug use or religious possession than a tale of physical pain: one side, as Kipling wrote so aptly, possessed; the other side, watching and taking notes.

Around mid-October (seven weeks or so after onset), I turned to religious texts, because the Buddha and Talmud and Christ talk about the head the way the migraines talked to me.

I got a big red Bible, and a big red and black collection of Buddhist writings, and kept them near the creasing sofa where I tended my migraines. And when the day was done and the headache receded, I lifted one or the other to my face and began to read.

One tells oneself, over and over, that the headache is just nerves and blood vessels, but the headache feels so much like an event within the mind that one becomes obsessed with the idea that the mind must be a physical place. It is an obsession characteristic of the migraining imagination, and one which Buddha loved to use as a test to train the still-supple souls of his protégés.

Get the Buddha in here first, in fact, that smug Buddha. He's the man for pain. It seems to me that the migraines accomplish much of what Buddhist teachers hope to accomplish for their pupils with meditation. They clear the mind wonderfully. During a migraine (the worse the better, of course), you will not be thinking about food cravings, or sexual desire, or work anxiety, or all those other worldly matters that calm breathing practices are supposed to sweep from the mind. You will be thinking about the migraine, but even this, somehow, seems right: the Buddhist teachers often recommend focus on some single mantra, some process, some conundrum, some object.

But you can't clear the mind of the migraine. There's no broom for that. For the Buddha, there is a *conditional mind,* the mind that wobbles through this world perceiving imperfectly and worrying about everything, and then there is the *essence of mind,* the timeless consciousness that we all share. This is, of course, incredibly migrainy, or, better, *hemicranic* (see, again, Kipling). In this formula, in my head, it is hard not to *perceive* the migraine as the essence of mind: it is the thing that won't go away when nothing else is left. The Buddha tells us that communion with the essence of mind is enduring mind. The migraineur's embrace of the essence is decidedly more ambivalent.

Judeo-Christians approach the spiritual problem of pain from a different, equally sublime corner. The migraineur *should* take comfort in those broken skulls at Calvary—they are an invitation, a sign. In the Old Testament, God shows He is real, quite often, by hurting people—He speaks as pain, and there is something extraordinary in the contrast between His insubstantial state and these material proofs of His existence. The Bible, in fact, is a long history of humankind being punched in the face by God and being invited to think about what it means. The instinct to believe that the pain comes from somewhere, is inspired by something, likewise the idea that the pain exists to make a point, probably a moral one, is embedded deep in us, as C. S. Lewis writes:

> God whispers to us in our pleasures, speaks to our conscience, but shouts in our pains: it is His megaphone to rouse a deaf world. A bad man, happy, is a man without the least inkling that his actions do not "answer," that they are not in accord with the laws of the universe.

But take a closer look at the Bible. Look at who most appalls God: stiff-necked people, people with hardened hearts. As Elaine Scarry writes in an absolutely perfect phrase, God's "forceful shattering of the reluctant human surface and repossession of the interior" is where the Old Testament action really lies. God doesn't have an agenda: He just wants us pliant, humble, cracks us open like eggshells because that, really, is all we are. And pain is the agent that makes this happen.

It is only a small shift, in turn, to wonder if this predates the Old Testament, if it lies at the core of what the human consciousness does with the experience of intense suffering. The Buddha, as far from Western civilization as we can probably get, accepted that pain was inevitable, not a penalty for bad behavior. But he still offered ways to rise above it. The New Testament is about something else: God is no longer the "weapon" (Scarry here, too) but a being capable of feeling great pain. It's an extraordinary transformation. And the cross, sitting atop the headpan stowing place? The weapon transformed into the symbol of salvation, that transformation at the center of this major world religion, is all about pain and how we interpret it. And every time a migraineur says that she feels like a chainsaw is cutting through her head, or that a nail is being driven through his skull, that same transformation is being played out in miniature—not the crucifixion but the transformation of pain into an expressive, and therefore empowering, symbol of how much it hurts to be alive and to have a soul and a purpose.

Reading the Bible through migraine lenses, in fact, one is struck by how much it feels like the continuation, even the apotheosis, of the other ancient dramas of pain. Wasn't this really Christianity's own version of something already immanent in human history, something at the heart of the mythology of the Greek gods, the worship practices of Babylonia, the Egyptian god and goddesses and their *ges tep*? Something God-like in the headache, in the pain, something in the human that must make sense of the headache by giving it to their gods? Christianity—like every other religion—could simply not be complete until Jehovah, like Zeus or Horus, felt uncontrolled pain and the sense of helplessness that comes with it.

2

I started to notice that my reading habits were changing, were becoming odd and ocular. What mattered anymore wasn't narrative but patterns on the page, the movement of words, a dynamism that wasn't evident before, in part because my head hurt too much to focus long enough for narrative, but in part because my consciousness could suddenly come so clear so fast that for brief flashes I could look down into a complex poem, for instance, as if it were a tidal pool.

I liked it. One day, next to the big red Bible and the big blue Buddha book, I discovered a big paperback of the works of Emily Dickinson. I know I put it there mid-migraine, but was still surprised to see it in twilight, and even a little more surprised that my migraining brain could make such an inspired choice.

Dickinson, possibly the greatest American poet of all, rarely reported a headache, which would be totally characteristic of her and her era. She respected headache in others, though: "It is only a headache," she wrote of one belonging to her sister, "but when the head aches next to you, it becomes important." And she described so many different kinds of pounding inside the human head—a funeral inside the brain, the breaking of floors, the buzzing of flies, the driving of coffin nails—that a modern migraining reader sees a whole different level to her slant rhymes, and wants nothing more than to travel back in time and bring her a cup of hot darjeeling.

I felt a Funeral, in my Brain.
And Mourners to and fro

Kept treading—treading—till it seemed
That Sense was breaking through—

And when they all were seated,
A Service, like a Drum—
Kept beating—beating—till I thought
My mind was going numb—

And then I heard them lift a Box
And creak across my Soul
With those same Boots of Lead, again,
Then Space—began to toll,

As all the heavens were a Bell,
And Being, but an Ear,
And I, and Silence, some strange race
Wrecked, solitary, here—

And then a Plank in Reason, broke,
And I dropped down, and down—
And hit a World, at every plunge,
And Finished knowing—then—

Like the Buddha, Dickinson saw the mind as the seat of immense power. But Dickinson did not have the Buddha's circumspection: she craved transforming the mind into a physical place. She's got the step-by-step of the headache absolutely right, the movement from a soft pulsating pain ("treading—treading—") to a pounding throb ("beating—beating—"). She describes the traumatized responses of the self to what envelops it: the growing despair ("Sense was breaking through"), then the degraded numbness, then the otherworldly solitude, the self and the "toll" of pain together occupying some appallingly exclusive cosmos. And then, the final stage: the wordlessness, the thoughtlessness.

And her metaphors fall apart even as they inspire, which is exactly what they should do. Never mind that "Funeral, in my Brain," which is already good enough. Who is the "them" that lifts the coffin? Who or what, exactly, are those pallbearers? And is the funeral set in her mind or in her soul—and where, exactly, is that "here" that the pained self occupies near the end of the poem, alone with silence? And where does she go next, as she falls through all those worlds? What would a neurologist call it, and what drug might one prescribe for you to keep you from ever going there?

3
―――――――――

Once one decides to compile a migraineur's library, the choices are pretty extensive. But it's a weird collection, spanning millennia, genre, seemingly themeless, hard to categorize, even hard to stack, a reminder of how hard it is to herd the history of headache into the mainstream. Everything from two-thousand-year-old medical textbooks to medieval religious texts translated from Latin to semi-autobiographical novels by surrealist painters. Glossy art books. Thick biographies. Books of ancient incantation and of cutting-edge neurology. And lots of letter collections. For starters.

The practitioners of the old migraine were smart, tough men and women, sylph-like creatures that blurred into darkness and steam when no one was looking. They regarded caffeine not like a lover that brought warmth and energy in the morning, but as a savior. They were sensualists: pain will do that, but so will an intimate relationship to light and dark, to hot and cold, and to their smallest gradations. And they were staged characters, too, launching themselves from their dark studies and their concealed places into bright sunlit society, the pained and painless selves so manifestly different from one another that society itself was, well, a kind of metaphysical crisis: is this me, here now, with the Prince, or is this me, now, with my throb and my cup, with the radiant, life-giving steam?

And lastly, the practitioners of the old migraine were often occupants of a creative plane so bright, so willful and intense that, from this modern context, one almost has to shield one's eyes to look at it. Francis Parkman, for instance, the great nineteenth-century historian and Harvard professor, could barely read or write. The slightest bit of sunlight inspired blinding headaches in him, so the curtains in his study were drawn tight, candles were lit dimly, a special machine relieved the pain in his fingers as flesh met pen and pen met paper.

Giorgio de Chirico, the great surrealist painter, in his auto-biography: "All at once, on my right, on the other side of the street, I saw on the first floor balcony of a house a great black pall flying in the wind. It was like a flash of darkness in the bright light that flooded everything. I felt a sudden anguish and terrible presentiment."

Ulysses S. Grant had headaches throughout the Civil War, as if the conflict itself was making him sick (as it likely was). He tried to cure them by "bathing my feet in hot water and mustard, and putting mustard plasters on my wrists and the back part of my neck." But it didn't work. He didn't hide "those terrible headaches" from his staff and other generals, but he also refused their help. He declined their offers to ride him to battle in an ambulance, or to have them quiet their music on evenings when the sound caused him "fearful pain." He accepted the headaches; they meant something to him about the war, about his leadership. Would his unyielding determination to destroy the Confederates, the chief trait for which Lincoln named him commander of the Union armies, have taken such shape and drama if one-half of his brain was not warring with the other?

This would seem far-fetched if he didn't explicitly link the end of the war to the end of his headache, writing that "the instant I saw the contents of the note" that contained Lee's surrender, "I was cured."

That gorgeous slur in Elvis's voice, the sad, shinerish look around his eyes, the "thank you verra much" that lingers long in the American memory. We are all familiar with the stories of the cocktail of painkilling and sedating prescription drugs found in his system at his death. But what has dropped out of the tale of Elvis's "burnout" is the fact, confirmed by the National Migraine Association, that he was under intense treatment for migraine and hypertension in the last years of his life, even admitted to hospitals in Memphis in 1973 and 1975 for headaches and for aura. Those drugs swirling around his system during his last days were not, in other words, just treating decadence.

Virginia Woolf resisted diagnosis. Sometimes she had auras: "flashes of light raying round my eyes." Sometimes not. Sometimes her headaches were the event, the wave uncovering the sand, as she described that hellacious migraine in the summer of 1922. Sometimes they were the concierge, the first symptom that introduced a lost, bedridden season, those lost, bedridden seasons, in turn, forming a tragic strand that led to her suicide in 1941. In her diary on August 15, 1929: "This melancholy. . . . It comes with headache, of course." And: "60 days . . . spent in wearisome headache, jumping pulse, aching back, frets, fidgets, lying awake, sleeping draughts, sedatives, digitalis, going for a little walk, & plunging back into bed again—"

But she made her pain bend to language, not the reverse. In essays like "On Being Ill," in her letters, she found entrancing figures of speech for her ailments, found, in fact, an entire ethos. Like a scientist, she divided her "particular headache" into "3 stages: pain, numb, visionary." Pain wasn't ever just pain, it was "partly mystical," an "odd whirr of wings in the head," a "kind of vibration." Her mind, she wrote, "becomes chrysalis," "shuts itself up," as she lay "torpid, often with acute physical pain." And then, a kind of preconscious creativity: something "suddenly . . . springs," then "ideas rush in me; often . . . before I can control my mind or pen.'"

"I feel my brains, like a pear, to see if it's ripe," she told her sister in 1910. "It will be exquisite by September."

Nietzsche, unsurprisingly, revered his migraines: "Amid the torments brought on by three days of unremitting headache," he wrote in *Ecce Homo,* his autobiography, "I possessed a dialectician's clarity and very cold-bloodedly thought out things for which, in healthier circumstances, I am not enough of a climber, not cunning, not *cold* enough." It was a gorgeous rationalization. He first got migraines when he was nine— week-long headaches that kept him out of school, that struck the right side of his head, that made him feel different from other schoolchildren, apart from the world itself: describing his "constant headaches" in 1861, then seventeen, he wrote, "I never really become fully conscious . . . everything around me seems to be like a dream."

As he grew, the headaches persisted: as many as 118 in a calendar year, in elegant patterns, nine-day skeins, ten Sundays in a row. His letters filled with complaints, as migraines combined with other syndromes. To his mother on October 19, 1878: "I am sitting here, wracked in pain." In his diary, winter 1882: "I was made to suffer enduring torments and to be burned to death over a slow flame." He saw auras, or what seemed like auras—"a profusion of fantastic flowers" against the screen of his closed eyelids—and read them as symptoms of "incipient madness."

Nietzsche left his chair at the University of Basel because of the pain, starved himself (bad idea), took prescriptions for cocaine and other sketchy drugs. And as he lapsed toward madness, he made terrible jokes that might not have been jokes but emblems of his resignation: "He told me of his terrible headaches," Marie von Bradke wrote in 1886, "and that an acquaintance—from India, I believe—had given him a poison to take, after which he lay on the ground as though dead. He also told me that he had tried other poisons, too."

And before then, what madness? Michael H. Hart offers us the possibility that Nietzsche's "headaches had the highest likelihood of influencing the course of human history." Would Nietzsche have dreamed so desperately of a Superman if he had not felt the need to transcend those three-day headaches? In turn, would Hitler have dreamed so hard of a master race if Nietzsche had not dreamed so desperately of a Superman? And so on.

Karl Marx, too, though the data is slight. Julius Caesar, though most likely he had slow brain cancer. George Bernard Shaw, George Eliot. Kipling, the easiest diagnosis in history. Alexander Graham Bell, Harry Truman, John Calvin, Madame Pompadour, Alfred Nobel: maybe, maybe. Composers: Tchaikovsky, Wagner, Chopin. Gustav Mahler had killers: "I have rolled with my eyes and grunted because of the pain," he wrote. His wife described them as "horrible hours of tragical agony," and interestingly, as "one of the self-intoxications of which he suffered until the end, and which are the cause of his last fatal illness." That she calls them "self-intoxications" is shocking; that she blames them for his death (from an unrelated blood disease), even more so.

He got them on trains, his only real cure walking for hours in train stations during layovers. He got them at home: only sleep would deter them.

Migraine ran in Charles Darwin's family: his grandfather, Erasmus, a physician, composed a long chapter on "megrim" in a medical book he called *Zoonomia*. Charles, in turn, complained of headaches from early middle age, one of a complex of ailments that dogged him until death. He had headaches that forestalled his wedding: "My last two days in London . . . were rendered very uncomfortable by a bad headache, which continued two days and two nights, so that I doubted whether it ever meant to go and allow me to be married." He had headaches that made his family life morose: "The children played in a depressed hush," one biographer wrote. He had headaches that made his "head whiz," that played their role in neurological breakdowns he described in cribbed notes as "partial memory loss 12 hours," or "sinking fits."

But he had headaches that helped him work, too, that provided him with "a very useful adjustment to his career," as one biographer argues. He fell ill, for instance, when he tried to read "metaphysics and religion." But not science. Better read some more science, then—and we all know what happened. Were Darwin's headaches a message from the deeper self to the surface, drawing him down the paths where his genius lay? In private, for instance, he complained of headaches that had "a mind of (their) own." Publicly, he wrote—in the wondrous *Expression of the Emotions in Man and Animals*—about the "involuntary transmission of nerve-force," wherein the nervous system, *just by the way it's built,* makes things happen that "from the first" are "independent of the will."

It's hard not to hear Darwin's "headache" talking in these phrases, the pain translated into theory, the theory making sense of the pain. Darwin understood that the failure of free will the headache both argues for and induces, the sense of something outside making things happen, was actually a cataclysmic closeness to the things inside.

4
————

The old practitioners kept me going, as rooms bobbed and weaved, as the inside of my brain twirled like a disco ball. I became a sylph, too. I tried to love the steam and the dark. Work, I told myself, was easy enough to fake. Luckily, I did have that release time, so there was less to counterfeit. Otherwise, I toughed it out, again and again, the toughing-it-out increasingly pointless and ceremonial, even as I sensed a knife's edge getting closer and closer. And the old practitioners offered metaphysical stability, a guidebook to see it all through.

I have to admit: I felt validation as I found the names of famous people who had migraine, felt comfort when I saw how they succeeded in spite of it, even because of it, contoured their genius around the pain, or used the pain as a catalyst. It was genuinely fun. Thomas Jefferson, during one headache-infested three-week period in 1790, composed a report on weights and measures in his head during the day, when the headache roared, and conducted the experiments and wrote the manuscript by candlelight once the headache waned. I saw the sense of this, was further comforted by the fact that Jefferson's headaches had the same daily pattern as mine. The migraine, I began to see, might be conceived as an intellectual problem: one that was not solved by an experiment, but healed by the use of one's intellect as a battering ram against the pain. No Zen allowed.

The deeper I dug, however, the scarcer the gold. At first, for instance, Vincent van Gogh gives us extraordinary anecdotes of a carnivalesque sensorium and the desolation it inspired. He describes the disappearance of the right half of his vision, the inversion of everything on the left. To Gauguin, he describes a self-portrait as "me . . . but me gone mad."

And he gives us the paintings, too. *The Starry Night,* with its whorls of light dancing across the sky, so stereotypically aura that it absolutely diminishes both headache and aura to even mention it. It is a postcard of a migraine. But *Rain at Auvers,* painted three weeks before he killed himself, is the real thing: a brown world, the haze created by a rainstorm beautifully matched to the haze of vision experienced mid-migraine. It's not an aura at all: it's a painting of light aversion. And the rain: rendered as slashing straight lines through the watercolor background, but slashing down in different directions, some left, some right, like no *real* rain. The whole canvas is not engulfed in disorder; the juxtaposition between normalcy and its opposite occupies your gaze, until it becomes your new order.

But what did van Gogh have; what was his diagnosis? He's not available for an appointment anymore. We can't send out his skull, moldering in that French cemetery, for an MRI. We can only reconstruct from diaries, letters, from the art itself, and this is not usually the way good doctors or readers work. And even if one could diagnose the dead, would one want to? Most critics and many general readers do not like it when a writer, artist, or musician's genius is too closely linked to illness. To make such claims devalues the artist and the art, many believe, and makes those artists seem like little more than stenographers for their genes. And what diminishes them, what makes their imaginations and wills seem less bold, diminishes us all: "All fail to prove their theories," writes John Pudney of Lewis Carroll's contemporary diagnosticians, who have found rich evidence of neurological disorders in their subject, "or to add much to the treasures of Wonderland."

All these reservations are true, unquestionably. But so what? Dostoyevsky confronted this argument with the character of Prince Myshkin, who, like his creator, suffered from epilepsy, and, like his creator, experienced "religious ecstasy" during the "seizures." "What if it is disease?" Myshkin asks:

> What does it matter that it is an abnormal intensity, if the result, if the minute of sensation, remembered and analysed afterwards in health, turns out to be the acme of harmony and beauty, and gives a feeling, unknown and undivined till then, of completeness, of proportion, of reconciliation, and of ecstatic devotional merging in the highest synthesis of life?

So what if van Gogh's art emerged from neurological illness? So what if Carroll transcribed his migraines and sent them down the rabbit hole? Is there a discount on genius when it is inspired by bodies so small they can only be seen by a microscope? There have been millions with temporal lobe epilepsy, if that's what van Gogh had (as Eve LaPlante surmises in *Seized*), and only one painted those canvases. There have been tens of millions, even hundreds of millions, with migraine: there has been only one *Alice in Wonderland*.

It might be both depressing and reductive to say that Dickinson's "I felt a Funeral, in my Brain" is about a headache. It is, but like many Dickinson poems, it is also about spirit, nature, sex, power, family, madness, and truth. It's about what Virginia Woolf meant when she told us that we may glimpse "undiscovered countries," the "wastes and deserts of the soul," from even "a slight attack of influenza"—if only we'd pay attention. Dickinson's genius is that she found a way to write about these larger things in such a way that she revealed the common configuration of experience across a range of what makes us human, and that head pain, amazingly, was banded together with these larger things. That the truth would blow off the top of your head, like orgasm, like pain, like God, like lightning, like beauty. Headache, Dickinson tells us, is one of the universals, or near it. The fact that artists with migraine and without can create migrainous art is not a point of intellectual confusion: it is the insight.

Researchers have considered this possibility for two centuries now, inching this idea to the center of the discussion of migraine and what migraines tell us about being human. Sir John Herschel, in "On Sensorial Vision" (1858), was entranced by the impersonal geometric forms of his own auras and speculated that they originated in "prototype(s) in the intellect." In 1942, Heinrich Kluver similarly speculated that there existed "hallucinatory form constants," both visual and deeper than visual, implying the presence of "some fundamental mechanism." Take mescal, *or* have a migraine (*or*, for that matter, a delirium from measles or tonsillitis), and you'd see the same "grating, lattice, fretwork, honeycomb," feel the same "experience of changes in size," the same "'splitting' of personality." More recently, Richard Grossinger has argued that auras "are psychosomatically like dreams," only more "primitive," not only "express(ing) uncompensated contents of the psyche" but "gaps in the body's neurohormonal equilibrium."

It is a small leap to include mystic vision and creative inspiration on this continuum. Hildegard of Bingen, among her many occupations (abbess, composer), was a doctor, and composed a medical text entitled *Causae et Curae*. She mentions migraines there, and the tone is impassive, if not ironic: she doesn't sound like a sufferer. But listen to her describe her religious visions and she captures a range of aura symptoms pitch-perfectly, sometimes adjoined to pain, sometimes not:

> Then I saw as it were a great multitude of very bright living lamps, which received fiery brilliance and acquired an unclouded splendor. And behold! A pit of great breadth and depth appeared. . . .

> I saw watery air with a white zone beneath it. . . .

> I could not see any light because of a clouding over of my eyes, and I was so oppressed down by the weight of my body that I could not raise myself. So I lay there, overwhelmed by intense pains.

Picasso, likewise, seems not to have complained of headache, although he was, by many accounts, an epic hypochondriac who easily could have. But he seemed to move from one exploration of the interior landscape of migraine to the next as he moved through his "periods": first, those great faces in the Rose and Blue periods, so flat, so isolate, their eyes so veiled and shinerish; then the dramatic, explosive configurations of landscape and body of his Cubist work.

The relationship between migraine aura and Picasso's work

is so intense, in fact, that it transcends any simple loop of cause and effect. Reading the case studies, one would sometimes swear that Picasso had invented aura, or, at least, the "illusory vertical splitting" that characterizes many auras (and that makes the phrase "splitting headache" more apt than one would think). Two European doctors, Michel Ferrari and Joost Haan, have spent years showing migraine specialists and their patients paintings of auras by migraineurs, and some of Picasso's portraits of women, "the face . . . painted two-dimensionally flat with a vertical split and shift of the eyes and other parts of the face." They report that neither doctors nor patients can distinguish the latter paintings from the former without "great difficulties."

Whatever their particular muses were, women and men like Hildegard and Picasso, like Woolf and Darwin, all went down the same deep well that the migraine sufferer reaches in a vastly less comprehensible way, tumbling down its walls— or falling down that acclaimed rabbit hole—wrecked, solitary, here. The brain speaks its elemental language to geniuses and to migraineurs alike. But only the former (unless, until, the rest of us take their example) can talk back. In this case, it is moot whether Dickinson had any headaches at all. It is moot whether Picasso did, or Carroll. What matters is that their cases, taken together, tell us that what we call mystic vision, or creative inspiration, may be vastly more promiscuous and accessible than we generally allow, and that illness may be a gate swung wide open. We ought to read migraine in Dickinson, not as an exclusive evaluation of what her poem really means, but because a lot of people have headaches, and she was smart and kind enough to respect their value. We ought to overlay migraine onto Picasso's work, not as an explanation for where he got his ideas, but because the coincidence is the thing itself, the deep and profound evidence that our minds might all be converging toward something rare and wonderful.

And we ought to admire them, and Carroll and others, for their elusiveness, for not naming names, because that is exactly the kind of truth that artists tell. It may be oppressive to our sense of creative genius to say that *Alice in Wonderland* is a migraine hallucination, for instance. But it is a slander to human nature, that strange grid of the ineffable, to deny it categorically.

5

We do not need to try to guess whether Charles Dodgson was having a migraine on that Fourth of July in 1862 as he and Robinson Duckworth rowed the Liddell children down the Thames to Godstow. Or whether he was simply unconsciously recollecting past migraines, or allowing recollections to infuse the story of Alice in Wonderland as he composed it, more or less spontaneously, telling it over Duckworth's shoulder as he rowed and little grave-browed Alice Liddell pretended to be the coxswain. Or whether the sunlight was giving him premonitions of headache as he rowed and talked, rowed and talked. Or whether he had a migraine, or some permutation of one, as he stayed up that night scrawling the first draft of his classic work, because little Alice had asked to see it right away. Or whether, as one inspired doctor has suggested, he was thinking about the migraine testimonies told to him by headachy children, turning Alice's illness into her Wonderland: "Visual distortions of the type described in the *Alice* tales," argues Richard M. Restak of George Washington University, "occur more commonly in child and adolescent migraine sufferers than in adults."

We can play detectives with the biographical materials. In his diary in 1888, Dodgson wrote: "This morning, on getting up, I experienced that curious optic effect—of seeing 'fortifications'— discussed in Dr. Lathan's book on 'bilious headache.' In this instance it affected the *right* eye only, at the outer edge, and there was no headache." The testimony is pretty clear, but maybe it points us to a migraineur, and maybe it points us to a hypochondriac. He owned a book, a medical textbook ("Dr. Lathan's") on migraine ("bilious headache"). He knew the term *fortification,* a staple used in describing the zigzag effects of visual aura. He knew the fact there was no headache was relevant. It wasn't the only illness he self-diagnosed: "epileptic, no doubt," he noted in that same diary after a faint or seizure of some kind.

Contemporary migraine experts have looked at his sketches, and they definitely see something. Podoll and Robinson, doing deft investigative work in the *Lancet* in 1999, produce a "carefully executed" pre-Alice "drawing" that Dodgson made of a small figure missing "parts of the head, shoulder, wrist, and hand . . . on the right side of the picture"—a "rounded border," they observe, "similar to that seen in a negative scotoma" (note that they say right side, as did Dodgson, in that 1888 diary entry). Others have noted the early sketches of Alice, her neck telescoping wildly, and—as did Lippman and other researchers in the 1940s and 1950s—recorded resemblance so strong to certain migraine hallucinations that the term "Alice in Wonderland syndrome" proved irresistible.

As interesting as these pursuits may be, however, they pale alongside and are rendered irrelevant by the simple act of reading the book. There may be no better literary representation of migraine in history—not the pain but the distorted and escalating sensibility. It is the first book a migraineur needs to read to dissolve the alienation; it is the first book someone without migraines needs to read if he or she is curious about what it's like. And it is the first book to use as evidence if one wants to argue that migraine taps a worldview, a deep pattern, available to migraineur and nonmigraineur alike.

The book is encyclopedic about migraine, so much so, in fact, that one wonders if it would have been possible for one man to have experienced so many of its different facets. As the book begins, Alice lolls on a riverbank on a "hot day," feeling "very sleepy and stupid," when Rabbit blurs by her. She pursues Rabbit down his Rabbit Hole and falls for three pages, "down, down, down," plenty of time to "look about her, and to wonder what was going to happen next." The stupor, the hot day, are premonitory enough, but the fall down the dreamy hole rings bells. Here are two of Oliver Sacks's case studies from *Migraine*:

> There seems to be a sort of hole in my memory and mind and, so to speak, a hole in the world.

> She says: "There is nothing there any more, just a blank, just a hole. . . ." She feels the "hole" is like death, and that one day it will get so large that it will "swallow" her completely.

The hole swallows Alice. When she lands in Wonderland, she quickly undergoes a series of bodily reformations, all catalyzed by drinking something from the famously inviting bottle labeled "DRINK ME," or eating the sugary little currant cake that says "EAT ME." In order, she shrinks down to ten inches tall, grows to nine feet high, cries "gallons of tears," feels intense confusion, recites a poem she has memorized and scrambles the words ("'I'm sure those are not the right words,' said poor Alice"), then shrinks again, nearly drowning in her own tears.

Everything that happens to Alice effortlessly matches symptoms that doctors for generations have recognized as characteristic of the onset of migraine. The abrupt crying, which up to 50 percent of migraineurs report in the early stages. The food triggers. The verbal and mental tumult. And the body? Here is tiny Alice:

> She waited for a few minutes to see if she was going to shrink any further; she felt a little nervous about this, "for it might end, you know," said Alice to herself, "in my going out altogether, like a candle."

Here are Lippman's Case 1 and Case 4:

> Very occasionally she has an attack where she feels small— "about one foot high," just before, or during the headache.

> I have a very peculiar feeling of being very close to the ground as I walk along. It is as though I were short and wide, as the reflection in one of those broadening mirrors one sees in carnivals, etc.

That last one, too, a bit Tweedledum and Tweedledee. Here is giant Alice:

> When she looked down at her feet, they seemed to be almost out of sight, they were getting so far off.

Here are Lippman's Case 3 and Case 5:

> When walking down the street I would think I would be able
> to look down on the tops of others' heads, and it was very
> frightening and annoying not to see as I was feeling.

> My head would seem far above my hands, far above table
> tops, etc.

For good measure, here's the Cheshire Cat:

> It vanished quite slowly, beginning with the end of the tail,
> and ending with the grin, which remained some time after
> the rest of it had gone.

And here's Karl Lashley, describing one of his own auras:

> Talking with a friend, I glanced just to the right of his face,
> whereon his head disappeared. His shoulders and necktie
> were still visible, but the vertical stripes in the wallpaper be-
> hind him seemed to extend right down to the necktie.

At this point, about one-third into the book, the explicitly
migrainy aspects recede: they are still there, though, back-
grounded, and that's what makes them so compelling. Mid-
twentieth-century psychiatrists and physicians loved the Mad
Hatter and the White Rabbit, who, to them, embodied classic
migraineur personalities: the White Rabbit, frantic, obsessed
with punctuality, the Mad Hatter, poignantly shy in public. But
it's deeper: it's in the alienation Alice feels as her body twists
out of her control, for instance. Here's Alice:

Who am I, then? Tell me that first, and then, if I like being
that person, I'll come up: if not, I'll stay down here till I'm
somebody else.

Here's Lippman's Case 3 again:

I wanted to run from myself, and several times thought that
I was actually doing so. I was two things—one leaving the
other behind.

And it's in the courage Alice finds as she adapts to her new
world and to the aberrant possibilities of her body. *Alice:*

Alice had got so much into the way of expecting nothing but
out-of-the-way things to happen, that it seemed quite dull
and stupid for life to go on in the common way.

And Lippman's Case 7:

After a few minutes of feeling large, the right half seems to
shrink until it is smaller than the left. This process has been
coming and going all day long. I know that it isn't really true
and keep on working.

Reading *Alice* during a migraine—a high-wire act, but not
if you can find a fairly mild migraine, after a day and a half of
pulsating pain across the left temple, maybe persistent enough
to inspire a little otherworldly disorientation—you will be
struck by how . . . *synchronous* it feels. It is not about the
thing; it is the thing. The way Alice's world slides into the sur-
real, from the moment she feels "sleepy and stupid" in the heat.
Even the fact that it's a sunny afternoon—there is something

about a sunny afternoon in a migraineur's world: "I felt that this summer afternoon had always existed," Sacks's Case 75 observes. The way, too, the hallucinations feel so real: "I get all tired out," Lippman's Case 6 observes, "from pulling my head down from the ceiling."

And all these characters, the Mouse, the Hatter, the King, Alice herself, who struggle to mean what they say, or say things backward, or trail off in midsentence, the ongoing debates over who is mad and who is not ("We're all mad here," the Cheshire Cat adjudicates). The sudden, shocking malice in the words of the Queen and the Duchess, all those "off with her head" orders (remember *Migraine Boy* and his grateful execution). But no debate is ever settled. No one is ever executed or convicted. Even Alice's equanimity in the face of the changes she undergoes, the confusion of Wonderland, is migrainy precisely because the madness is so even-handed, never leads to disaster, and never entirely perturbs Alice's sense of herself, whether she is nine feet or ten inches high.

Carroll has got everything here but the headache. He, too, seems to have respected its mystery. But, like every great author, maybe, too, he poked at that mystery, just to see if it would give. As the Mad Hatter testifies in the "who stole the tarts" trial in *Alice*'s Chapter 11, he grows suddenly confused and nervous, and utters a remarkably nonsensical phrase: "the twinkling of the tea." The King, startled, responds, "The twinkling of *what*?" to which the Hatter explains, "It *began* with the tea." It is all wonderfully kaleidoscopic, fragments of maybe diagnoses, perception blocking perception, just as it should be: the migraine starts with caffeinated tea, or ends with it; a twinkling across its surface, or the surface of any body of water, no matter how small, a routine aura. Sometimes a migraine even starts with a rift in the world where everything "twinkles": "rippling, shimmering, and undulation in the visual field, which patients may compare to the appearance of wind-blown water, or looking through watered silk," Sacks writes in that gorgeous neurological prose of his. The Mad Hatter's testimony is erratic, at best, and in a book where no one speaks all that lucidly, only the Mad Hatter is called out for it: "You're a *very* poor *speaker*," the King tells him. And he is. He is testifying about a migraine, and getting one as he testifies. Even in Wonderland, it is possible to be too far gone.

The Four Paths
of the Migraineur

But I, though I saw and heard these things, refused to write for a long time through doubt and bad opinion and the diversity of human words . . . until, laid low by the scourge of God, I fell upon a bed of sickness; then, compelled at last by many illnesses, I set my hand to the writing.

—HILDEGARD,
ABBESS OF BINGEN, *Scivias*

1

Emily, November 3: a sophomore, dark hair, dark eyes, fair skin with freckles, one would think, also dark—she's wearing a white sweater, an old-fashioned cardigan, black pants, there's a black-and-white schema to everything she does, and just under the eyes, where there's that familiar gray, shinerish thing. She looks like she just stepped out of an old movie and is just shaking off all the monochrome.

The first thing she wants to know is: Will she be able to go to law school? What's going to happen when she's got three hundred pages of reading and professors who don't hand out extensions the way they do in college, and a migraine hits? What happens when she's supposed to be in court and her head starts to pound?

Her profile: migraine once a week, more in hot weather, started when she was fourteen, across the middle of her head, the nose around the eyes. No aura. She's always been ahead of the curve, in terms of migraines, one of those kids with a parent who knew the score: her mother, remembering *her* mother's migraines from the get-go, was already asking her if she had bad headaches before she had her first one. She's already kept a migraine diary, has already tried several different drugs (one works, but she's only got a twenty-minute window to take it; one made her utterly listless, another made her too nauseous), has already cut out caffeine, most liquor, most sweets . . . hasn't mattered. That's the sad thing: she's already done her due diligence.

What she most wants to hear: that one can have a successful career. I tell her sure, that she'll be tougher, smarter, but she ought to learn a few ways to take it easy on herself, too. Talking to her, though, I get the distinct feeling she knows more about all this than I do. She has good advice: use a bag of frozen peas as your icepack. You can shape it any way you want, and the peas stay frozen a good long while.

That sick people often defy the terms of the contract described by Talcott Parsons, and don't seek the straightest path to recovery, might mean they are fulfilling some other contract, are taking some other path. There is the path of excessive stoicism, a toughness and a stupidity bred in us via our Calvinist roots.

There is the path of the excessive Buddhist, who uses the illness as an opportunity to transcend human frailty. There is the path of the sensation junkie, who regards the illness as an opportunity to feel more and more deeply. And there is the path of the workaholic, who uses the illness as a catalyst to work harder: "I could only avoid the shadows," Kipling wrote, "by working every minute that I could see."

I chose a combination of these paths—or, really, they were chosen for me, as if inevitable, and not without regret. I turned to writers and artists as my guides, when I might have been better off visiting a headache specialist. But it worked for a while: it was a way of having a community and keeping to myself at the same time. Soon, though, I recognized that I was looking for the wrong thing—a fact that was prodded into life by my conversation with Emily. If the statistics don't lie and roughly 12 percent of all men and women have migraine headaches, therein lay something disturbing: while the list of famous writers and artists with migraines is a long one, it does not add up to 12 percent of the longer list of famous writers and artists who ever lived. If anything, the migraineurs in the group amount to significantly less than 12 percent. For every Nietzsche, or Woolf, or Darwin, or de Chirico, there were countless more talented men and women who were defeated by their headaches, gifted men and women who never got a chance to nurse those gifts because they were too occupied to do anything but nurse their pain.

And let's not even mention what happened in the end to Nietzsche. Or Woolf. Or so many of the others. That migraine might not have caused insanity or death does not mean it was not complicit, which is what Mahler's wife was trying to say. "If pain could have cured us, we should long ago have been saved," George Santayana wrote, which is funny and obvious. But then he added, "Pain . . . has no resource; its violence is quite help-less and its vacancy offers no expedients by which it might be unknotted and relieved," which is not funny or obvious but devastatingly to the point the more one thinks about it.

At the same time, however, the very meaninglessness of the pain, to me, also created a sense of possibility. And the more random the pain, the more possibility. The violence may be un-stoppable, humbling. It may destroy you. But migraine doesn't really want to destroy you. It just doesn't know what it's doing. And we do. This is why, as much as it hurt, I could not take it seriously. It is not that what doesn't kill you makes you stron-ger, although let's be mindful that the man who famously said that was talking about migraines among his other ailments. It is the nature of the *it* that doesn't kill you that we have to envision: a thing within, a thing without, a thing we made, a thing imposed? A thing with a plan, or a thing with no plan, just a thing?

Migraines are powerful because they force one to contem-plate the great mystery of the boundary between free will and fate, between the thing we choose to do and the thing we're made to do. Why do couples argue when one complains of migraine and the other disbelieves, or believes, rather, that the migraineur can control the migraine? Because they are both right. Scientists play with this contradiction, referring to, for instance, "the spacetime continuum . . . which the patient with migraine both suffers and creates." But the great migraineurs understood intuitively that a creative act sometimes looks and feels like something you didn't want to do. They were all re-bellious thinkers—although, sometimes, surprisingly reserved ones, often disabled by what liberated them. And the migraine? It was implicated in their rebellions, in their shapings of new systems of thought and action that have changed the world.

Sometimes migraine was the catalyst. Sometimes it was the foil. Sometimes it was the jackhammer and the migraineur's mind was the rock.

And this is what I should have told Emily: it is not enough to tough it out. When migraine doesn't want you catatonic, it wants you making something new and won't rest until you do. Take, for example, Hildegard, an amazing, almost other-worldly example. Her early visions, which greatly resemble the descriptions modern men and women provide of their first auras, are linked to her voicelessness:

> I had sensed in myself wonderfully the power and mystery of secret and admirable visions from my childhood—that is, from the age of five—I concealed it in quiet silence. . . .

So the visions increase in scale, the pain in like scale, until insecurity and self-consciousness are driven from her:

> But I, though I saw and heard these things, refused to write for a long time through doubt and bad opinion and the diversity of human words . . . until, laid low by the scourge of God, I fell upon a bed of sickness; then, compelled at last by many illnesses, I set my hand to the writing.

Migraine may be episodic, but it entwines itself with a life and with the purpose of the life. It compels the message to the surface and compels, somewhat, its form. But to understand this fact, I soon learned, meant thinking in narrative terms, about a whole life, not in episodes. I can't tell you how hard this was, because chronic migraines simply make this sort of thinking close to impossible. But after a couple of months of persistent pain, I badly wanted to understand what my migraines were midwifing. More than that, I wanted to believe that they were midwifing something.

I can admit that, in my desperation, I might have tried too hard to impose a meaningful framework on my pain—finding the opposite possibility too soul defying to contemplate. But then I dug deeper into my library, and found that the great migraineurs did the same thing. Whether I wanted it or not, whether I had earned it or not, my destiny was bound up with theirs. I could only find for myself what I could convince myself they had found for themselves.

2

Anne Conway, who before she was married was called Anne Finch, was Thomas Willis's celebrity patient, the woman whose besieged tower never surrendered. There's a portrait of her, at least art historians think it is hers, a young woman in skirts so immense that she has to gather them in one hand to prevent herself from tripping, not so easy because, with the other hand, she holds a letter she is reading as she walks. The perspective makes no sense, because we can see the front of the letter, which means there is no way she can strain her neck far enough to read any more than a few lines at the bottom of the page. It is a picture of a woman reading for our benefit, not for hers.

The gown is off her shoulders. Strong nose, lidded eyes (remember, she is looking down, reading), dark curls down the side and one demonstrative bang across her small forehead.

She is clearly "beautiful," as Willis wrote, and perhaps "hot blooded," too. But she was also a reader, from a young age, working her way through her father's large library at Kensington Palace, marrying Edward Conway, a wealthy earl with another large library, inviting philosophers and religious men to Ragley Hall, their estate in Warwickshire, where they would write in quiet dells and she could chat them up.

She made herself erudite—intimidatingly bright, not easy for a seventeenth-century woman to do. She found a way to ask questions to bright men that stumped and flattered them at the same time. Henry More, theosophist from Cambridge, wrote that her queries on philosophy made him "not a little putt to my plunges." Thomas Baines, another philosopher, observed that she "passe(d) through the subtilest peeces of philosophy, without making many difficultyes," and speculated that her questions were so "intricate" because she already knew the answers.

In response, she was officially demure: "I could not have read what you have published of me wth out [*sic*] blushing," she told More. But really, she was not some wilting flower but a genteel challenge to conventional masculinity: "You write like a man," her father-in-law told her. More wrote that she was a "Genius" who had "not onely out-gone all" of her "own Sex, but even of that other."

But Willis, another of the great intellectuals of the time, was visiting Ragley Hall for a different reason. From the age of twelve, as she read and grew into "a right ffinch very proud" (as John Ward, vicar of Stratford upon Avon, described her), Conway got wrenching migraines. "Sometimes," Willis wrote, the pain was on one side of the head, sometimes on the other, sometimes all the way around. But when it was going, it took twenty days a month from her, in one-, two-, three-, or four-day runs. She hated light, hated sound, couldn't sleep (though when she could, she felt better), and couldn't eat.

That she was desperate and in pain was evident from the desperate and painful natures of the cures she sought. Willis wrote: "Remedies of every kind for the curing this headach, try'd in vain." She tried bloodletting, had arteries opened, had holes cut in her head so that the pain could "issue" out. She tried an "oyntment of Quicksilver"—mercury—itself life-threatening. Predictably, she was stoic in letters, expressing concern that "my complaints should fill so great a part of my letter."

And then, in her late twenties, she got smallpox, and her only child died, and the headaches became almost constant. Her husband wrote that "her sighs, and grones comes so deep from her, that I am terrified to come neere her." She spent as many as seven weeks straight in bed and was so weak and clumsy during these periods that it took two people to help her "set one leg before another."

By 1665, in her early thirties, she grew even more desperate for a cure. She wanted her head cut open; she wanted the pain out. Willis came around at this time and let more blood. William Harvey, another doctor, recommended "opening of the skull with a Trypanning Iron": she traveled to Paris to get the work done, but was talked out of it by Henry More. Her brother, John Finch, out of an almost deranged sense of devotion, traveled to Italy to learn human anatomy and surgery, and then returned to England and operated on her. Incredibly, she let him, and it must have hurt like hell. "The Lady Conway hath great pains in her head her sutures open," John Ward, another vicar, wrote. "Shee came into this miserie by a Brother of hers."

Once the wounds healed from her brother's "experiments," she tried other avenues. She devoured medical texts and was particularly moved by Robert Boyle's *Some Considerations Touching the Usefulness of Experimental Naturall Philoso-*

phy (1663). She tried his recommended remedy, a suspension known as Ens Veneris, and, dissatisfied, tried to get a batch of it from Boyle himself. She disregarded more popular cures, dismissing any prescription recommended by a "confident mountebank."

As the pain increased, however—now frequenting the right side of her body—she turned to more eclectic and spiritual solutions. She employed an Irish faith healer named Valentine Greatrakes, known then in the British Isles as "The Stroker": "My wife is not the better for him," Edward Conway told John Finch. She hired Francis Mercury Van Helmont, who fused medicine and religions ranging from Protestantism to Kabbalah in his practices, believing, as he wrote in *The Spirit of Diseases,* that "the Mind influenceth the Body in causing and curing of Diseases." Lord Conway spent six hundred pounds for his help and didn't seem to regret it, even if it didn't bring a cure: "I haue attained the satisfaction of doing that which is pleasing to my Wife in the highest degree."

Finally, as she entered her forties, Conway turned to Quaker theology, not for any cure, but for comfort. "They have been and are a suffering people," she wrote, "and are taught from the consolation (that) has been experimentally felt by them under their great tryals to administer comfort . . . to others in great distresse."

She died at the age of forty-seven, died a dissenting Quaker, which caused her family no little political problem. They embalmed her and put her in a macabre glass coffin. She was, clearly, a woman stuck in the wrong era. The men all knew that they were in the company of someone really extraordinary, and they were aware, too, that the mix of Conway's acumen with her distress was what made her extraordinary. They coveted her, in fact, and their covetousness (as exampled by her brother's surgeries, by her glass coffin) was part of the problem. Looking back, in turn, we can recognize so much of who she was and what she did from the biographies of other migraineurs, from the biography of migraine itself. In the months before death, bedridden and in constant pain, she tried to nurse a little manuscript into existence: "broken Fragments," Van Helmont, who found them, called what she wrote, the words barely visible on the page because of the weakness of her stroke with lead pen. Collated and edited, however, they appeared anonymously in Holland in 1690, and in England two years later, under the title *The Principles of the Most Ancient and Modern Philosophy*. It was, in all likelihood, the first significant philosophical treatise published by a woman in Western history.

And it was laced with a migrainy metaphysics. She argued that the "productions of the mind" had "body," that "Spirit and body," in fact, "are of one nature and substance." But Conway's genius lay in the clarity with which she said what made her see the world this way. It was her experience of unrelieved pain that persuaded her that life wore a psychosomatic tinge: "Why does the spirit or soul suffer so with bodily pain?" she asked.

> Why is it wounded or grieved when the body is wounded, whose nature is so different? . . . But if one admits that the soul is of one nature and substance with the body . . . then all the above mentioned difficulties vanish . . . the soul moves the body and suffers with it and through it.

Likewise, she meshed religion with mysticism, Bible with Kabbalah, showed unusual tolerance for Islam, inspired, again, by the examples of other sufferers:

The particular acquaintance with such living examples of great patience under sundry heavy exercises, both of bodily sicknesse and other calamitys (as some of them have related to me) I find begetts a more lively fayth.

In the end, you cannot divide the headaches from the art they help produce (or suffocate in infancy). And the wild treatment, the headlong dive across Europe, one's own skull as the canvas or the clay? In the end, you cannot divide the desperation to find a cure from the need to create, or from the intellectual desire that compels you to try and answer these damn questions, and not live with question marks.

3

Sigmund Freud was not yet forty when the migraines began, or, at least, when he began to write about them. He's not yet the iconic Freud, with the trim whitish beard, the forehead balding, one imagines, from all the intellectual activity just underneath the skin there, the analytical stare, the dangerous cigar. Instead, he's a little fatter, his hair is slick and black and hangs in lank bangs over the topmost part of his forehead, and he's got a beard so thick you can't even see his mouth.

He looks friendlier, uncertain, perhaps even a little haggard (he's got six young kids at this point). He's good at children's parties: for Mathilde's eighth birthday, he hosted one "20 individuals strong." At this point, he hasn't even decided that "psychoanalysis" will be his calling. The word doesn't even exist. But the migraines will help with that.

His first migraines are nonsymbolic events, just headaches, really, but persistent ones: "I was suffering from migraine, the third attack this week incidentally," he tells Martha Bernays, his future wife, in 1885. Content with dietary triggers for explanation, he blames "the Tartar sauce I had for lunch," takes some cocaine, "watch(es) the migraine vanish at once," and unsurprisingly finds himself "so wound up that I had to go on working and writing and couldn't get to sleep before 4 in the morning."

By 1893, though, he begins to intuit that diet isn't a good enough explanation. On May 30, another headache, another dose of cocaine—he calls it "cocainiz(ing)" and makes sure to hit both nostrils. But instead of wondering about what he ate, he starts to meditate upon how "young persons who must be presumed to be virgins and who have not been subjected to abuse" can still have "anxiety neuroses," and he concludes that they must possess "a presentient dread of sexuality." It is a migrainy, Darwinian stroke, to wonder how one can suffer pain without the experience that is supposed to trigger the pain, and it promises new directions in his thought.

By 1895, Freud is writing about his migraines more than any other ailment. By this point, he is supplementing cocaine with at least two of the new headache drugs, pyramidon and aspirin. He also befriends an ear, nose, and throat doctor from Berlin named Wilhelm Fliess, and they begin a correspondence where headaches are, arguably, the primary bond that links them.

For Fliess and many other European doctors during this period, headaches are caused by blocked nasal passages. He operates on Freud, some nasty cauterizing of the nasal mucous membranes and some work on the nearby bones. It doesn't help: Freud despondently describes "migraines rather frequent(ly). . . . I have rapidly turned grey." But Fliess also encourages Freud to think in other terms about his migraines, as "periodic" events timed to coincide with important emotional experiences. Freud, so inspired, starts to identify migraine triggers amid otherwise random events that match Fliess's schedule: the death of a sculptor whom he particularly admired, for instance; his daughter Mathilde's first menstruation, which gives him, he claims, "a migraine from which I thought I would die."

By late 1895, he begins to refine his perspective on migraine. He writes "Draft 1 Migraine: Established Points" and appends it to a letter to Fliess. The essay is notes, almost an outline, and displays flashes of the sensibilities he will later bring to bear on psychological matters. He composes closely observed descriptions of the *feel* of his migraines: "One has a sort of feeling that an obstacle is overcome and that a process then goes forward," he writes of their onsets, for instance. And, like Liveing, he implicates the nervous system more than the blood vessels. But he insists, too, that repression plays a leading role, that "migraine represents a toxic effect produced by a sexual stimulating substance when this cannot find sufficient discharge."

In the more personal passages of his correspondence, however, he's composing another story. There, migraine emerges as an extraordinary enemy and an extraordinary gift. A conflict emerges where he feels he should be writing about migraines, but he clearly desires to write about dreams. He calls the migraine work—all the scientific work, in fact—his "tyrant." Sometimes he sees his own migraines as a destroyer of self: "Well, my good spirits ended with a bad migraine on Thursday . . . everything has vanished. This nasty habit of my (mental) organization suddenly to rob me of all my mental resources is for me the hardest thing in life to bear."

At other times, though, his own migraines become the gateway through which he glimpses his extraordinary map of the human mind:

> Everything fine except for the three-day migraine. . . . During an industrious night last week, when I was suffering from that degree of pain which brings about the optimal condition for my mental activities, the barriers suddenly lifted, the veils dropped, and everything became transparent—from the details of the neuroses to the determinants of consciousness. Everything seemed to fall into place, the cogs meshed.

More emphatically, he begins to see migraines as part, if not the keystone, of the systems of repression and transference that he will subsequently claim as the basis of our dream worlds. He tells Fliess about "the most touching substitute relationship between my migraine and my cardiac symptoms and the like," a more nuanced version of the "analogy in fantasy" he earlier believed made migraine a symbolic forced deflowering.

For a time, the two words—*dreams* and *migraines*—compete against one another in his letters, one clearly rising, one falling: "My mood, too, is still holding up. Putting it all in the dream book must have done me good. A mild migraine—ill humor occurred on October 6." But something has changed. By 1899—not coincidentally, the year he publishes *The Interpretation of Dreams,* his "Dream Book," widely regarded as his breakthrough—he's got control of the migraines. He attaches to them surprising, counterintuitive adjectives: they are his "splendid migraine(s)," his "gorgeous migraine(s)." And he *employs* them: "My health has been excellent," he tells Fliess in 1900, "regulated by a regularly recurring slight Sunday migraine."

As Max Schur observes in *Freud: Living and Dying,* "Freud's interest in migraine as a psychosomatic symptom . . . receded" at this time. He stops writing about them, although they do reappear in letters from time to time, often linked to creative milestones: "Totem work ready yesterday," he would tell one correspondent thirty years later, regarding *Totem and Taboo*, "terrible migraine." But they don't matter as much, as if Freud stopped caring about them when he completed a phase of self-analysis that got him over many of his other phobias—his fear of travel, his obsession with death—a period of what Schur called self-induced "intense stress."

But this period of self-induced "intense stress" was what made Freud Freud—the period during which he mapped the psyche in now-familiar terms like *repression, transference,* and *subconscious;* turned to psychoanalysis as the means to heal wounds in the mind; and stopped listening to the "tyrants" who turned him away from the work he really wanted to do. Migraines spoke to him on the one hand like the voicelessness he feared—the graying hair, the pain that made him want to die—and on the other, like the whispers of his own desires. His migraines existed within a "mental economy," as Peter Gay writes, at the switching point between the somatic and the psychosomatic: as the physical manifestation of something emotional he was holding back, was being held back, pressing, almost physically, against the confines of that small space between the temples. Finally, they became the catalyst that made it impossible to live with the constant tension between defense and desire, and that prodded him in the direction of desire.

More than that, the study of migraine, for Freud, led naturally to the study of other less tangible interior dramas. The link between hemicrania and psychoanalytic theory is partly fanciful—but, from inside the migraining skull, where Freud lived it, it is also obvious. Would not the idea, no, the experience, that the head is throbbing—that, even better, half of the head is throbbing, as Kipling wrote so wickedly, while the other half sits calm and functioning—lead invariably and naturally to the idea that the mind, too, is divided into units like id, ego, and superego, some of which function while others are dissolved in chaos? For that matter, why overstate Freud's innovation? The idea that the mind is repressing something, and that something emerges as this throbbing in one-half of the head, is older than Freud, older than Christ. Is not psychoanalysis a kind of metaphorical trepanning, a virtual sawing open of the head to let out the bad stuff?

We forget this Freud, who refused to be beaten by his own pain. Like Anne Conway, like Plato, he recognized a link between repression and migraine, between the soul in pain and the body. But his genius was that he turned the thing against itself. He wouldn't, as Didion would say half a century later, make friends with the pain inside his head. He would put it on the couch instead, like it was his patient.

Lesson to migraineurs: practice psychoanalysis like the Buddha. Practice Buddhism like Freud.

4

Freud would have loved Thomas Jefferson as a patient, even as a confidant. Jefferson was practically an encyclopedia of repression: when his wife died, he destroyed her letters and mourned by riding his horse in solitude across the Virginia hills. Together they could have talked about their headaches, and how their headaches inspired them. Freud could tell Jefferson about his four years in the 1890s, during which he outlined the basic concepts of psychoanalysis. He could tell Jefferson about the three-day migraine he suffered in 1896, from which he emerged with the key ideas for *Interpretation of Dreams* in his noggin, almost like a reward for the pain.

And Jefferson, in turn, could tell Freud about his six weeks in April and May of 1776, the worst headache of his life, and how he awoke from it "almost a new man," as he told John Page, suddenly clear about the revolution and what it meant, the high so stupendous that his six-week headache was followed by a six-week period where he drafted a constitution for the state of Virginia and composed the Declaration of Independence.

Migraine pushed Jefferson, yet made him a plainer man: he looked forward to sailing on George Washington's sloop, he told his daughter, because the motion sickness would make him vomit and relieve his headache. At first, they came to him when his heart boiled over with loss. He got his first one, his first recorded one, when he was twenty-two and heard the news that the woman he loved was going to marry someone else. It lasted two days, and when it ended, he sat down at eleven at night and wrote letters to friends saying that his "scheme" was "totally frustrated." The great headache of spring 1776, "paroxysms of the most excruciating pain," followed the death of his mother, from a paroxysm of her own that took her away "in less than an hour."

He only got them every six or eight years, but they could kill an entire season, as one did in the winter of 1790–1791, lingering all the way until the following fall. Jefferson tried hot water, mustard plasters, calomel, cinchona bark, celebrated physicians, with little effect. He had two episodes, at least, while he was president, in 1802 and 1807. And like Freud, he recognized these episodes as cataclysmic, as a confrontation with, if not death, then something close to nothingness: "an attack of my periodical head ach," he told one correspondent. "I am obliged to avoid reading, writing and almost thinking."

If his headaches simulated death, however, and emanated from loss—and frankly, his inability to manage grief through any other means—they quickly became strategic: "The art of life is the art of avoiding pain," he would write years later, only partly tongue-in-cheek. He was a revolutionary, too, in this sense, that he understood the wisdom of locking himself away when others did not. In 1776, the other Virginian members of the Continental Congress simply could not believe that Jefferson had an "inveterate head ach" because of the death of his mother. They believed, instead, that he was shacked up in Monticello with his new wife, or that he had lost his nerve, at least briefly, about the rebellion.

Dramatically, Jefferson framed his arrival back in Philadelphia as a rebirth, as something more than six weeks back home: he told Page on May 17 that "I have been so long out of the political world." The long headache could easily have reflected the stress of that rededication and ended, as Woolf might have written, when he broke free from his pre-American chrysalis. But, in another sense, he took the headache to Philadelphia with him. Among political documents, the Declaration of Independence is the most migraine-imbued. Partly, this is because of its stunning after-the-pain clarity, Jefferson's upwardly arching dreamy rhetoric of freedom, where contradictions like love of freedom and ownership of slaves melt away—a political philosophy that, as much as Nietzsche's earthier dreams of Superman, stemmed from the desire to rise above some ineffable force holding one down, to beat the enigma of pain through prose and through thought.

But mainly the Declaration of Independence is migrainy because of what it asks: leave me alone. The Continental Congress cleaned it up, but the early drafts are oddly intimate, filled with scenes where the political story of America seceding from Britain fades into a more emotional tale where a disappointed hero bids farewell to friends and family who have breached their promises and who just now irritate him: "We must endeavor to forget our former love for them," he wrote, and the Continental Congress cut, "Be it so, since they will have it."

It wasn't the only time Jefferson came out of a headache with more political vision than the times could handle: a "six-day illness" endured in Paris in 1789 inspired a letter to James Madison that contained what Merrill Peterson has called "the most original and most radical idea in the whole Jefferson catalogue," a magnificently subversive and "self-evident" anthem claiming that "the earth belongs . . . to the living." Not a particularly migrainy sentiment, but the looseness of it, the almost drunken spirit it would take to declare all inheritance null, speaks to the exhilaration he felt when his head stopped "ringing," as he put it.

The headaches unmoored him from the scenes of Enlightenment calm that otherwise ruled his head, and when they left, made Enlightenment calm seem like the most divine thing one could imagine. He understood this completely, was deft enough in self-analysis (something for which he is not, generally speaking, given much credit) to understand. He sensed the rhythm: his famous statement that "a little rebellion, now and then, is a good thing, and as necessary in the political world as storms are in the physical," which means many things, is axiomatic of the kind of migraineur who's got control of his headaches, or at least passes enough painless time between episodes to put them in perspective.

And he recognized the migraine as a compelling passage-way between the enlightened, conscious, controlled self and the feral, unthinking animal within. He told this story once, in his *Notes on the State of Virginia.* Crossing the Natural Bridge, the renowned rock formation spanning a gorge near present-day Lexington, Virginia, Jefferson wants to walk to the edge and look "into the abyss." He falls to his "hands and feet" and crawls to the edge, a two-legged beast becoming a four-legged one, and describes a "painful sensation." It's a "violent head ach." And then, a lift, an exaltation, "delightful in the extreme . . . it is impossible for the emotions, arising from the sublime, to be felt beyond what they are here . . . as it were, up to Heaven." Man turned to beast; beast turned to angel. Or, if one prefers, the different clinical phases of a migraine, expressed in divine metaphor.

Sensation junkie that he was, Jefferson bought the bridge from a local farmer so that, presumably, he could feel like this again and again.

5

As these stories ran around my mind, as November crawled along with no cessation of daily migraine, I began to feel a certain exhalation, a sense of rhythm, a stirring, something that had nothing to do with pleasure. Oliver Sacks once observed that "a different form of consciousness is involved in creativity," "a much richer and stranger and more mysterious form of unconsciousness." I think that's right: a different set of rules, if rules at all.

To this day, I cannot tell exactly what migraine and creativity have got to do with each other, if migraine is a kind of creative activity, or a kind of thwarted, damaged creative activity. If it is the former, of course, then one might see how the same brain that makes the pain makes the poem—that brain is always percolating, always throbbing with something. If it is the latter, then one might see how the pain makes the poem necessary: migraine is chaos, a crowd of unassimilated ideas that lapses into faceless pain because it has to, because of the sheer top-heaviness of such nervous human surplus. The auras are amazing in this regard: "Has / the circus / come / to town?" Karla J. Dorman, a cashier and writer from Burleson, Texas, wrote about hers in a fine short poem. One does not invite the circus to town; one does not choose the size and color of its crazy lights; one does not hire its freaks. It just shows up, and the big burly men plant its tent pegs in your skull without a permit.

In either case—and I subscribe to both theories—I fell well and truly. In conversation, I became intermittently unresponsive, an irritating habit I have been unable to break: my mind, I hate to say, is sometimes truly elsewhere, as much as I'd like to bring it back. I lost weight in a cascade, a couple of pounds a week at first, and then fourteen pounds in two weeks in late October. My blood pressure dropped about twenty points—a good thing, actually, though probably not this fast.

Then came a real break in my lucidity—a good thing, too, although, again, not this fast. It was still a gentle fall, though. Migraine is "comorbid," contemporary doctors say, with depression. Men and women with migraines or depression, for instance, are more likely to contract the other, but no one is yet prepared to say exactly which is cart and which is horse—or whether both are carts and both are horses. But I was not feeling comorbid. I was not in rage, not in desolation. My mind felt like an abandoned house, all the furniture gone, the windows open, the wind blowing through, the shutters knocking in that absent way. This feeling was neither calming nor troubling. I was, I think, just exhausted by a specific physiological demand.

And then, in the end—this is late November, somewhere near Thanksgiving—one small, clear moment, a memory reconfigured so finely that if it were surgery it would have taken lasers to do it. There was no migraine this morning, but my mind was tense with anticipation that one would come. It was an itch, and, almost involuntarily, I felt that it had a vintage to it. I have often remembered what it was like to see those first auras when I was five or ten years old. I have often remembered that I wondered then how to describe them. But this time, I remembered something I had buried. I remembered, too, telling myself that when I could describe the dance of—well, how can I do this now—the swirling, racing, dotting, oscillating phosphorescent nodes that swam in front of my eyes, when I could describe what they looked like, what they felt like, how they made me feel—then I would be connected, I would be someone whose lived life and remembered life fit into one another like hand in glove. I suddenly remembered that the ability to turn this specific experience into words was a test, and it deeply mattered to me. There had to be a way to talk across the divide that kept me permanently estranged from others, as we are all permanently estranged from each other by the spectacular privacy of our own sensoriums. I couldn't help but believe that such a bridge existed.

I would concentrate when it was happening, I would think myself to sleep with this exercise, calling the nodes back to me. I never really knit together the sentences, though. Maybe I tried too hard, or maybe I preferred the challenge. The maybes line up like a catalog of my shortcomings both as a person and as a writer. But they do say something about how we respond to our auras and to our migraines, and to anything like them. Either we repress them or they demand the kind of attention that digs the kind of well out of which one might not climb so quickly or so deftly.

I was doing this when I was eight, when I was twelve, when I was sixteen. I remembered that, too, the longevity, the time spent. That little reconfiguration of my memory in November just amazed me. Even now, I have to talk myself into believing it: I just can't believe it took me thirty years to recognize the compulsion, the sense of obligation, the world-shaping triggered in me by that little trick of the light back in my bedroom in Jersey.

And if I didn't know that about myself, then what did I know?

I started to write, during my one or two clear hours every day, click-clacked out some sentences on my heavy-set Compaq laptop. The beginning scraps of this book. I can't say I wrote well. But that was never the point: from Freud, Jefferson, Conway, and their fellow old practitioners, I was never looking for creative inspiration. I was looking for something even closer to bone. For years, I loathed the use of the word *writer* to describe myself: I thought it was pretentious. I told interviewers that I was boring but that my subjects were interesting. I joked with students that I made editors pay me fifty dollars extra every time I used the first person.

A four-month migraine headache, however, changed all that. It's not that I became interesting—if anything, I am much less interesting than I used to be. But the migraine taught me what I suspect real writers know and have known all along: you use everything, or try to. I used to write in serene states, with a blue-sky mind. Now there are great storm clouds, a flash of lightning inside, whenever I get close to that thing, *that thing*, we are all trying to say. I am scared and excited in a way I didn't used to be, scared and excited by the sheer weight of nervous human surplus that lies just beyond these orderly words. I'm shaking as I type. I am looking over my shoulder.

Dickinson had it right: if one feels a funeral in one's brain, one had better write a poem about a funeral in one's brain. One has to do *something*. The alternative, really, is unthinkable.

THREE

Equally for no reason whatever, the vibration stops. Then one enquires why one ever had it, & there seems no reason why one should ever have it again. Things seem clear, sane, comprehensible, & under no obligation, being of that nature, to make one vibrate at all.

—Virginia Woolf

Opening the Case

One night as I was awakening from a particular vicious
(migraine), I dreamed that I had put my head in a suitcase
and was carrying it at my side.

—MOLLY BARR

1

The headache didn't go away, of course. Three months after
the circus came to my town and the big burly men planted
their spikes, business was still steady. The old migraine seemed
unyielding, ancient. And the old practitioners of migraines still
seemed like giant isolate figures struggling heroically to transform their pain into something monumental. As fall turned to
winter, however, and I turned forty-four hating the dawn as
much as if it were the face of evil itself, I experienced one particularly vicious migraine one early December morning.

There was no premonition this time, no aura. There was a
sick reaction, as if I were suddenly allergic to all light, all sound,
the world itself. Moving around the study, I fell to my hands
and knees, with something like real blindness, a headache on
both sides and the middle, a real shutdown. Briefly, I thought:

ah, so this is how it is for others. I got my wish. Then there was a sense that something was out of control, a panic, then a complete nausea that quickly brought me two levels closer to the surface. And then, what I remember best, a true vertigo, the bar across the base of the bed frame, horizontal in better times, turning methodically like the second hand on a clock, making it hard to figure out even how to lie down.

I remember trying to move—something involuntary in the urge to press forward—but even the small amount of dexterity required to crawl on hands and knees was beyond me. Next I was telling Siobhán—I'm not sure at this point who's moving where, or what room we are in—this one, this one is a bad one. But I'm also aware that I've not been persuasive making this point, that I'm really just whispering like this was a casual moment and I don't want to wake up Aedan, so she says, I have to give an exam today, and maybe this is the way she buys herself a minute or two to pull herself together. And I say, I'm not really sure I remember what I said here, and then I'm up and calling the doctor, but I can't press the buttons on the cell. And then she's up and calling the doctor, but it's early still, maybe (this I do remember) just a few minutes before the doctor's office is scheduled to open, a little too early to get anyone, a little too late for the on-call number, and we had learned to steer clear of the emergency room (we finally did take Aedan there once when he had a slight cough and were practically laughed back out their sliding glass doors).

It's not that I decided that I'd rather die than go to the hospital. But I remained aware, and Siobhán with me, through the panic and confusion, that migraine can't do anything lastingly bad to you.

The head pain receded slightly, or rather, I modulated to it, found its rhythm, accepted its residency, whatever. Siobhán took

Aedan to school and went to work herself. In my memory, I remember the expression on her face that morning, and I imagine a conscientious composition, a blankness of expression layered slightly with concern, a self-conscious effort. The army nurse mobilizing dutifully. And I hated it. I count on her for something else: she's from Northern Ireland, and like many of her friends from that country, she makes impatience endearing, even a burlesque of short-temperedness one can neither take seriously nor entirely ignore. Hands on hips. Roll the eyes. Smile. Or not. Sometimes she goes too far (another Irishism), sometimes not far enough: the imprecision of the sarcasm is precisely what makes it great. With that expression, though, where she showed only wan patience, I knew something was alien.

I lay in bed, the gray stillness, the mewing cat, the dirty laundry. As helpless as a newborn left alone in a room, I realized that toughing it out was really a form of self-immolation, the desire to beat the headache only making the headache worse, a long, slow road down. I decided I had better do *something* besides trying to endure the onset as if there were still no other options.

And oddly, at the exact moment where I decided to pursue the shortest possible path to cure, I felt the deepest possible fondness for all the erratic trajectories I had been courting. And then that fondness dissipated, knocked to pieces by something very hard and very plain.

A reader might well wonder why I took so long. In fact, I'm completely typical: according to the American Migraine Prevalence and Prevention Study, undertaken in 2004, only a little over half of those with migraine symptoms have been diagnosed with migraine and treat themselves as migraineurs. Almost four in ten think they have sinus headaches, three in ten stress headaches. And treatment is, at best, erratic. While almost everyone takes something, over half stick to over-the-counter medications that don't particularly help, like aspirin or ibuprofen. Only 12 percent actually take a medication intended to prevent migraine, although another 17 percent medicate themselves "coincidentally": without knowing it, they happen to take a drug for some other ailment that also treats migraine.

The reasons for such widespread maltreatment are buried deep in the stoic culture of the migraine, but resonate in modern ways. Migraines are easily mistaken for those other headaches, of course, for which treatments are more readily available. Many women remain fearful of skeptical physicians, spouses, and employers, for whom a headache complaint remains an expression of hypochondria or weakness. And because three out of every four migraineurs are women, many male migraineurs regard their own headaches as feminine, and downgrade them accordingly.

Institutions remain loath to change, too. Headaches are old; but the field is "young," as one medical author notes. Medical schools still rarely offer fellowships in headache care; many Americans must still drive hundreds of miles to see a board-certified headache specialist. Large grant-giving institutions, like the National Institutes of Health, still don't have categories for "migraine" and "headache disorder" in their funding and research benchmarks, or dole out much money for the cause: per sufferer, Robert E. Shapiro and Peter J. Goadsby calculate, the government yearly allocates thirty-seven times as much on asthma research, one hundred times as much for epilepsy. And insurance companies remain unsurprisingly calculating. Investigators at Saint Louis University have found that ceilings placed on insurance reimbursements for migraine pills compel many men and women on limited

budgets to diagnose themselves with exactly as many migraines per month as they can afford, no matter what their
left temples may tell them.

If progress has been slow in some areas, however, in others
it has been like lightning. In the past two decades, the medical
profession has dramatically altered our portrait of the migraine.
As Richard B. Lipton and Marcelo E. Bigal of the Einstein College of Medicine have noted, it's a "real disease" now. It can
be recorded, more or less, using imaging technologies that no
generation in human history before ours has possessed. It can
be mapped genetically. Its victims are also better mapped: it
no longer attacks individuals, or attacks them exclusively, but
strikes what epidemiologists label "vulnerable populations."
And there are dozens of treatments now—drugs found by accident and at least one drug found by design, diets that make
no intuitive sense yet tell remarkable stories about the links between heart and head, head and stomach. There are headache
centers, headache magazines, headache societies, headache
support groups. And, above all, there are new habits of mind,
a new migrainy worldview.

The new migraine had arrived. And I, like many others, had
been late for my enlistment.

2
———————

First, the neurologist's office: yes, I do think the neurologist's
office is a central part of the experience, or, at least, putting
the experience in perspective. My neurologist belongs to a
practice with a cheerful name located, of course, in a shiny new

office park set amid cornfields that rapidly disappear as more shiny new office parks are built. It is conveniently set between an MRI office and a dentist's office, each accessible through glass doors so anonymous that one has no problem whatsoever walking into the wrong office.

The waiting room always seems windswept and desolate to me, like an empty prairie, stacks of magazines blown into the corners and one or two patients sitting in the waiting room chairs, usually but not always elderly, struggling to keep their heads elevated, their eyes open, obviously in so much pain that any remaining vestige of self-pity about my own discomfort scurries away in shame.

When I first meet my neurologist, in fact—a woman so tall and healthy-seeming that one almost expects her to ride into the examination room on a horse, an impression augmented, no doubt, by the oversized leather Ralph Lauren purse she brings with her instead of a laptop or clipboard—my first question to her after she takes my history is this: on a scale of one to ten for pain, I'm like, a one or two, right? No false modesty here: it just hit me (and hits me still). And she nods but doesn't laugh, and then laughs a little. A slow double-take, really splendidly executed.

If I had walked into a neurologist's office thirty or forty years ago, we might have had a very different conversation, and my diagnosis and treatment would have taken a very different path. Since the 1960s, however, the migraine, like many other diseases, had been *reorganized*. Headache specialists who had banded together in small professional associations in the 1960s and 1970s now banded together into large international organizations—most famously, the International Headache Society (IHS), founded in 1981 to set "the clinical standards and diagnostic criteria" for head pain. In 1988, led by Danish headache researcher Jes Olesen, they fulfilled this mission, publishing an influential guide called the *International Classification of Headache Disorders* (ICHD-I), and a popular second edition in 2004 (ICHD-II).

Treatment also reorganized. Headache clinics and centers, pioneered by physicians like Arnold P. Friedman at New York's Montefiore Hospital in the 1940s and Seymour Diamond in Chicago in the 1970s, spread as far as Albania and Argentina, and to cities as small as Springfield, Missouri, and Stamford, Connecticut. Patient–physician support and education groups like ACHE were also founded, and medical journals dedicated to headache were published for the first time *(Cephalalgia)* or rose in prominence *(Headache)*. A political consciousness even emerged, as documents like the *Kyoto Declaration on Headache* (2005)—naming headache as one of the twenty most common disabilities afflicting humankind—circulated internationally, and groups like the Alliance for Headache Disorders Advocacy lobbied the U.S. Congress for increased recognition for headache research and education programs.

As with any significant cultural change, too, a new vocabulary emerged. The migraine was now defined as a *syndrome*, the aggregate of its symptoms, not just a headache. As a headache, however, "migraine" was the most compelling example of a "primary headache," a headache with no other source but itself. It was demarcated from its kissing cousins, the "tension-type headache," the "cluster headache," and the "chronic daily headache," and its high-quality knockoff, the "probable migraine."

And it was blended and stirred like microbrewed ale, the term *chronic migraine* (also called *transformed migraine*, among other names) coined to describe the hellish brew created when a migraine becomes an everyday or every-other-day event. Migraine, in other words, was no longer just an "episodic disorder." It was, as Bigal and Lipton wrote, a "chronic disorder with episodic manifestations." A "progressive disorder," too, something that could worsen. Possibly, even, an illness with an "anatomical" profile—not a thief in the night but an arsonist. A real disease, that is, whose "conceptual framework" for treatment, as Lipton argues, was changing. You always wanted to "relieve pain and restore function," yes. But now, too, you would also want to "prevent attacks and prevent progression." It turns out, maybe (a clinical maybe, not a literary one), that migraine *can* do something lastingly bad to you.

Old names receded; new names introduced themselves. In ICHD-I and II, for instance, the IHS renamed "classic migraine" the "migraine with aura," or MA. The "common migraine" became the "migraine without aura," or MO. Harold G. Wolff's mid-twentieth-century migraine had three stages, which he pragmatically called "preheadache," "headache," and "postheadache." J. N. Blau's 1980s postmodern migraine, however, possessed five nuanced phases: "prodrome" (now called "premonitory symptoms"); then "aura"; then "headache" (sometimes preceded by that splendid extra phase, the "free interval"); then "headache termination"; then "postdrome."

The migraine itself was subdivided into smaller, more carefully defined syndromes. Migraine was not just migraine, not just migraine with aura or without: researchers also isolated "the familial hemiplegic migraine" (half the body goes weak) and the "basilar-type migraine" (a long aura emanating from the brain stem and impervious to the usual drugs). The "typical aura without headache" was offered as explanation for why individuals like Hildegard and Picasso could create such precise renditions of aura without ever complaining of headache.

Despite the scientific tone of the nomenclature, however, headache classification still remained waggishly vague, a learned tribute to the polymorphous quality of migraines. This can best be seen, perhaps, in the ICHD-II. On the one hand, the IHS authors tell us, they present "explicit" criteria: no usuallys, no oftens. On the other, they add, "many different evolutionary patterns seem to be crossing each other": the same patient can be diagnosed with two different headaches, or one turning into another. The migraine itself can be fairly short (four hours) or fairly long (three days), but it's only a migraine if you've had at least five—otherwise, it's "infrequent episodic tension-type headache." And if you get a lot of them—more than fifteen per month for three months or more, eight per month that "meet criteria for migraine without aura or that respond to migraine-specific treatment"—you've got "chronic migraine," too.

The criteria are mix and match, like the menu at an old Chinese restaurant. You have "migraine without aura" if you have "unilateral location" and "moderate or severe pain intensity," or "unilateral location" and "pulsating quality," or "pulsating quality" and "aggravation by or causing avoidance of routine physical activity," or any other combination of two symptoms. And, not or: you have "migraine without aura" if the headache is accompanied by "nausea," or "photophobia and phonophobia" (fear of light and sound), or both.

Likewise, you have "migraine with aura" if you have any one of the following symptoms: "fully reversible visual symptoms," positive (you see things that aren't there) or negative (you don't see things); "fully reversible sensory symptoms," again, either positive ("pins and needles") or negative ("numbness"); or "fully reversible dysphasic speech disturbance," like Freud had. In turn, these symptoms ought to emerge in some sort of pattern, again, best two out of three. Your auras have to run for more than "5 minutes," for instance, but less than "60 minutes." But if they don't, you might still have a migraine with aura if you have one symptom that develops over five minutes, or "different aura symptoms" that "occur in succession" over more than five minutes. Or, or and/or: "homonymous visual symptoms" (partially blind in both eyes) or "unilateral sensory symptoms."

My neurologist, of course, doesn't pursue a case history with this kind of precision, and one suspects few neurologists, even ones with headache expertise, do—even the ICHD-II recommends the use of "free text" as a diagnostic tool. Instead, she does a gloss, looks for a few key symptoms, and moves on. "In 'real life,'" the British researchers Russell Lane and Paul Davies observe, "many patients do not fall into these neat categories." While acknowledging that the new wave of classification is vital, many doctors in practice seem to prefer other approaches. It's probably a migraine, as Lipton and others have argued, when the pain is disabling and fits a certain persistent pattern. Some doctors use well-calibrated scales to measure the intensity of a patient's pain: the Migraine Disability Assessment Scale (MIDAS), for instance, "is scored in intuitively meaningful units of lost days." The Headache Impact Test (the HIT-6) asks similar questions about the severity of the pain, the depth of your life's disruption. The ID Migraine does early screening: interestingly, its users have found that "the 3 best predictors" of a diagnosis of migraine do not include, for instance, aura, but "nausea, disability, and photophobia."

Other doctors, though, employ what one headache researcher calls the "dirty little secret" of headache diagnosis: the "actively complaining patient." On this scale, if you make it to the doctor and "actively complain" of a headache, it's a meaningful indicator that you've got migraine, or something that should be treated like one.

Despite the new names and new data (Davidoff estimates

"between 475 and 620" refereed articles on the subject are published yearly), the migraine remains "protean," two-faced, appealing to both the "lumpers" and the "splitters" among headache specialists. If the migraine of the American twentieth century was inspired by neurosis, by stress, by the psycho- side of the psychosomatic spectrum, the new migraine of the twenty-first century is part of the machine, "hardwired," in the parlance of the day. But those of us with the "wiring" do not constitute an exclusive club. For many headache specialists, in fact, to be "migrainous" is simply part of "normal brain structures." "Everyone," Lane and Davies argue, has the physiological stuff, even if "most people don't experience symptoms that are clearly identifiable as 'migraine.'"

For all modern efforts to define migraine, to clearly state its boundaries, there persists this anarchic, egalitarian impulse, making it little surprise that one of the breakthrough paradigms of the new migraine is the "convergence hypothesis." So named in 2002 by a group of headache specialists led by Roger Cady of the Headache Care Center in Springfield, Missouri, the "convergence hypothesis" argues that most primary headaches are essentially migrainous, "different points along the same physiological process," "escalating" in the direction of migraine if not stopped. "Headache" itself, for Cady and his coauthors, is not deviant, but what Emily Dickinson regarded it as: "a nearly universal experience," "the final common expression of a wide variety of assaults upon the human nervous system."

It is almost a political statement: headaches are democratic, and all headaches "converge" toward migraine. Different beginnings, different inspirations, all leading to one response, one loud, crude shock from the brain (and to the brain) as answer. The brain really doesn't care what turns it on. Some people simply have more on switches than other people. And what makes the switch go click still remains the great mystery.

3

Here's why migraine research remains as hard for contemporary researchers as it did for Hippocrates or Aretaeus: despite the discovery of drugs that can induce migraine, it remains difficult to catch someone mid-migraine, let alone solicit his or her cooperation. That seems pretty obvious. And here's why migraine research is easier than ever before: functional magnetic resonance imaging (fMRI), positron emission tomography (PET), and all the other forms of "functional imaging" that have revolutionized the study of the human body over the past few decades. It may still be hard to catch that migraineur and coax him or her into a bright lab. But it's never been easier to watch the brain in action and to see what is actually happening as the pain and the aura spread.

Combined with advances in microbiology, pharmaceuticals, and gene mapping, contemporary researchers have been able to use these various kinds of imaging to chart what they often call the "mechanism" of migraine. The word, however, is another false metaphor, implying more coherence than actually exists: as "mechanisms" go, the migraine, as it appears to modern physicians, is a collection of small machines that never really adds up to one big efficient one.

Let's start with the aura, which continues to puzzle researchers. Karl Lashley, drawing his own auras in 1941, and Aristides Leao, shocking rabbits that same year, performed visionary acts: numerous recent studies have confirmed the presence of "cortical spreading depression" (CSD) in patients as they aura, a surge of electrical current in parts of the brain, followed by a diminution of current in a larger part of the brain. What these studies cannot explain, however—and, in fairness, rarely try to—are the auras that do not match the CSD model, the ones that are wholly "positive," or "negative," or too long, or too short, or make you think that, like Alice, you are nine feet or ten inches tall.

Nor, for that matter, can these studies—yet—really explain the relationship between the headache and the aura: "Nobody has decided," Stewart J. Tepper, director of research for the Center for Headache and Pain of the Cleveland Clinic Foundation, observes. Some researchers believe there is no relationship, that pain and aura treat different pathways. Others believe that the aura is the start of all migraines, and that men and women who suffer migraine without aura are, in fact, experiencing ghostly "silent" auras. And others still believe that aura is the starter, but it operates on a kind of "rheostat": sometimes it's got the amps to gin up a headache and sometimes not.

Other researchers have mapped the headache, not the aura, also in cunningly industrial terms. Using PET and fMRI, several researchers—Weiller and his coauthors from the University of Essen in Germany, for starters—have argued that the headache originates in a "migraine generator," situated somewhere at the back of the brain, far away, in most cases, from where the throbbing will actually occur. This may sound counterintuitive to a layperson, but this is the way our trickster brains actually work: the entire nervous system is wired crossways, so a live nerve on the left side of the brain will trigger a headache on the right.

The disturbance, in turn, travels from the migraine generator down pain "pathways," which change with age the way the

Mississippi changes its course, explaining the reason why your migraines shift position from time to time. In time—in no time at all—the disruption turns on the trigeminovascular system, a kind of middleman that turns a disruption in the nervous system into an event that makes blood vessels dilate on the meninges, the protective covering that guards your nervous system and keeps your brain from rubbing against your skull.

The nerves there don't like the dilating blood vessels, so they release inflammatory chemicals, and it is this one-two punch—angry blood vessels, angrier nerves—that make the pain. And if the migraine generator stays turned on after the headache is over—and the PET and fMRI studies say it will in some patients—then you are going to get a lot of migraines until someone hits the off switch.

As unified as this mechanism sounds, however, it still doesn't explain whether and how the electrical disruption that lies at the heart of the weird vision and sound shows also inspires the head pain that follows. Let's look at this from a slightly different perspective: that of the nerve cells themselves, also called neurons, the tiny single-celled (more or less), uprooted tree–shaped (more or less) inhabitants of the migraine generator, the pain pathways, the meninges.

Normally, neurons stay "at rest," which is generally how you like them. But they can be "activated," or "fire," often in response to neurotransmitters like calcium or serotonin, chemicals that open up little doors in the cell membrane and allow a change in electrical differential to take place inside. Like a wire, the neuron conducts the electricity to its other end, where the neurotransmitter creates a new door to the next neuron, and so on, turning waves of neurons on or off across expanses of your brain. And firing neurons, or activating them, means that they make pain, or send along the message that makes pain.

Not all neurons are alike, of course—they're not even remotely alike. Like humans, some are excited by stimuli that
bore others. And some answer the door for certain visitors and
not others. They are well named, based on what neurotransmitters they receive—or, rather, what their receptors, those doors
on the cell membrane, receive—and what happens. Here, for
instance, are the names of serotonin receptors: 5-HT_2, 5-HT_{1B},
5-HT_{1D}, and so on. 5-HT_2 helps excite its home neuron when it
receives serotonin, which you don't want. Give a cell with the
5-HT_{1B} receptor some of that serotonin, though, and it reduces
the swelling on the blood vessels of the meninges, which you
do want. Give 5-HT_{1D} a shot of serotonin, and it helps cut off
the release of those inflammatory chemicals, again, something
you want.

Now here's where it comes together. One more approach:
genes. The idea that migraines run in families is a millennium
old. Here's what else is a millennium old: the idea that migraine
has multiple triggers and that the triggers are different from
one migraineur to the next. Contemporary researchers have
produced convincing studies that endorse the position of their
ancient and medieval ancestors, producing ample positives for
what causes a migraine. The difference now, however, is that
the entire enterprise is mapped on the double helix. Defective
calcium assimilation? There's a spot for that, and yes, that will
cause a migraine. Does your body inhibit serotonin for no good
reason? That's a mapped flaw, too. Like a bad street corner, a
certain "locus" attracts a bad crowd: "19p13," for instance,
has been described as a "hot spot" for migrainy genes, as has
"15q11–13," where many migraines with aura get their start.

The migraineur's gene map is not done, of course; if anything, scientists have barely begun that work. But it provides a
sense and a shape to the problem: migraine is what doctors call

"polygenic," which means that it can be inspired by a flaw on any number of genes. Some people have many of these flaws and some have one, and some, it would seem, have none. This means, essentially, that what might cure one migraineur should not be expected to cure another. And when one cross-references the tics hardwired into the body against the multiplicity of lifestyles, of exposures—and when one throws in the matter of the aura, and the bad stomach, too, let alone the half-dozen other seemingly disconnected symptoms—the problem of finding what causes a migraine and what stops it multiplies exponentially.

Sifting this data, medical researchers have lighted on a word to describe the brain of a migraineur: it is "hyperexcitable." That does not mean that the person is easily excited, only that his or her neurons are likely to fire much quicker and for much less inspiration. Some researchers argue that the source of hyperexcitability lies in genetic mutations, others in flaws in visual processing. Others theorize that the somatosensory cortex (the part of the brain that processes sensory info) of a migraineur is thicker than that of a nonmigraineur. Others still theorize that the difference is the mechanism itself. Rami Burstein and Moshe Jakubowski of Harvard offer the "unitary hypothesis" (not to be confused with the "convergence" one): "Different migraine triggers," they argue, "activate a wide variety of brain areas," lots of pathways getting lots of parts of the brain involved in lots of symptoms.

Peter Kropp, in the Department of Medical Psychology at the University of Kiel, tries to make a lovely point about all this: Maybe the difference, he argues, is that the brains of adult migraineurs still act like those of children. There's a "greater sensory openness" that children have during the period of "sensory imprinting." In grown-up migraineurs, that open switch never turns off. It sounds interesting. It even sounds nice. But it really isn't. It just means the chemicals move a little faster, the light bulb gets a little hotter, and sets fire, all too easily, to that cheap lampshade you inherited from your grandparents and wouldn't replace even if you could, which you can't.

In truth, the exploration of the modern migraine might be a linguistic quest as much as a scientific one. *Depressive,* as a noun, makes its subject sound passive, someone the depression acts upon. *Migraineur* makes one sound elegantly active (that touch of French, that spare *u* in the penultimate spot), like your headaches are something you craft, you polish, you practice. And what languid beauty lies in phrases like "free interval," "spreading depression," "galloping migraine," and, of course, "aura," a gorgeous old Greek word—the name of yet another weather goddess—that means "breeze."

Reading through medical textbooks—a hobby I much recommend—a layperson is struck by all the phrases that seem to promise more than they intend. Is it really possible that the language of neurology *needs* to be this expressive? Does the brain really have, can it really be clinically described as possessing, "eloquent" and "noneloquent" areas? Which parts of the brain are *most* eloquent, then? And can neurological disorders really achieve an "alarming crescendo"? Here's inimitable Karl Lashley, describing an aura:

> The scintillations have the form of distinct parallel lines, which cannot be counted but give the impression of groups of five or more. These seem to sweep across the figure toward the advancing margin and are constantly renewed at the inner margin, like the illusion of movement of a revolving screw.

My intuition is to think that language this refined is not innocent, that it shows how much the entire enterprise is about
naming the unnamable foreignness of that little-understood
organ between our ears, ironically, using itself, the only tool
we have with which to understand it. Maybe neurologists are
poets at heart, or maybe the brain, as a clinical entity, is more
poetic than we give it credit.

To understand migraine in modern terms means reading
through the advice you receive, though, *through* what the doctors and even the other migraineurs tell you, to the truth within,
which comes at you from crazy angles as if crazy angles were
the norm: that the "generator" of the pain should lie so far
from the pain itself; that "hyperexcitable" nerves must compel
retreat to silence and to darkness. But what kind of brain does
these kinds of things, and how do we reach it, really reach it,
and talk to it?

It seems clear that physicians write about brains that mesh
with the dominant paradigms of their time, that Thomas Willis's brain had a Newtonian feel, that the brains of the great
Victorians were all cogs and gears and waterwheels and a touch
of electricity and steam. By this standard, the new migraine
requires new metaphors. Drugwise, the practitioner of the new
migraine belongs to the same family as the epileptic (always
has, by the way) and the badly Tased (the badly Tased, in turn,
looks to the lightning strike victim for ancestry and lineage).
The hyperexcitable neurological system, in turn, is a computer
easily given to system error, awaiting its next reboot. Or better:
the migraining brain is an overloaded motherboard, the migraining brain its most visible breakdown. Has your computer
monitor ever failed and, in failing, it looked like a rainbow had
melted across your flowcharts or your prose? Like that.

One feels compellingly like a state-of-the-art entertainment appliance that took an electrical shock and won't quite work anymore. Circuits have failed, wires have fused together, cables have fallen under wet leaves somewhere in a deep forest, and a staticky hush has descended over your family room. The DVD player won't take the disc, or takes the disc but jerks horribly across the third, fifth, and eleventh scenes of every movie, always, as regular as dawn itself.

Or maybe the migraining brain is the scratched DVD itself: researchers at Leiden University in the Netherlands claim that MRI pictures inside migraineurs' skulls show many "subclinical brain lesions"—especially if the migraineur gets auras or a high frequency of migraines. It's hard to know what to do with this one: each headache a scratch on the DVD, until you can't watch the movie at all? Each headache a scratch on the paint job of your Hyundai? Do they slow down the car, make it labor on the straightaways, or do those scratches just rust, leaving the Hyundai still able to get you where you need to go? The doctors from Leiden warn us that these "types of brain lesions . . . increase the risk of adverse sequelae," like stroke and dementia. That is, they slow down the Hyundai.

None of these metaphors or similes really work, though, any more than the photographs on flickr or the paintings at the migraine art competitions completely close the gap that divides migraineur from non-, and the migraineur from himself or herself. As Scarry writes, "To conceive of the body as parts, shapes, and mechanisms is to conceive of it from the outside." The language of migraine is all outside. What is needed is the language of the inside. Such a language, though, such a language. We know the brain is not an orderly place, not a logical one, although one feels a certain optimism from the notion that it can be so confidently mapped and photographed. It feels like a machine, yes, but a very humble one, overwired and miswired by some previous homeowner who didn't want to spend the money on an electrician, and didn't mind if he had to flick a switch in the living room to turn on the garbage disposal.

But it's a soft machine, too, as the cliché goes. For all that electricity running through it, one also senses the wash of chemicals and blood within which the machine purrs and ticks and buzzes. A migraining brain, in turn, simply clicks itself on and off more often than a nonmigraining one. That's all. It is more subject to brownouts, certainly, and even blackouts. It *is* staticky, its barriers more porous, the divides between normal states of being more like demilitarized zones.

But all these descriptions: more systems, more outside. How to get inside?

Taking the Cure

No headaches AT ALL . . . it's worth not being able to
feel my feet most of the time.

—ASKAPATIENT.COM RESPONDENT, DESCRIBING
SIDE EFFECTS OF A MIGRAINE DRUG

1

We talk to the brain, we reach inside, through the cures we employ. And no better evidence illustrates the continuing mystery
of the migraine than the forms of treatment it has inspired in
a modern age.

As I walked out of my neurologist's office that first time, I
felt neither optimistic nor pessimistic. The diagnosis was solid
enough, if imperfect. Like most, I could be credibly, airtightly
diagnosed with two or three different kinds of headache, something "evolving": something "episodic" entering the "chronic
migraine" area, even slipping into "new daily persistent headache" (I learned about this one later), with a suspicion of "medication overuse" to keep things lively.

That was all fine: the blurriness of definition was, in many
ways, more assuring than a quick diagnosis. But the conversa-

tion around the outskirts was vague. I was sure of my neurologist's medical authority and her compassion (and nothing she did or said subsequently would change that), but she wore that medical authority and compassion lightly, relegating me to that gray postmodern world of "this might work" or "you might try this" and "check back later."

This was the outline of what she prescribed. First, she recommended a drug, Topamax, that anti-epileptic drug prescribed to men and women with frequent migraine (my GP had placed a sample in my wet palm three months before, but I had ignored it). It would take a month or two to ramp up, and I might not be really happy for a while, but it worked a lot of the time. Second, she recommended that I keep the Imitrex around, for more urgent occasions. Third, she recommended that I keep taking atenolol, my blood pressure medicine, which was actually often prescribed for migraine: my "coincident" medicine, it turns out. Fourth, she recommended that I keep a migraine diary, a *real* log of my headaches and what might be triggering them. She was not militant about this, and even looked at me sardonically when I mentioned buying a little blank diary for the purpose.

Fifth, she mentioned, without endorsing, other avenues I might pursue, none of which included reading the medical textbooks and scholarly articles I was already poring through. Rather, these included alternative practices, such as acupuncture and biofeedback, and even herbal remedies. And, last, she also suggested—and let me get her expression right here, because it was not skeptical but well in the territory of detachment—that I might check out some of the headache remedy books I could find on the shelves of my local chain bookstore, and see if they had anything that helped me.

In retrospect, I would come to admire the thoroughness of

this list of recommendations. She had not covered *everything,* but she had provided a fine gloss on many of the remedies currently available to migraineurs. Migraine has many possible sources. By that logic, however, it also has many possible treatments. But just as headache researchers remain cautious about saying how all the parts of migraine fit together, their sense of history keeps them fairly wary about the idea that migraine cures are a conscious work of humans: "The word 'serendipity' appears repeatedly when the history of" migraine-preventing drugs is described, writes Elizabeth Loder of the Brigham and Women's/Faulkner Hospitals in Boston, because so many of them were discovered without "concerted, purposeful effort." By accident or design, the acute or "rescue" treatments—for when the migraine hits—have worked pretty well. But the preventive options, the "prophylaxis," have only achieved "about 50% reduction in frequency of attacks in approximately 50% of the patients," as one headache specialist observes—a huge improvement, but nothing you'd want to count on. The best prescription, then, is often a lot of prescriptions, doled out in a when and a how that makes medical sense.

My three drugs of choice, for instance, provide a fair example of the way modern migraine drugs work and how they came to be known as migraine drugs at all. Imitrex is the brand name for sumatriptan, a leading member of a family of drugs called triptans, developed in the mid-1980s by a researcher named Pat Humphrey and that stalwart of modern medicine, a team at a large pharma firm. Triptans were the game-changer, the single class of drugs explicitly devised to treat migraine as it happens, proving, in Humphrey's words, that "migraine truly is an organic disease and not just the figment of imagination of 'neurotic' patients."

Here's what a triptan does: remember serotonin receptors 5-HT$_{1B}$ and 5-HT$_{1D}$, those doors on certain nerve cells? A triptan opens them and makes those cells do what they do best, in the former case reducing the swelling of blood vessels where it hurts, in the latter reducing the release of inflaming chemicals. Some do it fast (Imitrex, for instance, or Relpax, an eletriptan), within an hour or two, and some do it slow (Frova, a frovatriptan), over four hours, but all work with dramatic effectiveness.

Here's what they don't do, though: stop an aura, or work that well if you wait too long to take one. Some people find that one triptan works, but another doesn't. Some people find that it takes a couple of tries before one works. Some people—a substantial minority, at least—find that none of them work. And some people—those with bad hypertension, a family history of heart disease, or diabetes—find that they fiddle with the size and shape of their blood vessels a little too much to be entirely safe.

Atenolol, in contrast, is a beta-blocker, synthesized to treat hypertension, and for use after heart attacks. Like other beta-blockers, there is no clear reason why it helps people with their migraines, and the fact that it helps any migraineurs at all was discovered only by "serendipity" in the 1960s when doctors prescribing propranolol (now sold, usually, as Inderal) discovered that it helped prevent migraines as well as lower blood pressure.

Perhaps the reason this class of drugs works on migraineurs is the simplistic one: beta-blockers slow a person down, and so relieve the sources of stress that inspire migraine in certain individuals. Or perhaps the answer is more clinical. Remember 5-HT$_2$, the serotonin receptor that helps excite nerve cells and cause migraines? Beta-blockers, as the name implies, block the impact of betas, which are adrenaline receptors, and cut down adrenaline effects throughout the brain, including—possibly—one that trips 5-HT$_2$ into action.

Topamax, lastly, is topiramate, an anti-convulsant drug approved by the Food and Drug Administration in 1995 to treat epilepsy. Nine years later, however, persuaded by several large studies and vast anecdotal demand, the Food and Drug Administration also approved the drug for migraine, and it is now estimated that four million Americans take it daily, often because the other drugs have not worked.

And yet no one exactly knows why Topamax *does* work. In part, that is because the relationship between epilepsy and migraine remains vague—the two syndromes share symptoms like visual disruption and the death-like neurological shutdown, which is why, for instance, Van Gogh could produce paintings so reminiscent of migraine auras while likely suffering from something else. And, in part, Topamax remains a bit of a mystery because anti-convulsants, as Robert A. Davidoff has written, do so many things that it's hard to tell what's doing the trick. On the cellular level, Topamax might be working on some other receptors the way triptans work on the ones for serotonin. Or it might be working on the ion channels—the gateways into nerve cells that help control the flow of voltage rushing around the brain—slowing down their action or even blocking them like beta-blockers inhibit the activity of adrenaline from cell to cell.

Of course, these three kinds of drugs really only nick the iceberg. Besides anti-hypertension drugs like the beta-blockers, triptans, and anti-convulsants, American migraineurs are also taking antidepressants, a practice begun half a century ago when the link between migraine and neurosis was the hot diagnosis. They are also taking narcotics like Vicodin or Demerol (which they probably shouldn't be). Other migraineurs are treating

themselves with anti-inflammatories and analgesics and vaso-
constrictors alone or in interesting mixtures (Excedrin Migraine,
for instance, is part aspirin, part acetaminophen, and part caffeine), barbiturates, other anti-epileptic medicines, or methysergide, the 1960s-era drug still sold under the brand name Sansert.
Calcium channel blockers work like Topamax theoretically does,
and impede the ion channels in cells that like to change their
current when they taste calcium.

Magnesium is a popular alternative to pharmaceutical remedies: "Migraines occur when the blood vessels of the brain act
erratically," Jay S. Cohen writes understatedly in *The Magnesium Solution*. "Magnesium causes them to relax." The store
of herbal remedies is also vast: many men and women, for instance, swear by massive doses of B_2 vitamins, or butterbur,
an aster plant with a long medicinal pedigree that is also often
used to treat asthma and allergies.

Among alternative remedies, biofeedback has many adherents: learn how your body works and then teach yourself to
regulate it, often, in the treatment of migraines at least, by learning how to control the heat in your hand. Maybe it's the relax-
ation therapy that produces results, but maybe it's the sense of
confidence many biofeedback patients feel when they discover
they can control parts of their bodies that formerly seemed
uncontrollable: "It may thus be the case," E. B. Blanchard and
coauthors wrote with emphasis in 1997, "that it is the experience of apparent success at an ostensibly relevant task of high
credibility that leads to . . . (headache) relief."

Likewise, some studies have endorsed the idea that acupuncture relieves migraine, especially, as researchers at the University
of Padua observe, if you supplement with a good rizatriptan (aka
Maxalt). Let the practitioner of Traditional Chinese Medicine
(TCM) diagnose the cause of your ailment, sometimes inter-

nal but often external, "an invasion," Ruth Kidson writes, "by the essential characteristics of that factor, resulting in a disease that reflects those characteristics." For headache, wondrously, the most common invasion is that of wind, "always moving, insubstantial, and agitated." Let the acupuncturist find the beleaguered meridian and slide in the needles at the right points: *Angle of the Head,* maybe, at the "corner of the forehead." Or *Wind Pool,* "at the back of the neck." Or *Yang Brightness,* "between the eyes." Restore the balance between yin and yang. Shut down the bad *qi.* Restore the good *qi.*

If half of migraine treatment consists of active therapies, however (preventive or "rescue" or both), the other half consists of passive therapies, a short or long list of the things you oughtn't do, oughtn't eat, oughtn't see. Almost every persistent migraineur is aware of this strategy: keep a diary, search for "triggers." And almost every migraineur is aware of the limits of this approach. Sometimes triggers are obvious and scarcely require a diary. Light. Weather changes. Menstruation. Stress: an "aggravating factor," according to the International Headache Society, just so we're clear—it doesn't make migraine, but makes you do things, like not eat, that do.

But sometimes triggers are not obvious, not at all. Because there is no clear gestation period that turns trigger into throb, for instance, there's no way of knowing, except through repeated mistakes, that yesterday's chocolate was the inspiration, and not Tuesday's steak, or this morning's low sun shining through the trees, or this afternoon's hell-bent conference call, or a cunning combination, again, of two out of three.

Migraine researchers have done significant work in this area, but the list of potential triggers only seems to grow longer. Two hundred years ago, a migraineur in treatment was ushered away from buttered toast and chocolate. But contemporary migraineurs need to worry about an extended list of foods, from staples like corn, eggs, and wheat for some sufferers to preservatives like MSG and nitrates for others. They need to worry, too, about ambient modern triggers like the air conditioning or the cleanser the night crew at the office used to clean the carpet.

And yet while all these triggers have been proven to produce a headache in some migraineurs, few triggers have been shown to produce a migraine in more than a fraction of migraineurs, so there are few sure guesses and few opportunities to make an easy call, to impose a moratorium, and get on with your life. Even the sure things are not sure things: researchers have found that roughly 60 percent of all migraineurs identify weather change as a trigger, but half of those identify the wrong weather change, blaming falling barometric pressure when they should blame rising, or a cold blast when it's dry air they should vilify.

Likewise, while two-thirds of all women with migraines identify menstruation as a cause, only 15 percent have migraines *only* during menstruation, complicating the chain of cause and effect. In many cases, it seems, change itself is the culprit: not the kind of weather change, but weather change at all. Not the amount of stress, or the amount of estrogen, but the sudden rise and fall.

In certain cases, the trigger is not even necessarily a trigger. While many physicians still cite chocolate as a major provocateur, for instance, some prominent migraine specialists argue that a craving for chocolate is actually a premonitory symptom, and that the candy stands guilty as charged only because it was standing in the wrong place at the wrong time. In other cases, the trigger is a mistake. Sunlight, for instance, causes migraine headaches in some people the way it makes others sneeze, an electrical signal sent by the optic nerve to the brain in response to bright light and misinterpreted by the overzealous trigeminovascular system as a different kind of threat completely.

Even more remarkably, triggers seem to be culturally particular. French migraine researchers, testing a French population, found widespread complaints about white wine and chocolate. British researchers, testing their own countrymen and women, found red wine and cheese to be the more potent triggers. Such anomalies might point to flaws in the studies, but more likely, they point to something mysterious about the human temperament that migraine reveals. It's not the chemical in the wine that triggers the migraine generator, but something else inside the wine entirely, something in what the wine means to the drinker—something that might change by region, by individual, by culture, that simply obliterates the border between the somatic and the psychosomatic.

From this diversity of therapies and diagnoses, all of which seem to work but few of which work fully, a conversation has emerged. Some diseases have a clear cause; others have a clear cure. The treatment of migraine, however, in any individual case, amounts to a treatment about treatment itself—about *how* one wants to use drugs, about *how* one wants to change one's life, about *how* one wants to sift through all this data that modernity produces.

This is, in fact, the barely hidden agenda of the convergence hypothesis, one of the reasons it speaks so potently to contemporary headache specialists and their patients. It is not just a clinical evaluation of the nature of headache, but a response to an overabundance of research and classifications. Patients are "confused," Cady and coauthors note, about "what is and is not migraine." Not sure whether they are migraining, patients "wait and see," when all evidence suggests that nothing beats a quick triptan before whatever you might be having escalates. What "converges" in the convergence hypothesis, in other words, are treatment recommendations.

In reality, despite the impression of diversity, a consensus has emerged about what you should do with your new, improved modern migraine. Go to the bookstore, and that's where you'll see this conversation most vividly—both the richness of it and the consensus. Since the mid-1990s, just as there has been an explosion of research into migraine, so, too, has there been an increase in the number of books on migraine written for laypeople and offering different kinds of "breakthrough" cures.

Just as grant-giving institutions like the National Institutes of Health still don't classify headache and migraine as separate categories for funding purposes, however, major bookstores make you work: no section for headache or for migraine, either, though there are sections for asthma, for chronic fatigue, for depression. Chronic illness—you probably know this—is a new, essential genre, a few books there, medical advice, step one, personal advice, step two, uplift (don't overdo it), step three. But migraine is still hard to find. Sprinkled in the section entitled "Illness," or "Pain Relief," you are likely to find three or four titles, and likely these: *What Your Doctor May Not Tell You About Migraines: The Breakthrough Program That Can Help End Your Pain,* by Alexander Mauskop and Barry Fox; *Living Well with Migraine Disease and Headaches,* by Teri Robert; and most popularly, *Heal Your Headache: The 1-2-3 Program for Taking Charge of Your Pain,* by David Bucholz.

On the surface, these books promise iconoclastic cures, time-tested outside the traditional medical establishment. And the cures are sometimes as iconoclastic as promised. Mauskop (director of the New York Headache Center) and Fox, for instance, make a substantial case for a three-pronged semiherbal cure featuring magnesium, the blood vessel relaxer; riboflavin, which helps energize those listless mitochondria; and feverfew, a kind of wannabe sunflower that also works, theoretically, to slow down serotonin.

At the same time, most of these volumes also offer a strikingly similar set of observations and reference points. Some of the advice is common sense; some of it is centuries, if not millennia, old. Find a good doctor—not just a GP (nothing personal) or a neurologist (the GPs of the nervous system) but a true headache specialist. Acquire good sleeping habits and eat more regularly (we might as well be reading Ben Franklin's *Autobiography* here). Simplify your life. "Educate yourself," Teri Robert, a patient advocate, herself a migraineur, recommends: Emerson could literally have not said it with fewer words.

But there is something else, too, a description of a way of life, heartbreakingly close to the prescriptions for living from addiction programs, inverted, maybe, or maybe lacking the moral component of those programs' dicta. If the practitioner of the old migraine specialized in Zen and will, the practitioner of the new migraine is a specialist in counterintuition. As I listened to my neurologist (not a headache specialist, but no dozer), as I read these books, as I (platonically) searched my soul, I found that, to be cured, I would have to stop toughing it out. I had to learn, too, that just as the nervous system sends its messages crosswise, everything that can save you can hurt you, too, because that is the great and indefatigable truth of migraines.

My migraine cure, in fact, was grounded in faith. I would give up painkillers that authentically killed pain with only nominal evidence that they also caused it, and give up pleasures with only nominal evidence that they inspired pain, in the hope

I could work my way out of an insidious network of double-crosses and rebounds (this is, in fact, Bucholz's first step). I would have to make peace with Imitrex, that splendid pill that healed my throbs every time but gave me new ones if I downed three in a six-day period.

And I would have to make peace, too, with caffeine (my older brother's solution, by the way), which can stop a migraine in ten minutes and start one twelve hours later, which seems to help some people and simply destroy others. Likewise, some exercise is good, and some exercise is bad—one just has to *feel* it. In fact, an extraordinary number of the things most deft at stopping the blood vessels in one's brain from dilating are also adept at starting them up again, usually after an interval of time sufficiently random to conceal their complicity in the second act.

One can meditate on what quality in the contemporary age yielded this wisdom to our medical personnel. I like to think that we are simply very paranoid and very clever, able to trace evil closer to its origins than any generation that preceded us but no more able than our ancestors to uncover its roots. Ironically, though, this has led to treatment being more scattershot and not less. The advice to find your triggers, and eliminate them, is routine. But since researchers, practicing neurologists, and how-to writer-doctors all acknowledge that the triggers are harder to catch than the Road Runner, many of them gravitate (a gentle pull, but unmistakable) toward the essentially practical recommendation to cut a broad swath across all the potentials. No alcohol, no chocolate, no diet drinks, no "high-sugar events," my doctor told me. No bananas, no peanut butter, no smoked meats, all the tobacco you want, all the *stale* bread you want, the books argued. Wear sunglasses a lot, because you can never be sure which sunbeam is the toxic one.

And if the headaches are particularly bad, and if you are the sort who takes advice particularly seriously, the solutions are direly prophylactic. Try to keep things quiet, not just during the headache, but before and after. Maybe you should give up sex—there is such a thing as a "benign orgasm headache"—although doctors from the past often argued quite the opposite. And remember, change is the enemy. Try not to let your weekends be too different from your weekdays: that's the "weekend migraine." Watch your vacations: that's the "vacation migraine," aka the "Maui migraine." Keep that stress level nice and steady, not too low (there's a "let-down migraine"), not too high. And maybe you don't want to move around too much. You still won't know why electricity gathers inside your head as if inside a thunderhead and then releases itself like lightning across your cerebrum. But maybe your headaches will go away, or, at least, become something with which you can live.

2

———

I start in mid-December. A languorous fall has left some leaves on the trees, some heat in the air. The nights are quiet: I spend the evenings in our family room listening to the clear echoes of branches brushing against the house, wind dashing the tall oaks, rains falling heavily and then dissipating. The temperature is dropping, though—and then this night, the first night of winter. Inside, a low pain lies over my right eye like a thin cumulus cloud at sunset, tilted slightly. Not too bad, but a sad inevitability.

First, I began the bans. No drugs but Topamax, no foods

but those on a tight list. I was barely eating anyway, but this was still hard. All the *verboten* is a primary reason so many people find it hard to give up their migraines: "wine, chocolate, caffeine," a friend mused to me, as I reeled off the list of forbidden substances, "why don't you just kill yourself?" But I became a hermit in wide open spaces anyway, attentive to every dose of every stimulus, newly aware of how head and stomach meet and match. I took each ban in turn and found myself missing each in different ways. I didn't miss beer and wine very much, but hated being the only person not drinking in the room: drunk people never buy the migraine claim, I have found, and will *never* stop trying to buy you a shot. I missed everything about the taste of chocolate and soon found myself cheating it in wanton little doses.

What every migraineur learns, though, and no one more than those migraineurs who choose to give it up, is a deep respect for caffeine. Pope's cure still holds sway in modern America: there must be millions of American migraineurs who weigh their coffee with devout seriousness, knowing that the slightest uptick or downturn in their daily intake will trigger an equally devout migraine. It is small wonder, considering the option. Giving up caffeine is almost bad enough to make one reconsider the headaches, in part because the withdrawal causes headaches almost indistinguishable from the original.

I managed the decaffeination headaches, which felt familiar enough. But I was surprised at what happened afterward: a listlessness appeared that was, from a metaphysical standpoint, even worse than the pain. The real danger of caffeine comes when you discover just how much of your work it has been doing for you, and how helpless you are without it.

I entered a phase that starred wearying passages of neurological disruption—not quite headache but something disturbing enough to deprive sleep. A little shake, especially if some mildly, benignly exciting event should intervene, like a decent football game on the television, the blood rushing only a little bit, but enough that I would feel it down one arm, and dreaded having to pick up anything with that hand. But a really exciting football game—let's say, Patriots–Colts, AFC Championship Game, February 2007, 38–34—I'd have to watch something like that through a shroud of pillows and blankets and at a tilt, Joseph Addai knifing through the beaten-down Patriots defensive line for the winning score looking, to me, like a man running straight up into the air.

Soon, though, the pain and the listlessness abated slightly, and a kind of clarity availed. My world was hypersensitive, full of astonishing bonds. Five M&M's on my tongue felt like heaven, ten on the tongue a sharp jab to the temple from the migraine deity, a reminder not to tempt fate. For the record, these responses to chocolate were almost undoubtedly psychosomatic, and characteristic of the paranoia that affects anybody who tries to unravel the secret code of their triggers.

I began to self-consciously regard my life as a series of aversions—I wasn't sure if I was the monkey that had been trained to avoid the electric shock, or if I was merely a new variation on the Stockholm syndrome, my captor the headache itself, with whom I bonded and made myself one, as we all do with our pain sooner or later. But it all kept me loosely on the straight and narrow. No matter how much I wanted that glass of Kentucky bourbon (with spring water, like James Bond wanted in *Goldfinger*), I could remind myself that its warming taste would produce a very specific migraine—thin and stretched taut at a sixty-degree angle across the left half of my skull, like an achy, cockeyed trampoline implant.

Of course, the diet was just the chaser, until the Topamax

slowly worked its way into my system, 25 milligrams, then 50, then 100, over two months. It was unpleasant, the Topamax listlessness doubling down with the caffeine withdrawal until I was one big lockjaw. Like many modern objects, I found my cure complicit with the illness. When one's drug of choice is commonly nicknamed "dopamax" (or "stupidmax," which I like a little more), then there is really no invention left in the observation that one has merely exchanged one form of dizziness and confusion for another.

But the dizziness and confusion was, at least, of a new order. I did not care for the nosebleeds (horribly, only when I was really happy), the sore knee, the numbness, the dulled appetite: the Topamax menu of side effects is truly arcane. But I grew rather fond of one Topamax side effect: as my mind searched for a word, that word and all of its second cousins competed wildly for my attention. It was like a mad scientist surgically grafted a pocket thesaurus inside my brain.

Gradually, though, within a month, the headaches began an orderly retreat—or, rather, took up new, subdued positions. I no longer had to pretend that I heard conversations that I did not hear, saw things I did not see. The tower of iridescent light packed its crystalline bags and went to go bother someone else. I tried to keep all the triggers below a threshold, treating them like a cumulative, like the doctors and the books told me, and to keep the drugs steady. And I began the rebuild, the reappearance: learned to revere, again, the high-pitched shout of my kid's pleasure, the roughhousing, the whole carpet-level-and-just-above worldview of a child. Put the ice pack back in the deep freeze, maybe a little too early, in all honesty. Put an end, or at least a tapering, to Babysitters Passing in the Night. Took up my place on the sofa for the daily tell with Siobhán, and learned to revere, again, the soar and bounce of her voice and her quick, sifting mind. Then found my way back into the right bed afterward.

But inside I was buzzing and humming like R2D2 in *Star Wars*. I'd wake up at one with a jolt; I'd wake up at five seeing plains of bright light. Driving to school, my fingers would tingle as they gripped the wheel. Playing video games with Aedan, my left arm would fall asleep for half an hour. Sometimes at night, I would wake with a start, my lips gone numb like someone had rubbed them with cocaine.

And headaches: I gathered a collection of small ones, the way other people keep figurines. The clear one that feels like cracked porcelain around the rim of the nose. The wriggling one that feels like torn fiber optics under the left temple. The strange, empty one that makes me feel like the front upper left part of my head has completely disappeared and been replaced by crisp air.

The beep of the microwave oven as it is tapped, 3, 2, 0, start, producing a corresponding stab above the left eye, a gentle one, tap, tap, tap, tap, each a fraction of a second after the corresponding microwave beep, the way that thunder just follows a near lightning strike. Then the stabbing pain that remains for five minutes, just under the skin, remote, electronic, like something the microwave set off inside me. The weather changing again, a heavy, dank overcast, the great tall oaks in our neighborhood shedding fat brown and red leaves, so many of them they scud across the sky like bats flying in their crazy radared formations. Then a quick wind, a swirl of leaves, a blast of rain for fifteen or thirty seconds, and the headache disappears like Dracula.

And, wow, some nights it's almost like music. Mid-evening in March, darkening sky all afternoon, and around ten, the lights in the house all down save the glow from my computer screen, the second ball scene from *Pride and Prejudice* playing on DVD, and then a throb of pain right-center forehead, really hard, the head jumping forward a little, then twice again in the next minute or so (Darcy dancing with Elizabeth, camera pans, Bingley watching Jane). Then a calming, then another throb, enough to make the right side of my head feel like it's melting on its rightmost border. And then, five minutes later (Mr. Collins proposing to Elizabeth), the sky flashes outside. Then it rumbles, and then it rains. And this synchronicity between the storm inside and the storm outside, I have to tell you, is simply enthralling. We are talking, the deep parts of my brain and the deep parts of the sky. Or rather: they are brothers, talking. I'm just an onlooker. I can see their lips move, but I can't hear the words.

Migraine Parties

We are all potential migraineurs.

—PAUL DAVIES AND RUSSELL LANE,
Migraine

1

Shortly after New Year's, 2007: three weeks of Topamax have made me dull as unbuttered toast. But the headaches are already *lighter,* not at all the sensation I expected.

Right now: two or three times a day, a premonition, a cold flush across the front of the face, dizzy but walkable, and freckles of pain where a real headache might develop. But I'm learning: the migraines don't trigger if I get lots of (but not too much) sleep, if I eat as little as possible (not a fast, which, as Nietzsche showed us, would be a mistake) across as bland a spectrum as possible. Bowls of brown rice are as reliable as can be, and apples, for some reason, maybe one vegetarian burger a day for protein, some pretzels, some salad. I yawn a lot, need to lean my head against something from time to time (how convenient that the world is full of walls and columns). But I don't get the attack.

A feeling of otherness, a feeling of sharpness, at the same time. Like a general phobia, a misanthropy, but a clarity, too.

I still don't know what's starting them, though. Weather? Food? A natural human craving for misanthropy and for clarity?

Returned to the social ramble, somewhat. Siobhán pleased. A dinner party: eight people in a group sitting around the fireplace with paper platefuls of lasagna on their laps. Four volunteer that they have migraines—three quite severe, one occasional. A fifth volunteers that he doesn't, but that his father has been unable to stop his for four decades, gets them from as innocent a stimulus as a long elevator ride. Imitrex is praised, although the side effects are not—a young woman says she feels a constriction in her chest every time she takes it, and still needs to be convinced she isn't getting a heart attack. A man in his forties, who had been diagnosed with sinus headache and took Sudafed daily for five years, an utter waste of time.

A slight, teasing argument starts between a married couple, the woman who gets occasional migraines (her eyes light up when she discusses her first aura, of the wavy line variety) and the man whose father has migraines. What brings on your headaches, then, she asks him? Not eating, he says, now shyly acknowledging that he has some kind of persistent headache.

This kind of conversation sucks the life out of the room. It goes excitedly for about ten minutes and leaves a silence in its wake, much like spreading cortical depression or the aura it inspires. Just a real party killer, and I feel abashed starting it, knowing how things will turn out.

2

Winter, early spring: this was the season of Migraine Parties. Unintended, of course: no one plans a Migraine Party. I would go out to some social gathering, someone would ask me what I had been doing, I would answer (and what else was there to say), and a little convo would evolve, sometimes one-on-one, sometimes with enough momentum to take over half the party until the topic lost steam. Nonmigraining men (and remember that women outnumber men three to one among the migraining populace) were often quizzical: to many of them, the idea of migraine was simply not that plausible. For some, it was clear that the migraine had been deployed against them in marital strife, the phrase, "you're giving me a migraine," used literally and without irony as the silencer. I felt for them: in my opinion, blaming the spouse is like blaming the doctor, when one should be blaming someone, something, else.

But the word *tough* also echoed through these conversations, as part of the same roughly amiable query: *Wasn't it just a matter of being tougher?* Given that the men who asked this question were mostly academics, hardly the most machismo subset of American men, I wanted to laugh and say, *How tough do you think you are?* ironizing accent marks around "tough," of course, that ridiculous word.

Women were more understanding. It was no problem to talk to some stranger about chocolate bars (never the whole bar, she'd say), or coffee, or a lifetime of different regimens. Most researchers are careful to point out that there is no clear reason why women get more migraines than men. Falling estrogen levels during menstruation are a prime mover, as are the hormonal rhythms of women's lives, a fact that allows women the dubious opportunity to track their migraines through life changes in a way men cannot: migraines multiply in women after first menses, recede during pregnancy, and recede again after menopause. But visit a few Migraine Parties and you will see plenty of anecdotal evidence supporting another explanation for why it seems that so many more women than men get migraines: women own up to their migraines more often and more readily.

In fact, my social world, like my neural net, was also full of astonishing new bonds. I enjoyed my new migrainy friends, my dopamax peers, and the bitter, asynchronous jokes we made to one another. I saw a new tragedy that I had never seen before, overlaid upon the story of the world I already knew. It was a nonerotic, everyday kind of suffering, to be sure, a limited kind of political revelation, but I prized it.

I found, to my surprise, that I had grown a new, erratic second sight, which gave me the ability to sometimes tell when someone else is having a migraine. This is the tell, the giveaway: there is a squint around the eyes, a craving for quiet, for dark, almost involuntarily exhibited in the muscles of the face. Sometimes, if you look hard, you can actually see the migraineur develop dark rings under the eyes in the space of a half-hour.

Shortly, I was comparing tells with other migraineurs. One teacher shared a story in which she had to tell a student to *go now*—a student for whom the symptoms of migraine were so obvious that they became disruptive in a classroom. For her, the most evident symptom was a loss of visual acuity. You'll hear this a lot. It's not that the migraineur looks blind, stares vacantly, for instance, or is unable to focus, but that the eyes seem to be engaged in some other activity not visible to the nonmigraineurs in the room. The migraineur is staring at something not visible, or looking around something that is not visible, or wincing at light which, to everyone else, seems normal, or even subdued. The first symptoms, of course, describe someone experiencing aura; the last, someone with light-hatred, the sun-pain.

Some migraineurs know what to do. The wife of a friend who excuses herself in the middle of parties, her departures as whispery as the leave-takings of Poe heroines: "Your husband and my wife both have migraines," her husband will purr seditiously to your wife, "let's be wine-drinking partners after they go home early." Your child's principal, who works in a darkened office at midday. Many do not know what to do, though, and when I could, I'd usher them into dark rooms, or chauffeur them to their homes, or at least scold them away from their toxic cans of aspartamed soda pop and their tall traitorous Starbucks.

And then there are others, the ones who present themselves with an austere but intense self-sufficiency, who dismiss your offers to help and just keep blinking. They are the ones who "have tried everything"—you'll hear this phrase often at a Migraine Party—and who will intone the list of the everything they have tried in bleary sing-songs. These are the top-flight amateurs of migraining, and as they talk, as the shiners under their eyes almost seem to turn to radiant, one senses that they are marking time, looking for some rhythm between the times their heads are free and the times they are not, and in that rhythm they no longer find any particular tragedy.

3

Another party—a renovated farmhouse on a county road north of the city, fallow fields on one side, red barn on the other, one horse, one big dog (setter), and a chest full of turtle shells, snake skins, and tiny animal skulls that captivates Aedan. Mid-afternoon, eight people, brownies served on individual plates with forks, and four are talking about their migraines, three sitting on the elevated fireplace mantle, a fourth on the coffee table, she, a local veterinarian, gray hair and Ben Franklin glasses, tan, tucked-in faded green tee and blue jeans. When I tell her I have migraines, she gets up purposefully and takes my arm as if I had no more sense than one of those big dogs she normally treats, and says, pulling and tugging my flesh to these instructions: "Thumb pointing up, three finger widths down from the elbow joint, dig your finger into the muscle belly." She digs. "Does it hurt?" she asks. It does. "That's headache stress," she says—"not a migraine, but you are thinking you might get a migraine." Since I am feeling migrainy at that very moment (those brownies on their plates suddenly looking very ominous), I find her diagnosis appealing.

She points to another spot, between the eyes, it's *Yang Brightness:* "When you feel a migraine, here's the spot. I carry around a set of needles, and when I feel a headache coming on, in they go. I've walked into stores with a big needle stuck between my eyes, forgot it was there." Then she pauses and says, "The more you rub (or poke, or stab: I can't remember the verb she used) these places, the better your migraines will get."

The hostess: since she was seven, flashes for aura, for two hours, even, before the headache. Now, once a week or so, and lately, at 2 or 3 A.M. She doesn't like the drugs (frowns viscerally when I mention Imitrex), doesn't think they work. Instead, she takes a twelve-ounce Coke, or maybe two (so like Pope and his nighttime coffee regimen), and that's what works best. Her description of her headaches: she reaches her hands out as if she is gripping something, calls them her "hold onto the side of the ship" headaches. Fiercely dislikes people who call them just headaches.

Her husband, a gentler variation of what I've heard from other men, the ones who often think they are too tough to get migraines: he is understanding and he is not. "When I first started going out with her," he says, "I thought she was going to be one of those, 'I have a headache'—you know." Then he rolls his eyes and smiles gently, and leaves the thought unanswered. Was she?

Together they give intimations of what migraine can do to a relationship—but, like great artists, the beauty of their public appearance together is that they only give intimations. He is diplomatic but betrays a little edge. She expresses rolling-eye frustration toward those who say that she just has headaches— I'm repeating this because she does. He seems to acknowledge that he was once one of those, and it somehow adds to her list of grievances, another thing, as a man, he doesn't get. As a man, the migraines are added to his list of things he can't understand but is expected to understand, and he adds that to his list of grievances. And yet here's the beauty: they *seem* stronger for it. You want to ask them how they did it, but you know, like great artists, they'll only smile, look away, and certainly never tell you. Because it's the Zen koan of marriage, after all, better not said aloud: the test, as Plato wrote, is its own answer.

What I liked most about the Migraine Parties was that they reflected something larger. There are support groups almost everywhere, and clearinghouse Web sites like knowyourhead ache.com that can help you sift through the more than one hundred fifty thousand hits a Web search on words like *migraine* or *headache* will generate. It is true that only about half of all

American migraineurs know what they've got. But two decades ago, according to the American Migraine Study, a massive, on-going survey of tens of thousands of men and women, that fraction was even worse—closer to one-third of all migraineurs than one-half.

Still, I enjoyed the small, unsolicited intimacies better, the casual proof that something big was happening. When the story of the migraine is the story of the love affair between a migraining brain and a dark room, the story turns inward. But when the migraine is a social event, then one must approach it from a different perspective. And if the private migraine contin-ues to dominate—and those statistics showing that many mi-graineurs seek neither diagnosis nor treatment argue strongly that it does—one of the most interesting phenomena of the new migraine is that it is more public, like it used to be in the days of the clay crocodile and the dour trepanner.

Almost everything I discovered at the Migraine Parties re-flected what was, and wasn't, changing about the public dia-logue on migraine. According to the American Migraine Study II, for instance, roughly 12 percent of the American population can be diagnosed with migraine, a community that grows as the country grows: 23.5 million in 1988, 27.9 million in 1999, around 35 million today, in 2009. Until you start meeting mi-graineurs everywhere you go, though, hiding in plain sight, you can't appreciate the scale of the problem: if more than one out of every ten men and women is a migraineur, then that means that more than one out of every five families in America (23 percent to be exact) has got a migraining wife, husband, or kid, or more. And while half of those men, women, and kids have not got it too bad ("mild or moderate disability"), about half report that the headaches create a serious impairment in their ability to work, to keep house, to raise the kids who might, in turn, grow up to report their own mild or moderate disability to some future researcher.

Epidemiological studies—research that examines how many, and who, are likely to contract a disease or respond to a treatment—have calculated the financial cost of all this. Someone who gets migraines will file twice as many medical claims, and spend 1.6 times as much on health care, as someone who doesn't. Together, the migraining community in America creates 112 million days of bed rest every year and burns twenty billion dollars' worth of productivity. Almost one out of every ten days of work lost to illness in America, in fact, is headache inspired.

Something else the Migraine Parties tell us: when you consider that most of the people with their heads down, their eyes averted (or sunglassed), are women, that many men still see head pain as something one might defeat with a dose of the stoic, one can easily see how the intersection of migraine and gender is a flashpoint. One prominent headache specialist observes that he couldn't get a grant for headache research as late as the 1980s because granting panels didn't see headache as "a significant problem" but as a "women's problem," "all in their heads." What changed, he notes, was in part the invention of the triptans: sometimes it takes the drug that cures a disease to convince people that a disease exists. But something else changed, too: what Paula Kamen, author of *Out of My Head,* calls "the revolutionary phenomenon of online openness" about women and illness, a near-perfect vehicle for revising the cultural profile of a disease like migraine.

The migraine blogs, for instance: they're not just all written by women, but they're gendered down to their titles, *migraine girl, migraine chick* (which features "migraine Barbie," who gets little sympathy from the nonmigraining Barbies alongside

whom her blogging creator poses her). There's chronicbabe
.com, too: the "mothership" of the pain blogs. Run your eye
down the comments section of the *New York Times*' new
migraine blog: the blog authors are equally divided between
men and women, but the respondents (one of whom describes
them cumulatively as "migraine nation") are overwhelmingly
women. The celebrity endorsers, the self-identified migraineurs
who, for both callow and selfless reasons, put their faces on
triptan ads, are almost all with-it actresses or female tennis
players (Monica Seles, Serena Williams).

Men *are* coming around. But more slowly. If the history of
the migraine in America were well told, Elvis Presley would oc-
cupy a place as essential as the one he occupies in the history of
rock-and-roll. Instead, ironically, his reputation in death suffers
due to our communal inclination to undervalue the headache
in its masculine form. More recently, though, many men have
engaged in a cultural shift, played out in the forum of American
life most dedicated to the ethos of toughness: big sports. Troy
Aikman, who won three Super Bowls as the quarterback of the
Dallas Cowboys, now acknowledges a lifelong problem with
migraines: "Mine primarily starts around the temples, and then
it radiates more to the back of my head." He acknowledges, too,
that many men still won't own up: "For men out there, there
seems to be a stigma about these things." The lore has altered,
as well. Terrell Davis won the Super Bowl Most Valuable Player
Award in 1998 despite a migraine that left him "blank(ing) out"
halfway through the game: "I noticed I couldn't see," he subsequently told interviewers. Kareem Abdul-Jabbar, famously,
suffered through migraines during the 1982 and 1984 National
Basketball Association Championship Series. Headache: Game
Five, 1982, six points and four rebounds. Postdrome: Game
Four, 1984, thirty-two points, eight rebounds.

Part of the drama of contemporary epidemiological studies, though, is that they change the profile of illness itself. It's not about individuals anymore, not exactly. A Victorian medical author—even a mid-twentieth-century one—was much more likely to draw conclusions about an illness from a handful of detailed cases. To a modern epidemiologist, however, illness no longer belongs to individuals but to groups, to classes, to races, to populations, especially vulnerable ones, and to people who already suffer from something else.

There are socioeconomic studies, for instance: unquestionably, men and women from lower socioeconomic classes get more migraines than men and women with greater wealth and status. Some researchers argue the presence of a downward spiral: the migraines make it harder to work, to make money. Others argue that the problem starts earlier, that there are more migraine triggers and aggravating factors for kids living in poverty than in wealth.

Then there are racial breakdowns: African-Americans seem to get migraines about one-third less than white Americans, and Asian-Americans seem to get them even less. One might be inclined to ascribe these differences to cultural factors, but population studies from Africa and Asia argue that genetic history might be the decisive factor: Japanese men and women seem to get no more and no fewer migraines than Japanese-Americans; Africans, no more and no fewer than African-Americans. But no one really knows.

There are the studies of comorbidity, always modest about telling us what causes what but not about what kind of company one illness might be keeping on some dark street corner. Migraine and depression, for instance. The mid-twentieth-century psychiatrists did have a point, but they didn't dig deep enough: depression can also be inspired by erratic serotonin intake, suggesting that the same chemical flaw that makes the head pound can sometimes, through a different chain of cause and effect, lay it low. Migraine and phobia and panic, yes: bipolar disorder, substance abuse, no. These are the ways that migraine can't kill you but might help. Epilepsy (this one's obvious) and MS (this one's not). If you have high blood pressure, observe Drs. Preza, Ciraku, and Haxhihyseni of the Headache Centre of Tirana, in Durres, Albania, among others, you have a 50 percent greater chance of having migraine, too. If you have migraine, note a group from St. George's Hospital Medical School in London, you are twice as likely to have asthma.

And if you have migraine, argue researchers all over the world, and if you are a woman and you are under forty-five (and maybe, too, if you are over forty-five), your stroke risk almost doubles. The numbers, when you see them, are not shattering: fifteen out of one thousand without migraine get stroke, for instance, thirty out of one thousand with. When it comes to comorbidities, it's important to take that grain of salt. But take it with caution: actress Sharon Stone, for instance, mistook a brain aneurysm for one of her frequent migraines, and now warns migraineurs to pay close attention to any headache that doesn't feel like the usual banging.

Likewise, it's worth noting that the whole idea of vulnerable populations is not static. Migraine generators are within and without: migraine hates turbulent change, and the modern world is full of turbulent change. Swedish researchers, for instance, have interviewed groups of émigrés from Latin American countries: political exile, they have found, causes migraines. So, as a lingering aftereffect, does torture. Observers reporting on conditions in the T. Don Hutto Residential Center outside Austin, Texas, report that migraines are among the leading ailments cited by the refused asylum seekers (and their children) detained there. The recipe is simple: vicious levels of anxiety about the future, combined with poor food, bad sleep, dry air.

But the best-researched migraine generator in the contemporary world is perhaps the most obvious: the war in Iraq, where "headache," as two neurologists posted in Baghdad tell us, is the "leading cause" of "neurologic assessment." According to Captain Brett Theeler of the Madigan Army Medical Center in Fort Lewis, Washington, soldiers returning home after one year of duty are reporting staggering incidences of migraine: 37 percent meeting International Headache Society criteria, or "probable," as opposed to 5 percent before their tours. And their migraines, once acquired, are hard to shake: "Our data suggests the soldiers continue to have migraine after they get home," Theeler observes, "and they may be more severe."

It makes a cynical kind of sense, and matches up with what we know about what makes migraine, and how we measure it. The Iraq War, after all, provides plenty of stress—more than it needs to get the job done, but what migraine generator is known for subtlety? Plenty of dramatic weather changes, too. And plenty of sunlight. That's two big migraine triggers and one big aggravating factor. There's a sample population, too, the American soldiers, that places a high value on toughness, as a result of which fewer than 3 percent of those diagnosed have sought treatment with triptans, preferring to self-medicate with ibuprofen, acetaminophen, or aspirin.

And something else about that sample population: for the first time in their lives, many of them are receiving careful, regular medical care, so it is hard to say whether they are getting migraines for the first time or reporting them for the first time, whether they are part of an epidemic or a shift in the recognition of the illness. But what else do these statistics tell us? What other lessons await some imaginative army neurologist posted

in a theater of war? What lessons about the crude language of
the brain lie there, too? If something like trepanning makes
visible the violence of the migraine inside the skull, might not
migraine return the favor and offer a means by which the brain
dramatizes to itself the violence it witnesses outside? Should
we really be surprised that there might, in fact, be a migraine
epidemic, at least in certain parts of the globe, among certain
peoples? And who can treat this? In the world of the new migraine, there are Migraine Parties that send you an invitation,
and there are Migraine Parties that send you an eviction notice,
warrant, or stop-loss in lieu of invitation. But there is no short-
age of Migraine Parties.

4

What epidemiological studies can't create, and understandably
so, is a three-dimensional portrait of all the cross-eyed marriages and half-assed careers created by all those days of bed
rest, all the truncated workdays, all that lost housework. In
retrospect, I was relieved that Siobhán (and Aedan, for that
matter) had not offered intense solicitousness and had also not
turned away. Siobhán allowed me to see the migraine as something I could not control in part but also as something I was
making for myself—a genuine disability on the one hand and
a day's worth of dirty dishes left for someone else to clean and
put in the washer on the other.

And yet we never agreed, really, and she'd tell this story differently. When it was happening, we didn't talk about it, in that
way—we diagnosed the ailment, but not what it meant to us.

And when we talked about it afterward, as part of the rebuilding, she said, "You could still watch TV, surf the Web, drive a car, didn't exactly look dead to the world." She said—and here I'm paraphrasing a bit—there was absolutely some kind of psychological component, some compulsion, about which I wasn't straight to her or to myself. If I ask her now if she wishes she had treated me any differently, she answers smartly, "Until you started doing this book, no." But she remains a bit of a skeptic, as much as I remain a believer. And she also says: "We never said anything we would regret later. It was clean at the end." And she's absolutely right about that: we both made it fairly easy for me to be sick, and to recover, too.

In retrospect, I think this disagreement is about right. I'm not even sure it's disagreement so much as a plain acknowledgment of how pain divides us and how, amid the layers of triggers and treatments and genetic explanations, there is no one single key to tell you if migraine is something you make or something you can't help. And love, and marriage: in my social contract, the beauty of love lies in the fact that you don't compel the consent of the one you love. But you do stick, because tenderness requires only a wholly different kind of consent. Was she unkind, was I self-absorbed? I'm not the right person to answer that. But did she make sacrifices for me, and did I change for her? I believe she did, and I did. Did we communicate well, do we communicate well now? A migrainy, Darwinian answer: families don't say everything they should, don't do everything they could, but are still rewarded with blissful moments where they understand each other without the need for conversation, and equally blissful moments where they help each other just by being themselves.

But what would have happened if my headaches had not gone away? What happens if they come back? Walter F. Stewart, director of the Hood Center for Medical Research, observes that over the last five to seven years, clinicians are focusing more and more on the many-named *chronic migraine*—the episodic that turns routine. Its modus operandi: it comes like a thief (or arsonist) every day for six months or so, then goes. Until it returns. Sounds about right, doesn't it? So what if? Here's how I imagine the conversation: part of me wants to tell Siobhán to take Aedan, get the papers, start with someone new. Another part says: don't leave me, please. I'll be better again, I promise. In reality, though, this is what I'll probably say, over and over, in familiar variations: just give me an afternoon in bed, an hour, close the blinds, turn off the light. And, in reality, they'll probably give me that afternoon, that hour, over and over, with some combination of solicitude and impatience, bemusement and frustration.

And yet—obviously—we've been ridiculously lucky, a nine or ten on a scale of ten for luck. Many migraineurs don't have our time, our money. Many migraineurs have migraines that go on for decades or that intrude themselves uncontrollably. Many migraining spouses (and their children) have the burden of being neither too caring nor too cold—for decades. Emma Darwin, who waited patiently until Charles's head stopped pounding so that they could wed, once wrote that nothing "marries one so completely as sickness." But she placed a limit on her willingness to play nurse, also writing, "It is a great happiness to me when Charles is most unwell that he continues just as sociable as ever." As difficult as an episodic or even transformed migraine can be, its burden is slight compared to the quasi-permanent intervention of an illness that requires solitude on an institution, like marriage, which requires its opposite.

Multiply this circumstance into the tens of millions now, one in five marriages, and one can see what an epidemic event is taking place in the private places of our society. Studies tell us contradictory stories. Some researchers report that the clear majority of migraine spouses are considered "supportive" or "sympathetic," as opposed to "resentful" or "unsupportive." But other researchers estimate that the damage is widespread, that the divorce rate among marriages in which one spouse has chronic illness, for instance, is 75 percent. The rate of anxiety and depression among the caregiving spouses is also high, as if such illnesses were literally contagious.

The clichés of a migrained marriage: vacations are canceled; Saturdays disappear as the migraining spouse stays in bed and the non-migraining spouse drifts absently around the house, too solicitous to leave, too bored to stay and not resent it. The uneven division of chores. And sex—this from a migraineur's husband, in some dark bar—and sex! The eyes looking upward, half rolling, in amazement, or as if to seek a break from God. And lastly, the vast agenda-setting power of the migraine itself, the questions it demands. If you have migraine, it's fifty-fifty your kid will, too. If you and your spouse both have migraines, it's three out of four. Should you have kids at all then, for instance? How many? And how much guilt should you feel about the ones you've already had?

The calm moments are still nice, maybe even nicer. But the fights stink, because a migraineur can't fight worth a damn, so there's no chance to clear the air. So finally, maybe, husband and wife both lose interest in the drama, which may not be a bad thing. But the disappearing never really stops: "If my wife is mine for ten days in the year," Balzac's "General R—" in *The Physiology of Marriage* tells another French military leader at a party, in language so contemporary one almost looks for the dot-com address, "it's about all she is . . ."

And the domestic never really heals up: if the migraineur

feels tortured by the ordinary and wants to unmake the world, the non-migraining spouse takes that as a taunt. Tiptoe, always tiptoe, the non-migraineur learns, until a new emotion develops, and it's resentment, yes, but it's longing, too. Tap the bed, just a little, just to see if your wife's nervous system is really so torqued that she can't stand it, maybe because you hate it, maybe because you hate her just at that moment, maybe because you just want it to go away, maybe because you really want to touch her instead, and this is the closest you can get.

The rudeness, I think, is almost inevitable. Migraineurs hate the rude thing; it always gets their attention, and it gets some of that resentment out into the open, so it's two-for-one. So say what you're thinking: *you're sleeping your life away. These migraines seem to come at awfully convenient times, don't they? It's your fault. You didn't pray enough; you didn't take care of yourself; this is just a way to keep your distance from me.*

But these couples won't divorce. The divorce, if it comes: perhaps the migraineur instigates. She's got a hunch that it's her husband causing her pain: "Getting a divorce," writes one commentator on the *New York Times* migraine blog, "cured my migraines!" Maybe she's right, and maybe it's the Babylonians with their reed surrogate all over again, a modern ritual for transferring the pain from head to effigy: divorce the spouse *and* divorce the migraine. Perhaps it's civil, the migraine hurting the marriage, but everyone's reasonable, the migraineur understands, the non-migraineur understands. But sometimes it's not reasonable, it's not civil, it's just the end, the last straw, the migraineur out of reach, the non-migraineur twisted out of recognition. No friends left, all the money gone. A scene in an emergency room. A court order.

In truth, though, both sides are probably right. And Siobhán's and Aedan's and my story is just one on a spectrum.

Support *is* a virtue, and that absolutely needs to be said. But love is not just about support, even in those cases where one spouse is a born nurse. Even in sickness, let alone health, romance is mad and senseless, and people fall in love because of triggers as hard to isolate as migraine triggers, and they stay married because of something that's as deep, untouchable, and polygenic as a migraine generator. There is no guidebook, nor should there be.

Weather

There is a sort of elation about sunlight on the upper part
of a house.

—EDWARD HOPPER

1

The next autumn: a trip, a surprise trip for Aedan, to a farm
outside of town where there are rides, corn mazes, a dinosaur
(a crane, actually, draped in a dino costume) that chomps on
pumpkins. The migraine has already taken hold, but maybe a
trip out, etc. etc. But that turns out to be a total mistake. The
utter nausea that accompanies a car trip, especially if one is
driving: hand over the keys, close your eyes, or fasten your
eyes on the brake lights of the car in front, try not to feel the
jogging of the car on the pavement, the swelling inside, the
movement of the throb inside the brain. Couldn't be worse.
The kid wants to sit on your shoulders—"No," the wife says,
"your daddy has a headache." Couldn't be worse than that.

But there is something to the movement from dark spaces to
light ones, from closed places to windy ones. The farm, on the
south side of the city, in the shadow of the beltway, on a windy

fall day, the crunchy gravel road, pony rides, the giant straw mountain, the kids on the pedal go-karts, these things somehow comfort (the dinosaur is painfully loud, though, scares the kid—*come here, boy,* the teenager working the dino's voice like the Wizard of Oz pipes malevolently). Take a break, get out of the sun. Sit in the car, the Honda Civic, like so: in the driver's seat, head turned to the right and down so that the forehead nestles against the side of the passenger seat, the kid's hoodie draped over your head to block out the light. This is pretty good: you can go to sleep like this. You can just get home, take the drug you should've taken hours before when you weren't certain you had a migraine, and be awake and alert enough to play ball in the driveway with the kid before the sun goes down.

2
_____

Sometime in summer 2007, I gave up the Topamax and gave up most of the monkish habits, too. I was supposed to give up the Topamax: many prescribing physicians like to give it an eight- or nine-month run, like a good but not great Broadway show. But the decision to discontinue still felt personal. One afternoon, at a meeting with my superior and her superior, in answer to a professional query that presented only the slightest anxiety, I stood up from my chair, pointed my finger, and declaimed an answer that would have been entirely rational if not for its antic delivery. I knew the drug had made me do that. My experience with migraine had taught me to accept that I couldn't always control my body and its responses to simple stimuli. But this was different. I'd trust a migraine with that kind of authority over my nervous system, but I was sure as hell not going to trust that little pill.

Giving up the monkish habits was human nature, of course. Almost everyone does—you'll give them up if the treatment works, and you'll give them up if it doesn't. Even the how-to-cure-your-headache books that recommend such habits also recommend that, sooner or later, you should reintroduce yourself to some of your favorite sins. I reintroduced myself to milk chocolate, to Kentucky bourbon, to bold (but not shimmering) sunlight. I declined caffeine (mostly), getting drunk, and a few other easily avoided sundries. This tempered monkishness, I reasoned, combined with the occasional Imitrex, ought to keep the migraine at bay.

And the migraine came back. It didn't come in lockstep at dawn anymore, more like on cat's feet two or three times a week, almost a year to the day it took up occupation (migraines can be seasonal, can come every fall, for instance). I still loathed its onset but had to acknowledge that it was tempered, as my response to it was tempered, a friendship, a compromise, an old marriage where neither party feels obliged to change that much for the other. More than that, I had to acknowledge that our relationship (for I was now thinking of it as a relationship) had changed over the past year. I still wasn't sure if I was dealing with a thing inside me or a thing outside me. But it didn't seem to matter anymore.

When dealing with a shape-shifting disease like the migraine, the best treatment is some combination of self-knowledge and a really good, trustworthy pharmaceutical. But if one was forced to choose between those two forms of treatment, one should never hesitate to choose self-knowledge first. And what saved me this second fall (make of that pun whatever you'd like) was a fuller recognition of the limits and possibilities of my own body. I learned to recognize the symptoms of onset more quickly, picking up telltale codes across my face, in the tips of my fingers, during the mid-morning hours of a migrainous day. This activity was unquestionably paranoid, since what might constitute a "sign" could vary horribly: perhaps a yawn was a little too sharp, a page of reading a little too illegible. But it was an effective paranoia, and it had a bright side, too: it compelled me to recognize all the signs of good health that mingled amid the warnings, from the waning of a sore shoulder to the intermittent blessing of clear vision.

And I learned how to respond. I could freeze a migraine in onset if I beat a hasty retreat from sunlight, or if I ate warily from the point at which it began, or if I took a red hot shower at the right instant. I adapted the lessons offered to me by my friends at the Migraine Parties, and found that the cost of a little medicinal caffeine (doled out like medicine, in doses measured by ounces) was slight compared to the reward. I tried Excedrin Migraine if I caught the migraine early. I saved my Imitrex if I didn't. If it had been a few days since the last Imitrex, I ate it hungrily.

More than that, I recognized that migraine was kind of a dance, if a violent one, as much martial arts as waltz, and that the best cure was to remain light on my metaphorical feet. There was a time for retreat to a dark room, and there was a time for a flood of creative activity, which the migraine demanded, even when I didn't. But the anxiety I felt about retreating from the world and the people I loved too frequently made more migraines, too. If the migraine responded poorly to change, it demanded balance and nuanced attention to the flow of life, to the topography of love, of creation, and of strategic withdrawal from which we all shape our everydays. It will ruin

many of those everydays. But it will also force you to live well
during the in-betweens.

3

In leaning toward this new appreciation of the migraine, I was
greatly helped by the reflections of modern doctors on this ancient condition. Maybe it's their newfound ability to photograph the brain as it works, or maybe it's just the tenor of the
age (or maybe they just see stupendous numbers of migraine
patients), but many contemporary headache specialists are unusually disposed to make migraine seem like something pretty
normal, not deviant.

In some cases, though, individual researchers are willing to
go further—not just to say that migraine is normal, but to see
that it has a reason for being and to explore what that reason
might be. I surrendered the Topamax in the summer of 2007
because I did not like what the drug did to me: I could feel that
physically. But a physical feeling becomes an action only when
it is activated by the right ideology, and in many ways the decision to go mostly undrugged and accept the migraine as part of
my life required some kind of permission slip. And for that—
that second migrainy August in 2007, the humidity warping
all the papers in my study, the reading cure in its last, crucial
stage—I want to thank the doctors who could actually argue a
positive, yet unsparingly unsentimental, idea of the migraine.

Elizabeth Loder, for instance, has proposed that migraines
make sense if we look at them from an evolutionary perspective—
and if we alter any perception we might have that the machinery

of evolution works any better than, say, the corporate and technical decision-making that produces a new computer operating system. As Loder notes, it is possible that migraine is an imperfection in humankind upon which natural selection has not yet contrived its magic. As likely, however, migraines are not useless. If they were, they would have disappeared long ago. Migraines compel you to eat better and to sleep regularly. They compel you to avoid stress, which can do far worse things to you than give you a headache. In a man or woman with stroke-prone genes, the genes that provoke migraine might not be God's error, but God's early warning system, saving your life with the occasional shaft of pain that compels you to live better. And those blood vessels that dilate too easily, that trigger-happy trigeminovascular system? They might be saving you from some worse "vasoconstrictive emergenc(y)," the kind from which you won't awake refreshed in a few hours.

And lastly, migraines make their owners "exquisitely responsive to a variety of environmental stimuli," which might be useful if some of those stimuli are toxic, or might trigger worse problems, or might upset the social fabric. Thousands of years ago, migraine might have compelled women to retreat to dark, quiet places to rear children—in which case, the reason more women than men have migraines now is an evolutionary hangover. And it might have compelled men away from "novel or complex environments," namely, places where "predators or other dangers" may have lurked—in which case, the reason I have migraines is that I had an ancestor who wasn't sufficiently respectful of the territorial claims of saber-tooth cats.

All these observations, however, make the system seem more elegant than it actually is. Diseases and abnormalities are saved if they help prevent something worse, or sometimes, something equally bad, but they remain diseases: most famously, men and women with the sickle-cell gene have been shown to be less susceptible to malaria, a fair if far from perfect trade-off.

Likewise, even those diseases that provide benefits are rough-edged instruments of salvation, set to "hair-triggers": evolutionary theorists Randolph M. Nesse and George C. Williams liken "regulation mechanisms" like migraines to household fire alarms that go off every time the toaster oven chars a piece of toast. The price of saving you from the fire even once cannot be undervalued, but you still wish you could rewire the sensor that detects danger when there's hardly any at all, that sees your own private apocalypse in every bit of stress and every dapple of sunlight.

But even *this* description makes the system seem more elegant than it is. In fact, migraine, like a Zen koan, might be the answer to its own question. Just as it compels its owner to resist and loathe any change on the spectrum from emotional to chemical to meteorological, it may itself be the halfhearted, unrefined product of the changes undergone by our species since the beginning of migrainous time. Perhaps, for instance, the inside of us has changed, but not as smoothly as one might hope. In fact, from an evolutionary standpoint, the brain is a jalopy built from new parts and old. And migraine might be caused by the bad communication between the parts that evolved long ago (down on the brain stem, of course, where researchers have unearthed the migraine generator) and the parts that have evolved fairly recently (up in the meninges, where the blood vessels dilate and the nerves get angry). Picture a computer running pieces of different iterations of its operating system, or better, a new operating system with an old, inadequate memory chip—from before Moses. From *way* before Moses.

Or perhaps it is the outside that has changed. Migraine was a mechanism built to limit its owner's exposure to sound and light and novelty during an epoch when there was less of each, and is now ineptly suited to the modern environments of everyday life. Picture Tokyo today. Now picture it three thousand years ago. In which locale would you rather have a migraine?

As I read these articles (Why is it so hard to make reading feel like action? Inside the mind it feels like nothing but), August gathering force, the papers warping more, the dead ladybugs gathering on the sill, I felt like my cure was coming to a close. It was a good cure: the story of the migraine, after all, is one where scientific inquiry and imagination meet, and where mind and body commingle promiscuously, so a diet of reading and somatic self-knowledge covered all the bases. But it was a terrible cure, too, and it was in these starchy evenings in my drooping study where I recognized the mistakes I had been making, and that would keep me from ever learning to live alongside the migraine.

I had assumed, for instance, that the human body wanted to be perfect, and that every imperfection was an affront. I now understood that the human body could be systematic without being perfect. I realized, too, that most of my cure was a mistake, although a mistake only one little sidestep from the right course. I had been looking for a language to describe migraine, to fight it with my own words, when what I should have been doing was listening to the migraine and learning to understand the crude language it was speaking to me.

This had little or nothing to do with Zen solutions, with making friends with the migraine, with toughing it out, with any pragmatic social contract for good health and good society, with, even, the counterintuitive approaches demanded by contemporary regimes of monkish habits and discreet pharmaceuticals. And it had little to do with the nagging issue of who, or what, if anything, was talking to me when the migraine called out in its crude, raw language. All I needed to do was regard the migraine problem as a problem in translation, me and the migraine in Venice, each gesticulating freely with our hands, me trying to find out on which track the train to Firenze was arriving, and the migraine trying to tell me.

I really cannot emphasize enough how subversive this little metaphorical step felt to me. Elaine Scarry had argued that talk of systems and machines was a way of looking at the body from the outside: so what, then, did it signify that I suddenly saw pain itself as an older version of myself? As a neurotic medical advisor, taking my temperature, watching my diet and my sleep, measuring my anxiety, and then blasting a fire alarm in my ear for six or seven hours until I got the point? As a doddering old man, really, who rarely smiles, who can't show his love, but is so devoted to my survival that he drives me entirely to distraction? And as an example of how God and the central nervous system, when they work, work crudely and with a cruel sense of humor?

Because now, more than ever, I could envision its language as something I could hear with human ears. It talked to me, finally. I could live with it, especially if it paid its half of the rent. I knew it compelled creativity, but I didn't know why, because I wasn't listening. But then I was, and I understood its crude language and how I had been hearing it without understanding it. So many migraine symptoms are death-in-miniature, for instance—the torpor, the pain so great it shuts off thought, the hatred of all sensation that drives one into the darkest, smallest place—that migraine stimulates its owner to create, to make, to fight the drift dustward. It's like a condensed harbinger of the grim reaper, and it puts people on their skates. It sure put me on mine.

And what else? What about the auras, for instance? From

the perspective of my reading cure, it was hard to miss the fact that contemporary scientific observations had acquired a newfound relevance. Read the researches of contemporary headache specialists through the prisms composed of the works of Picasso, the writings of Carroll, through the histories of cubism and surrealism themselves if you'd like, through the labors of countless others whose art and writing and music seems to speak a common mysterious language of abstract forms. Consider, too, those twentieth-century doctors who tested mescal or LSD (devised as a migraine cure, incidentally) to conceive the observation that, when people hallucinate, they hallucinate in a shared lingua franca of zigzags and Alice distortions. What the modern doctors confirmed for me was what I wanted to believe, that migraine, despite the way it urges the average migraineur to seek all manner of solitude, also sends a powerful message about what we all share. What "converges" in the "convergence hypothesis," deep down, is us. What "unites" in the "unitary hypothesis": us.

And what else? The "exquisite" sensitivity to changes in barometric pressure, the external inspiration for so many of my migraines? I experienced perhaps two hundred headaches in my life that immediately preceded the coming of a thunderstorm before I appreciated the obvious: the headache could actually be a signal that a thunderstorm was coming, a warning to seek shelter, its pain and hatred of light and sound a compulsion, as well, to seek shelter. If so, it was a signal dumbly out of time, something ancient, the wrong nervous language for a world where shelter is everywhere. And as such, it was a clear and unmistakable message of another order, proof that what is old stays with us, stays with us past its usefulness, stays with us not just in the culture but in the body, too.

It is no surprise, then, that a migraineur looking for answers might look to the past, might look to history for answers, without knowing why or even knowing the question. But the migraine pushes you further: its language of phonophobia and photophobia turns every migrainous event into a withdrawal not just from contemporary culture, but from culture itself. You turn off the light, you turn off the sound, you run from the saber-tooth: "Prehistory," de Chirico wrote in a brilliant, untitled manuscript, "is taut in me like a vibrating string." But there is a point to all this turning away, right, an evolutionary mandate for such a state of mind? We crave privacy perhaps, our bodies sending us a signal that the crashingly loud, strobing culture we have built is not a thing of nature. Turn back, the body says, or at least: don't forget. But what of the auras, and the visions, and the elevated, almost spiritual passages, the re-writing of normalcy? Aren't there also evolutionary mandates for these states of mind? Don't we need them? You tell me.

The language of the migraine, and of the brain, it turned out, wasn't so crude after all.

4
———————

The future of migraine therapy. The official line: "The more we learn about the clinical features and pathophysiology of mi-graine, the closer we are to finding a satisfactory monotherapy," Drs. Kalra and Elliott from Louisiana State University observe. "Until then," they add, "recognizing that mixed mechanisms underlie migraine symptoms, rational polytherapy can be use-ful." The unofficial line: the ironic beauty of a complicated, awkward, completely human illness is that, on the way to "satisfactory monotherapy," we make more cures, not less. In particular, scientists are looking carefully at calcitonin gene-related peptide (CGRP) inhibitors—what one researcher describes as the "new era" of migraine drug. CGRPs dilate blood vessels along the meninges and flourish during migraines. The drug that shuts them down may fix migraines as often and longer than triptans, and without tripping warnings for patients with heart problems.

And researchers are also looking at what Stewart Tepper calls "outside the box" solutions. For chronic migraineurs, for instance, they're looking more closely at botulinum toxin type A—Botox. It seems to paralyze hyperactive nerve cells the way it paralyzes muscles and may provide a compelling alternative for patients who have "compliance issues" with pill regimens. For acute sufferers, "transcranial magnetic stimulation" is showing promise: a small device you press to the back of your head when you sense that aura, two quick magnetic pulses that fight the electrified hyperexcitability of your nerve cells on its own terms.

Maybe Galen was right about that electric torpedo fish after all; maybe all the trepanner needed was more supple knives and something worth inserting into your forehead.

The best migraine music, no doubt: with apologies to the famous musical migraineurs like Tchaikovsky, Wagner, and Mahler (especially Mahler), I prefer the contemporary. And not, as you might think, the quiet stuff: mid-migraine, the most twee folk song sounds like death metal turned up to 11. And not (with apologies to the great Jeff Tweedy of Wilco, among others) even songs written about migraines, or during migraines. Migraine songs are not about migraines, but they are about disorientation. Like Dickinson's poems, they animate the brain as a place, as a living thing, where feelings are expressed far (in

brain geography terms, which amount to little more than centimeters) from the feeling's source. The music churns, feedback
and static—the migraine is not classical, it is not hip-hop, it is
definitely punkish—a growl in the guitars, looping feedback
and static and then some lo-fi drums, and then a voice, too
loud, too jittery, too high, on edge, fast and then faster. The
White Stripes:

> These two sides of my brain need to have a meeting
> Can't think of anything to do

Or, lower, the Old 97s:

> White Noise swells in my head . . .
> I would give anything not to feel so jagged

The best art for bringing on a migraine: a tie between
Edward Hopper and Georgia O'Keeffe, and no close third.
Hopper and his love of the morning light, his devotion to the
"elation" that a shaft of sunlight can bring at just the right
time, is migraine thinking turned so perfectly inside out that it
almost makes sense again. The only person who loves sunlight
more than someone who loves sunlight is someone who must
ration it.

And O'Keeffe? What migraineur wants to face her sun-
drenched desert landscapes without the thickest, greenest pair
of Polaroids?

And yet, during the maturing phase of her career, the O'Keeffe
becoming O'Keeffe phase, when asked what inspired this painting or that, she responded, roughly, I saw it in a headache.

Paint what you know, she might well have said, especially if
it looks like something you *shouldn't* know.

• • •

In the end, I am thankful that so many of my migraines are inspired by weather, because that reminds me that the opposite of the politics of isolation is a politics of oneness, and the migraine is telling you to practice both. The meteorological contract migraine offers is a tumultuous one, stacked with plenty of codicils for which you can have no use: one loses the desert, the heat, the high sun, the dry air. Worse, one loses a sort of oneness with the nation: America is a land of sunshine, and we just don't respect clouds and gray. We associate happiness with bright expanses of sunlight, and recognize light as a solvent for misery. It's even at the heart of our meteorological eros: we all long for the eyes closed, the head upturned, lying on the sand on Long Beach, any Long Beach.

I'd rather meet the morning sun without ambivalence, the way I used to; I'd rather feel the electricity of an oncoming thunderhead in some less hyperexcitable way. But I'd be foolish not to appreciate that "exquisite sensitivity" (another splendid turn of phrase from a doctor's pen, by the way) has a peculiar magic, and that there are moments in my everyday now that make broad, flat sunshine seem mundane. The drive to Aedan's school, for instance: straight north to south, the leaves down from the trees, the sun just over the horizon, the tree trunks to our left making it blink and blink as it follows our car, leaving delicate fluorescent traces across my vision later that enthrall and completely chill me.

The migraine is my companion now, and I simply can't live without it. It has become my geography, my compass. It comes to Ireland with me when we visit Siobhán's family: the nuanced but never-ending gradations of weather characteristic of the Ulster countryside, for instance, produce nuanced but persistent headaches, most located in the left temple, some over the left eye, oppressive, clumsy, but short in duration, cruising across the noggin from brow to temple like airport runway lights in cascade. The high cerulean sky one finds on the northern tip of the island on a rare sunny day, where the ozone seems particularly thin, the blue almost royal blue, not yet purple but closing in, the sunlight just entering some more profound place on the UV spectrum. That sky can inspire a headache that feels like a cave-in, as if the brain were clay and everything suddenly just slid down the center, enough pain to make me wobble and sidestep like an Oliver Hardy soft-shoe, and then enough elation afterward to make one love the landscape to the point of tears, the black mountains tumbling down toward the cliffs, which themselves tumble down to the sea.

And the roads, those corkscrew Irish roads, lined with hedgerows that, as your little rent-a-car hurtles along, telescope into an unthinkable narrowness. The approaching Eurocars, the little ones, more like waterbugs than oncoming vehicles, dart impossibly through the tunnel your vision creates. One blink readjusts everything so that a three-dimensionality establishes itself, configurations of trees and mountains and appropriate background and foreground. But the hedgerows still play with the migraine, the hypnotic persistence of them, hill after hill, turn after turn, until you realize that they wave and weave just like your auras, interpose themselves on the land the way the aura interposes itself on your field of vision, in parallels so precise that it is electrifying.

And it comes with me to California, too. San Diego, on a family vacation: a long day at Seaworld, but who knows what it can be—a chocolate chip cookie unevenly shared with Aedan, the shimmer off the water in poor old Shamu's pool, that early vacation tension, the letoff, that famously yields up migraines. Then the driving, those rollercoaster boulevards all over Torrey Pines, the lowing California sun pinwheeling from left to right to center, the right hand turning the steering wheel, the left adjusting and readjusting the sun visor, always a couple of seconds behind that first enervating flash of sun, those beautiful shadowy canyons providing relief so intense that it actually borders on joy.

Or this: standing on the cliffs of the Torrey Pines State Reserve, three hundred feet above the beach, a wide, wide swath of ocean at one's feet, a huge brutal slice of that ocean shimmering in front of the westward-leaning, not-yet-sinking mid-afternoon sun, and eagle-eyed Siobhán sees something just to the right of that brutal, dizzying shimmer, a minuscule-by-contrast flash of something gray surfacing and blowing mist into the air, sinking and rising and blowing mist and turning and submerging, and who in their right mind is going to turn away from a whale just to avoid risking a migraine?

And so you get the migraine, of course.

Fundamentally, though, my migraines are Midwestern, homeland, heartland, whatever: a great building tension that matches the backdrop of barometric pressure in the atmosphere, then the blowout that matches the great thunderstorm, then the threat of tornado, then the calm and the cool. And sometimes, on an odd Tuesday or a Thursday, when the wind is blowing all the way across America from the Rockies, acquiring along the way every gemlike molecule of pollen and dirt that exists from Denver to Terre Haute, and bringing with it a drop in the Fahrenheit or a touch of thunder, the old migraine returns, faceless and intransigent. It is indifferent to every effort I have made to keep my head down and stay out of trouble. It ignores the drug. It ignores the ascetic diet. There is no counterintuitive modern logic to shield me from this thing. There is no logic at all. It responds only to cures that existed six thousand years ago, to darkness, to ice, to steam, and these aren't really cures—when this headache visits, I'm no more human than the feral cat that waits out its injury underneath a bush. And I'm not remotely interested in politeness to other living beings. And, weirdly, precisely because it defies modernity, because it defies society, this migraine also feels as if it bears no human origin, as if it bears no relation either to human creativity or to thwarted human creativity. No crowd of ideas, images, and thoughts await concatenation and order, or collapse. This headache exists outside of human history.

Which is the one thing I like about it. Like a recovering addict, I almost want to say: I would not miss the migraines. But I would miss the places the migraines took me. As an electrical storm rages outside my window, a second electrical storm rages inside my temple; as the earth's atmosphere dilates and the tiny vessels inside my brain dilate in tune, can it not be said that, between and among the throbs, I am being taught a very profound cosmic lesson by a most visceral and heartfelt teacher?

And even through the pain, I'm grateful for that lesson. In the end, I think, no story about migraine can only be the story of the pain. There is the story, too, of this lesson and this gratitude, and of the longing like addiction, all joined to the pain and yet rising from it like a phoenix.

Migraines are not, I think, explicitly spiritual events. But the only way I outlasted my migraines without at least temporary derangement was to accept a lesson that mimics the spiritual so closely that the difference scarcely matters and may, in fact, not be difference at all. And that lesson is, when it comes to mind and matter, the windows really are wide open, the wind really is whipping the shutters, and the doors, in fact, are blown clean off. Most of the time, I'm in charge. I can't avoid that. But if God or the central nervous system wants to punch me in the side of the face, or plant a warped kaleidoscopic vision where I should be seeing half a stop sign, there's nothing I can do about it, nothing I want to do about it, nothing left to do about it but gape (in a metaphysical sense, of course) at the wonder of it all. That is the migrainy worldview: the migraines scour you, humble you, then they make you all dreamy and a sensation junkie, stuck in an imminent future tense always a little more alive than you ever desired, a memorable place if not a beautiful one, a place to build, if one can build castles in air. And I believe I can now, and I thank the headaches for that. This is a story about pain, the great, cowardly indescribable. But joined to that pain, rising from it like a phoenix, it is also a story about hope—hope blasted, then hope twisted, and then, finally, just hope.

February 22: a new snowfall the night before, three inches or so, icy cold so the flakes don't cohere, they just sit on the ground like a coat of fur. We have stayed inside, blinds partially drawn, so when I walk outside with Aedan—he to move toy bulldozers and snowplows through the new snow and admire the tracks they make—I am completely blinded. I mean, it is shocking: I am not used to being this blinded, my eyes long to shut, and even before I can shut them, I feel the visual world go dark with shafts and nodes of phosphorescence. I turn around, go inside, find a pair of sunglasses, blue and wraparound, and come back outside, but now, a different sensation: I am, I think, about seven feet tall. I am keenly aware of a new angle on things, a strange outburst of length in my calves and thighs. It lasts for about fifteen minutes. At first, I want to rebel against it, but then I think, why not, it's no stranger than the strangeness of snow and sunlight and no less natural.

Aedan has surprised us lately with some interesting news: he sees "colors" in front of his eyes, whether his eyes are open or closed, and only "sometimes." He says: "I see yellow here and here and here and here and here and here and here and here and here and here and here and here and here and here," as his finger points in the air at one place and then another, or draws a wavy or zigzagging line in space.

He says that he sees pictures, too: "a brachiosaurus herd," or his painted hand, and not all of it—only "here and here and here," and here he is touching parts of my hand to demonstrate what parts of his hand are visible: just the tips of the fingers. Aura, maybe: maybe he'll be a silly billy after all. Fifty-fifty. If so, he's already better at describing it than me, and I had a forty-year head start. If not—well, it's hard to say where his imagination stops and his vision starts. It's harder to say it matters.

I ask him if he ever gets a headache. He says, "Once." "For how long?" I ask. "What is that time between a second and a minute?" he asks back.

I ask him if he likes seeing the colors, and he says very much. He also says he can see God sometimes: an old man in a red shirt and blue pants, long gray beard, a cane, and a friendly face, like "a straight line."

What is the job of the father here? Not much, I think. Show him the ropes, all the ropes, if he needs them. That's what this book is for, in case you hadn't guessed. But what else? Why tell him what he already knows?

Notes

Author's Note

ix *If I met you* See Robert A. Davidoff, *Migraine*, vii: "the average neurologist is unaware of the strides made in understanding head pain." During interviews for this book, both headache specialists and patient advocates stressed this advice (Teri Robert, interview, July 9, 2008), and stressed, as well, the idea that family physicians and even neurologists were not well-versed in new developments in headache treatment, and often preferred not to treat headache patients at all. This, however, runs somewhat counter to my own experience, where a neurologist, not a headache specialist, led my successful treatment.

Introduction:
A Man with Patches on His Head

1 *"If a man, with patches on his head"* Charles Darwin, intro. and ed. Edward O. Wilson, *The Voyage of the Beagle*, 129. Qtd. in Elizabeth Loder, "What Is the Evolutionary Advantage of Migraine," 624.

3 *Describe it* See Robert A. Davidoff, *Migraine*, 55: "In their initial phases, the discomfort of many migraine attacks is characterized as a mild or dull, deep, steady ache or sensation of pressure . . . it may then develop the throbbing quality described by patients as 'pounding,' 'hammering,' 'beating,' or 'banging.' Between 47% and 82% of patients indicate that their head pain has a pulsating quality."

3   *I get up*   Ibid., 55: "Sometimes the pain is so subtle that its existence is only perceived when the head is rapidly moved or when the patient bends over."

3   *I've got three options*   Ibid., 57: "Placing an ice pack on the scalp or neck decreases pain intensity for some migraineurs, although others favor the application of heat to the head. Still others may gain some pain reduction from a hot shower or bath."

6   *Then, one August week*   Ibid., 45: "Not infrequently, patients awaken in the morning to discover that a headache is developing . . . there appears to be a circadian variation in the onset of migraine attacks; most seem to develop early in the morning." See also 77: "Most commonly, the headache gradually increases in severity as the day progresses, reaching a peak in the afternoon."

9   *"damp, drizzly November"*   Herman Melville; notes, James D. Hart; design, Andrew Hoyen; illus., Barry Moser. *Moby-Dick or, The Whale*, 2.

9   *It is a nerve-storm*   See Edward Liveing, *On Megrim, Sick-Headache, and Some Allied Disorders: A Contribution to the Pathology of Nerve-Storms*. Respect for Liveing's work appears to be widespread among contemporary headache specialists. See, for instance, Oliver Sacks, *Migraine*, 138; Russell Lane and Paul Davies, *Migraine*, x–xi, 11.

10   *light*   Russell Lane and Paul Davies, *Migraine*, 73, 76.

10   *caffeine*   Stewart Tepper, *Understanding Migraine and Other Headaches*, 68, calls caffeine "the double-edged sword." Robert A. Davidoff, *Migraine*, 99, reports, "10% of patients indicate that their migraine headaches are produced by the consumption of coffee or a caffeine-containing product." See also John F. Rothrock, "The Truth About Triggers," 500.

10   *menstruation*   Stewart Tepper, *Understanding Migraine and Other Headaches*, 17.

10   *a chocolate bar*   Robert A. Davidoff, *Migraine*, 98.

10   *cigarette smoke*   Ibid., 78.

10   *the last migraine itself*   More than a clinical distinction. For instance, Oliver Sacks, *Migraine*, 161: "A migraine can become a response to itself."

10   *It affects three times more women than men*   See, for instance, Stewart J. Tepper, *Understanding Migraine and Other Headaches*, vii, 16. Robert A. Davidoff, *Migraine*, 14. Walter F. Stewart, Richard B. Upton, and Joshua Liberman, "Variation in Migraine Prevalence

by Race." Walter F. Stewart, Richard B. Lipton, D. D. Celentano, and M. L. Reed, "Prevalence of Migraine Headache in the United States: Relation to Age, Income, Race, and Other Sociodemographic Factors." The gender difference among migraineurs is axiomatic: references appear in every textbook, virtually every epidemiological study. The racial differences are less referenced.

10 *And the list*   Russell Lane and Paul Davies, *Migraine*, 66: "The processes involved in terminating a migraine attack are even less clearly understood than the events underlying initiation."

10 *"lie down"*   Joan Didion, "In Bed," in *The White Album*, 172. A terrific essay: that I sometimes use it as a foil in this book should not be taken for disrespect. Quite the opposite.

PART ONE

13 *"The pain"*   See H. Isler, H. Hasenfratz, and T. A. O'Neill, "A Sixth Century Irish Headache Cure and Its Use in a South German Monastery."

Ancient History

15 *"And screened in shades"*   Alexander Pope, ed. Cynthia Wall, *The Rape of the Lock*, 73. Qtd. in Stephanie Patterson and Stephen D. Silberstein, "Sometimes Jello Helps: Perceptions of Headache Etiology, Triggers and Treatment in Literature," 76.

18 *the face animates, the voice races*   See, for instance, Oliver Sacks, *Migraine*, xv: "Many patients with migraines—especially young patients—have no idea what is happening to them, and may be terrified that they have a stroke, a brain tumor, or whatever—"

18 *Animals don't get migraines*   See, for instance, Seymour Diamond and Mary A. Franklin, *Headache Through the Ages*, 12: Migraine symptoms are "totally subjective and there is no animal role model in which we can conduct research."

18 *"The animal, if in exercise"*   Qtd. in Edward Liveing, *On Megrim, Sick-Headache, and Some Allied Disorders: A Contribution to the Pathology of Nerve-Storms*, 2.

19 *"clutching her head and groaning"*   Qtd. in Elizabeth Loder, "What Is the Evolutionary Advantage of Migraine," 630.

19   *"within 15 min"*   Ibid.

19   sag-gig . . . *"sick-head"*   Samuel N. Kramer, trans., *Enki and Ninhur-sag*, 11. Qtd. in Seymour Diamond and Mary A. Franklin, *Headache Through the Ages*, 16. H. Isler argues that, while these references may only have "their literal meaning," or refer to other ailments. H. Isler, "Retrospect: The History of Thought About Migraine from Aretaeus to 1920," in J. N. Blau, ed., *Migraine: Clinical, Therapeutic, Conceptual and Research Aspects*, 659–660. Stephanie Patterson and Stephen D. Silberstein, "Sometimes Jello Helps: Perceptions of Headache Etiology, Triggers and Treatment in Literature," 76. Jeff Unger, "Migraine Headaches: A Historical Perspective, a Glimpse into the Future, and Migraine Epidemiology," 367. The original claim seems to be W. C. Alvarez, "Was There Sick Headache in 3000 B.C.?" 524.

19   *Babylonian and Assyrian incantations*   Andrew George, e-mail correspondence, Sept. 26–Oct. 3, 2008, describes the Akkadian *di'u*. See also R. Campbell Thompson, ed. and trans., *The Devils and Evil Spirits of Babylonia*, vol. 1, xi. JoAnn Scurlock and Burton R. Andersen, trans. and comm., *Diagnoses in Assyrian and Babylonian Medicine: Ancient Sources, Translations, and Modern Medical Analyses*, 59–60, 692.

19   *"holder . . . hand"*   JoAnn Scurlock and Burton R. Andersen, trans. and comm., *Diagnoses in Assyrian and Babylonian Medicine: Ancient Sources, Translations, and Modern Medical Analyses*, 311, 312.

19   *"Head disease"*   Benjamin R. Foster, *Before the Muses: An Anthology of Akkadian Literature*, vol. 2, 861. R. Campbell Thompson, *The Devils and Evil Spirits of Babylonia*, vol. 2, 65–67, provides an older translation, which is widely quoted in migraine texts. See, for instance, Seymour Diamond and Mary A. Franklin, *Headache Through the Ages*, 14. Alan Rapoport and John Edmeads, "Migraine: The Evolution of Our Knowledge," 1221. Arnold P. Friedman, "The Headache in History, Literature, and Legend," 670. G. W. Bruyn, "Migraine Phylakteria: Magic Treatment of Migraine," 32–34. In the migraine textbooks, *di'u* is usually called *ti'u*, based on an outdated source, and is regarded as primarily headache. In the scholarship of Assyrian and Babylonian scholars, however, it appears that *di'u* is regarded as more elusive but probably an early symptom of enteric fever, or malaria. It does not appear that those scholars, however, regard migraine as having other symptoms besides headache.

19 *Treatment included*   R. Campbell Thompson, *The Devils and Evil Spirits of Babylonia,* vol. 2, 57–59. G. W. Bruyn, "Migraine Phylakteria: Magic Treatment of Migraine," 33.

20 *The ancient Egyptians   Ges tep* could also be cluster headache. Jes Olesen et al., *The Headaches,* 1. J. F. Borghouts, *The Magical Texts of Papyrus Leiden I 348,* 9, spells this *gs-tp.*

20 *The* Papyrus Ebers   Seymour Diamond and Mary A. Franklin, *Headache Through the Ages,* 16. Russell Lane and Paul Davies, *Migraine,* 3. Stephen D. Silberstein, "Historical Aspects of Migraine," in Stephen D. Silberstein, M. Alan Stiles, and William B. Young, eds., *Atlas of Migraine and Other Headaches,* 13–14. The "clay crocodile" anecdote is popular. Alan Rapoport and John Edmeads, "Migraine: The Evolution of Our Knowledge," 1221. Ralph H. Major, "The Papyrus Ebers."

20 *"seemed to see"*   Qtd. in Seymour Diamond and Mary A. Franklin, *Headache Through the Ages,* 18; Russell Lane and Paul Davies, *Migraine,* 4–5; Macdonald Critchley, "Migraine from Cappadocia to Queen Square," 28.

20 *"For they flee"*   Qtd. in Seymour Diamond and Mary A. Franklin, *Headache Through the Ages,* 19–20. See also Russell Lane and Paul Davies, *Migraine,* 5, who describe him as the "first to distinguish cases of what we would recognize as migraine from other types of headache." Stephen D. Silberstein, "Historical Aspects of Migraine," in Stephen D. Silberstein, M. Alan Stiles, and William B. Young, eds., *Atlas of Migraine and Other Headaches,* 14. H. Isler, "Retrospect: The History of Thought About Migraine from Aretaeus to 1920," in J. N. Blau, ed., *Migraine: Clinical, Therapeutic, Conceptual and Research Aspects,* 661. Alan Rapoport and John Edmeads, "Migraine: The Evolution of Our Knowledge," 1222. Macdonald Critchley, "Migraine from Cappadocia to Queen Square," 29–30.

20 *A century later*   See, for instance, Macdonald Critchley, "Migraine from Cappadocia to Queen Square," 30. Russell Lane and Paul Davies, *Migraine,* 7.

20 *"hemicrania"*   Stephen D. Silberstein, "Historical Aspects of Migraine," in Stephen D. Silberstein, M. Alan Stiles, and William B. Young, eds., *Atlas of Migraine and Other Headaches,* 14. H. Isler, "Retrospect: The History of Thought About Migraine from Aretaeus to 1920," in J. N. Blau, ed., *Migraine: Clinical, Therapeutic, Conceptual and Research Aspects,* 661. Alan Rapoport and John Edmeads,

"Migraine: The Evolution of Our Knowledge," 1222. Macdonald Critchley, "Migraine from Cappadocia to Queen Square," 30.

20 *It's a French word* Russell Lane and Paul Davies, *Migraine*, 8. See also George M. Gould, "The History and Etiology of Migraine," 7. Seymour Diamond and Mary A. Franklin, *Headache Through the Ages*, 20.

20 *"Antaura arose"* Qtd. in G. W. Bruyn, "Migraine Phylakteria: Magic Treatment of Migraine," 35.

20 *In the legendary Greek myth* Jes Olesen et al., *The Headaches*, 1. Russell Lane and Paul Davies, *Migraine*, 3–4.

21 *"Give me your head"* J. F. Borghouts, *The Magical Texts of Papyrus Leiden I 348*, 18. See also Jes Olesen et al., *The Headaches*, 1.

21 *she treated headache* See *Ancient Egyptian Medicine: The Papyrus Ebers*, trans. Cyril Bryan, intro. Elliot Smith, 39–40, 59–60. Seymour Diamond and Mary A. Franklin, *Headache Through the Ages*, 17.

21 *"liable to be increased"* Paulus Aegineta, trans. and comm. Francis Adams, *The Seven Books of Paulus Aeginata*, vol. 1, 355. Qtd. in Seymour Diamond and Mary A. Franklin, *Headache Through the Ages*, 26–27; Russell Lane and Paul Davies, *Migraine*, 13.

21 *"bread or toast"* Qtd. in Fred Rosner, "Headache in the Writings of Moses Maimonides and Other Hebrew Sages," 316.

21 *"in comfortably-warm"* Qtd. in ibid., 317.

21 *The Talmud* Ibid., 317–318.

21 *"electric torpedo fish"* Qtd. in Seymour Diamond and Mary A. Franklin, *Headache Through the Ages*, 23. Diamond and Franklin also describe the treatment as a "precursor to electrotherapy" (23). See also Paulus Aegineta, trans. and comm. Francis Adams, *The Seven Books of Paulus Aeginata*, vol. 1, 359.

21 *Indians in the Americas* Seymour Diamond and Mary A. Franklin, *Headache Through the Ages*, 58–59. Arnold P. Friedman, "The Headache in History, Literature, and Legend," 675.

21 *Seventeenth-century Europeans* Seymour Diamond and Mary A. Franklin, *Headache Through the Ages*, 57, 58.

21 *"drug for the head"* Plato, *Charmides*, 8, 22. Qtd. in Stephanie Patterson and Stephen D. Silberstein, "Sometimes Jello Helps: Perceptions of Headache Etiology, Triggers and Treatment in Literature," 76.

22 *"Mar Nestorius"* Qtd. in G. W. Bruyn, "Migraine Phylakteria: Magic Treatment of Migraine," 32.

22 *Medieval Irish Catholics*   Seymour Diamond and Mary A. Franklin, *Headache Through the Ages,* 41–42.

22 *"bullaun stone"*   H. Isler, H. Hasenfratz, and T. A. O'Neill, "A Sixth Century Irish Headache Cure and Its Use in a South German Monastery."

22 *"Cool(s) the noxious fluxes"*   Ibid.

22 *"You will gain . . . my head"*   Ibid. I have taken some latitude with these legends.

22 *"migraine"*   These prayers are translated and summarized in G. W. Bruyn, "Migraine Phylakteria: Magic Treatment of Migraine," 36–38.

23 *trepanning*   Often called *trephining.* Alan Rapoport and John Edmeads, "Migraine: The Evolution of Our Knowledge," 1221. Arnold P. Friedman, "The Headache in History, Literature, and Legend," 670.

23 *Abulcasis*   Macdonald Critchley, "Migraine from Cappadocia to Queen Square," 31. Macdonald Critchley, "Bygone Remedies for Migraine," 171. H. Isler, "Retrospect: The History of Thought About Migraine from Aretaeus to 1920," in J. N. Blau, ed., *Migraine: Clinical, Therapeutic, Conceptual and Research Aspects,* 663. *Abulcasis* is the westernized version of Abu al-Qasim Khalif ibn al-Abbas Al-Zahrawi.

24 *Wagner and Nietzsche*   George M. Gould, "The History and Etiology of Migraine," 14. Freud, too: Max Schur, *Freud: Living and Dying,* 98.

24 *"migraine with aura"*   "The International Classification of Headache Disorders," 2nd ed., 25.

24 *Rest, simple diet*   See Seymour Diamond and Mary A. Franklin, *Headache Through the Ages,* 120: "Simple diets have been recommended for centuries. . . ." Stewart Tepper, *Understanding Migraine and Other Headaches,* 68: "It seems a deceptively simple observation: keeping regular living habits can be extremely important in keeping the headaches down."

24 *The Egyptians*   Russell Lane and Paul Davies, *Migraine,* 3.

24 *Pliny recommended*   Arnold P. Friedman, "The Headache in History, Literature, and Legend," 671. Macdonald Critchley, "Bygone Remedies for Migraine," 171, writes that "from the earliest times, local applications to the aching head or neck has been advised."

24 *"pain upon my forehead . . . will be well"*   William Shakespeare,

Othello, ed. Norman Sanders. Cambridge: Cambridge UP, 1984: 126. Qtd. in Seymour Diamond and Mary A. Franklin, *Headache Through the Ages,* 53. Qtd. in Macdonald Critchley, "Bygone Remedies for Migraine," 171. Qtd. in Stephanie Patterson and Stephen D. Silberstein, "Sometimes Jello Helps: Perceptions of Headache Etiology, Triggers and Treatment in Literature," 78. "Sometimes Jello Helps" is an excellent review of references to migraine among literary characters, an avenue I have chosen not to pursue in this book.

24 *Plato, of course* Plato, *Charmides,* 19. For the link between Plato and modern psychotherapy see, among others, Jes Olesen et al., *The Headaches,* 1.

25 *But no one should be surprised* Jes Olesen et al., *The Headaches,* 1: "Prehistorical trepanned skulls found in Egypt have been explained as relics of brain surgery for headache, but no further evidence supports this claim, although scraping the forehead down to the bone to make it bleed was a headache remedy among the fellahin up until the twentieth century." See also Stephen D. Silberstein, "Historical Aspects of Migraine," in Stephen D. Silberstein, M. Alan Stiles, and William B. Young, eds., *Atlas of Migraine and Other Headaches,* 13: "Trepanation continues to be practiced today." Malcolm C. Lillie, "Cranial Surgery Dates Back to Mesolithic," 854.

25 *The migraining head* Joan Didion, "In Bed," in *The White Album,* 169: "I wished only for a neurosurgeon," Joan Didion writes, "who would do a lobotomy on a house call."

25 *There is a splendid print* Reprinted in Seymour Diamond and Mary A. Franklin, *Headache Through the Ages,* 65.

26 *Ice and steam and pressure* See Elliott A. Schulman, "Breath-Holding, Head Pressure, and Hot Water: An Effective Treatment for Migraine Headache."

Enlightenment, Part 1

27 *"The influences from these three sources"* David Werner, "Healing in the Sierra Madre," 65. Qtd. in Arnold P. Friedman, "The Headache in History, Literature, and Legend," 678–679.

27 *"typical aura without headache"* "The International Classification of Headache Disorders," 2nd ed., 28.

27 *What I didn't know then* Russell Lane and Paul Davies, *Migraine,* 93: "Some patients experience auras without headache for most of

their lives before some event precipitates more typical attacks with headache."

28 *They make one think* Russell Lane and Paul Davies, *Migraine,* 11.

30 *And then, a headache, only not* See, for instance, Oliver Sacks, *Migraine,* 18. See also Robert A. Davidoff, *Migraine, 57.*

31 *Thomas Willis* Widely quoted. See, for instance, Alan Rapoport and John Edmeads, "Migraine: The Evolution of Our Knowledge," 1222. An excellent analysis of Willis on headache can be found in Hansruedi Isler, "Thomas Willis' Two Chapters on Headache of 1672: A First Attempt to Apply 'New Science' to this Topic." Isler argues that Willis "anticipate(s)" both "Wolff's hypothesis" and "Blau's complete migraine" (97).

31 *"father"* Russell Lane and Paul Davies, *Migraine,* v.

31 *"Headach"* Thomas Willis, *Two Discourses Concerning the Souls of Brutes,* 105.

31 *"Nervous Fibres"* Ibid., 107.

31 *"water() . . . upon"* Ibid., 106.

32 *"a venerable . . . hot Blood"* Ibid., 124–125.

32 *"above twenty years"* Ibid., 122. This is probably the most famous case study in the history of migraine: it is cited in virtually every retrospective article and book. For instance: Macdonald Critchley, "The Malady of Anne, Viscountess Conway," 44; Macdonald Critchley, "Migraine from Cappadocia to Queen Square," 33–34.

32 *Their portrait of migraine and the body deepened* References to the contribution of astronomers in migraine literature are widespread. See, for instance, Jes Olesen et al., *The Headaches, 5.* Russell Lane and Paul Davies, *Migraine,* 10. H. Isler, "Retrospect: The History of Thought About Migraine from Aretaeus to 1920," in J. N. Blau, ed., *Migraine: Clinical, Therapeutic, Conceptual and Research Aspects,* 669.

32 *John Fordyce* Russell Lane and Paul Davies, *Migraine,* 18. Macdonald Critchley, "Migraine from Cappadocia to Queen Square," 36.

32 *Samuel Tissot* Russell Lane and Paul Davies, *Migraine,* 19.

32 *"wipe . . . body"* Robert Whyte, *Observations on the Nature, Causes, and Cure of Those Disorders Which Have Been Commonly Called Nervous, Hypochondriac, or Hysteric,* preface, 61, 305–308.

33   *"welcome stupor"*   Qtd. in Macdonald Critchley, "Migraine from Cappadocia to Queen Square," 32.

33   *"effect like the motion"*   Qtd. in Hubert Airy, "On a Distinct Form of Transient Hemiopsia," 253.

33   *"a singular kind of glimmering"*   John Fothergill, "Remarks on That Complaint, Commonly Known Under the Name of Sick Head-ach," 120–121. Qtd. in Edward Liveing, *On Megrim, Sick-Headache, and Some Allied Disorders: A Contribution to the Pathology of Nerve-Storms,* 76.

33   *"He opened the door"*   Macdonald Critchley, "Migraine from Cappadocia to Queen Square," 35. Seymour Diamond and Mary A. Franklin, *Headache Through the Ages,* 121. Macdonald Critchley, "Bygone Remedies for Migraine," 173.

33   *"would imagine that a cavity"*   Macdonald Critchley, "Migraine from Cappadocia to Queen Square," 34.

33   *Different names abounded*   For "sun-pain," see George M. Gould, "The History and Etiology of Migraine," 8. For "sick-giddiness" and "blind-headache," see Edward Liveing, *On Megrim, Sick-Headache, and Some Allied Disorders: A Contribution to the Pathology of Nerve-Storms,* 7, 8. For "cephalalgia" and "cephalea," see Francis Adams, commentary, Paulus Aegineta, trans. and comm., *The Seven Books of Paulus Aeginata,* vol. 1, 352. "Cephalea" is now often spelled "cephalgia." Constantinos Trompoukis and Konstantinos Vadlikolias, "The 'Byzantine Classification' of Headache Disorders," 1063.

34   *"red migraine"*   Qtd. in Russell Lane and Paul Davies, *Migraine,* 20.

34   *"white migraine"*   Ibid.

34   *"melted butter"*   John Fothergill, "Remarks on That Complaint, Commonly Known Under the Name of Sick Head-ach," 108.

34   *They devised*   Macdonald Critchley, "Bygone Remedies for Migraine," 172.

34   *"'Italy'"*   George M. Gould, "The History and Etiology of Migraine," 21.

34   *"apply cloths dipped in water"*   E. F. Haskell, ed. R. L. Shep, *Civil War Cooking: The Housekeeper's Encyclopedia,* 378. See Jan R. McTavish, *Pain and Profits,* 13.

34   *"whenever a slave"*   William Glasgow, "On Certain Measures for the Relief of Congestive Headaches," 262. Qtd. in Jan R. McTavish, *Pain and Profits,* 14.

35 *Mary Boykin Chesnut* Jan R. McTavish, *Pain and Profits*, 9. Macdonald Critchley, "Bygone Remedies for Migraine," 172.

35 *Laxatives* For calomel and cannabis, see Seymour Diamond and Mary A. Franklin, *Headache Through the Ages*, 119, 122; Jan R. McTavish, *Pain and Profits*, 23–24. See also Macdonald Critchley, "Bygone Remedies for Migraine," 174.

35 *Champagne* Jan R. McTavish, *Pain and Profits*, 24.

35 *In Pennsylvania* Ibid., 12.

35 *In the Bahamas* Ibid.

35 *"ludicrously strange"* Charles Darwin, intro. and ed. Edward O. Wilson, *The Voyage of the Beagle*, 129.

35 *"apply about six leeches"* Qtd. in Jan R. McTavish, *Pain and Profits*, 14.

Victorian and Modern

36 *"I'm very brave generally"* Lewis Carroll, *Through the Looking Glass*, in *Alice in Wonderland* and *Through the Looking Glass*, 239. Qtd. in Arnold P. Friedman, "The Headache in History, Literature, and Legend," 662. Qtd. in Seymour Diamond and Mary A. Franklin, *Headache Through the Ages*, 78.

38 *"the night-side of life"* Susan Sontag, "Illness as Metaphor," 3–4.

38 *Edward Liveing, if we trust his portraitist* Edward Liveing, *On Megrim, Sick-Headache, and Some Allied Disorders: A Contribution to the Pathology of Nerve-Storms*, preface.

39 *"A man of high intellectual attainments"* Ibid., 35–36.

39 *He acknowledged* Russell Lane and Paul Davies, *Migraine*, vii.

39 *"abrupt transition"* Edward Liveing, *On Megrim, Sick-Headache, and Some Allied Disorders: A Contribution to the Pathology of Nerve-Storms*, 35.

39 *"shudder(ed)"* Hubert Airy, "On a Distinct Form of Transient Hemiopsia," 247. Qtd. in Edward Liveing, *On Megrim, Sick-Headache, and Some Allied Disorders: A Contribution to the Pathology of Nerve-Storms*, 114.

39 *"I can't tell you why"* Edward Liveing, *On Megrim, Sick-Headache, and Some Allied Disorders: A Contribution to the Pathology of Nerve-Storms*, 17.

39 *His patients forgot words* The idea of the "crude language" of the brain is inspired by this from Oliver Sacks, *Migraine*, 223: "In

migraine, the symptoms are fixed and bounded by physiological connections; but its symptoms can constitute, as it were, a bodily alphabet or proto-language, which may secondarily and subsequently be used as a symbolic language."

40 *"I am not at all disposed"* Edward Liveing, "Observations on Megrim or Sick-Headache," 366.

40 *"The malady"* Ibid., 365.

40 *Cocoa and caffeine* Seymour Diamond and Mary A. Franklin, *Headache Through the Ages,* 122. Macdonald Critchley, "Bygone Remedies for Migraine," 173, 174. On Gower's mixture, see Stephen D. Silberstein, "Historical Aspects of Migraine," in Stephen D. Silberstein, M. Alan Stiles, and William B. Young, eds., *Atlas of Migraine and Other Headaches,* 16.

40 *Within ten years* An excellent history of the development of these drugs can be found in Jan R. McTavish, *Pain and Profits.*

41 *"ten adult doses"* Qtd. in Jan R. McTavish, ibid., 109.

41 *"almost"* Ibid.

41 *"Migraine: Established Points"* To Wilhelm Fliess, Oct. 5, 1895, *The Complete Letters of Sigmund Freud to Wilhelm Fliess, 1887–1904,* ed. Jeffrey Moussaieff Masson, 142–144.

41 *Freud, who had originally treated* A. Karwautz et al., "Freud and Migraine: The Beginning of a Psychodynamically Oriented View of Headache a Hundred Years Ago," 23.

41 *"forcible defloration"* Qtd. in A. Karwautz et al., ibid., 24.

41 *While Freud's essay was not widely read* For a broader discussion of Freud's influence on twentieth-century migraine diagnosis, see A. Karwautz et al., ibid. Jan R. McTavish, *Pain and Profits,* 165–166.

41 *"acted like magic"* Qtd. In Jan R. McTavish, *Pain and Profits,* 80.

41 *By the 1920s* For phenobarbitone, see Macdonald Critchley, "Migraine from Cappadocia to Queen Square," 37.

41 *And another German chemist* Jan R. McTavish, *Pain and Profits,* 164. Stephen D. Silberstein, "Historical Aspects of Migraine," in Stephen D. Silberstein, M. Alan Stiles, and William B. Young, eds., *Atlas of Migraine and Other Headaches,* 19. Alan Rapoport and John Edmeads, "Migraine: The Evolution of Our Knowledge," 1223.

42 *In 1938* A summary of this experiment can be found in Russell Lane and Paul Davies, *Migraine,* 26–27.

42 *"smoking drum"* Ibid., 26.

42 *"scintillations . . . scotoma"* Karl Lashley, "Patterns of Cerebral Integration Indicated by the Scotoma of Migraine," 337–338. See also 332, 333, for a description of the experiment and sample of the sketches. Lashley identifies that rate of movement as 3 millimeters per minute on 339. See also Russell Lane and Paul Davies, *Migraine,* 27–28.

42 *"spreading cortical depression"* Aristides Leao, "Spreading Depression of Cortical Activity in the Cerebral Cortex." Some pigeons and cats were also used (359). See also Aristides Leao and R. S. Morrison, "Propagation of Spreading Cortical Depression." A summary of Leao's experiment can be found in Russell Lane and Paul Davies, *Migraine,* 28–29. An overview of the "Spreading Depression Theory," which is now generally accepted, can be found in Martin Lauritzen, "Pathophysiology of the Migraine Aura: The Spreading Depression Theory." See also H. A. G. Teive, Pa Kowacs, P. M. Filho, E. J. Plovesan, and L. C. Wenreck, "Leao's Cortical Spreading Depression: From Experimental Artifact to Physiological Principle," 1457–1458.

42 *By the 1930s* See Robert A. Davidoff, *Migraine,* 17–18. In this review, Davidoff argues that "available evidence implies that many personality features one finds in migraineurs are a consequence of migraine pain, rather than features that originally increased their vulnerability to migraine attacks."

42 *"an inappropriate"* Robert M. Marcussen and Harold G. Wolff, "A Formulation of the Dynamics of the Migraine Attack," 256.

43 *"a well dressed group"* Harold G. Wolff, "Personality Features and Reactions of Subjects with Migraines," 895, 899, 904.

43 *"harbored strong resentments"* Qtd. in Jan R. McTavish, *Pain and Profits,* 166.

43 *In fact* Robert M. Marcussen and Harold G. Wolff, "A Formulation of the Dynamics of the Migraine Attack," 251.

43 *"firm, well-placed breasts"* Walter C. Alvarez, "Some Characteristics of the Migrainous Woman," 2178, 2183. Qtd. in Oliver Sacks, *Migraine,* 123.

43 *"'goody-goody'"* Harold G. Wolff, "Personality Features and Reactions of Subjects with Migraines," 898.

43 *"complete amnesia"* Jule Eisenbud, "The Psychology of Headache: A Case Studied Experimentally," 592–593.

43 *"low and out of sorts"* Ibid., 610.

44 *"average in business"* Caro W. Lippman, "Certain Hallucinations Peculiar to Migraine," 346–347.

44 *"one foot high"* Ibid., 347.

44 *"look down"* Ibid., 348.

44 *By the 1950s* Jan R. McTavish, *Pain and Profits*, 4, 162.

44 *"Many physicians"* Robert S. Kunkel, "The American Headache Society: Looking Back," 681.

44 *"by default"* Qtd. in ibid. "No one wanted to see these patients" is Kunkel's paraphrase.

44 *They gave their migraine patients* Ibid., 683. Elizabeth Loder, "Prophylaxis: Headaches That Never Happen," 694–695.

44 *And, in the late 1960s* Robert S. Kunkel, "The American Headache Society: Looking Back," 683.

45 *Vascular theories* This debate between vascular and neural theories is much discussed in migraine literature. See Russell Lane and Paul Davies, *Migraine*, 24.

45 *Neurological theories* See Russell Lane and Paul Davies, ibid., 29–30.

45 *Even psychiatric researchers* Wolff's contributions to headache study were signal, and multidisciplinary. See, for instance, Jan R. McTavish, *Pain and Profits*, 170; Russell Lane and Paul Davies, *Migraine*, 27.

45 *As historian Jan R. McTavish* Jan R. McTavish, *Pain and Profits*, 10.

45 *That large numbers* Ibid., 11.

45 *In the early twentieth century* Ibid., 2–3.

45 *"something, such as"* Ibid., 2.

45 *"as the result"* Ibid., 3.

46 *constellation* "Constellation" is used frequently to describe the grouping of symptoms in migraine. See, for instance, Robert A. Davidoff, *Migraine*, 44.

PART TWO

47 *"Do not undervalue"* Mark Twain, from "Pudd'nhead Wilson's New Calendar," *Following the Equator*, 517. Qtd. in Seymour Diamond and Mary A. Franklin, *Headache Through the Ages*, 86.

Tongue-Tied

49   *"English, which can express"*   Virginia Woolf, "On Being Ill," 194.

51   *Then his face returns*   Robert A. Davidoff, *Migraine*, 47: "Some individuals have had only two or three episodes in their entire lives."

51   *But Woolf makes it sound*   Elaine Scarry, *The Body in Pain*, 4–5, refers to "this absolute split between one's sense of one's own reality and the reality of other persons": "physical pain does not simply resist language but actively destroys it." 13: "To have pain is to have *certainty;* to hear about pain is to have *doubt.*" 54: "A fifth dimension of pain is its ability to destroy language."

51   *In desperation, Scarry notes, men and women yield*   Ibid., 15.

51   *"Hell even my own"*   Butterflylady150, comment for Timewarlord, "Anatomy of a Migraine," youtube.com.

52   *"I'm the crash"*   "Weathering Migraine Storms," Deborah-weatheringmigrainestorms.blogspot.com, Dec. 11, 2007.

52   *"someone crying"*   Butterflylady150, comment for Timewarlord, "Anatomy of a Migraine," youtube.com.

53   *"rebound headache"*   Stewart Tepper, *Understanding Migraine and Other Headaches*, 41–42, 45. Also called "transformed or chronic migraine with medication overuse." Russell Lane and Paul Davies, *Migraine*, 67. Robert A. Davidoff, *Migraine,* 77, refers to "chronic daily headache—so-called transformed migraine." Davidoff notes that "one epidemiological investigation has estimated that patients with transformed migraine constitute 2.4% of the general population."

55   *"the outward spread"*   Hubert Airy, "On a Distinct Form of Transient Hemiopsia," 250.

55   *"The printed letters"*   Sir John Herschel to Hubert Airy, May 4, 1868. Qtd. in Hubert Airy, ibid., 252.

55   *"All words and letters"*   Hubert Airy, ibid., 257.

55   *"My head is aching awfully"*   To Mrs. John Tavenor Perry, May 22, 1882, Thomas Penney, ed., *The Letters of Rudyard Kipling, Vol. 1, 1872–89,* 20.

55   *The therapeutic and diagnostic value*   Klaus Podoll, interview, June 18, 2008: "Yayoi Kusama is the best example for this. She has explicitly referred to her art as a therapy which has spared her becoming insane."

55   *the National Headache Foundation, for instance*   The 2003 Mi-

graine Masterpieces can be found at headaches.org/NHF_Programs/ Migraine_Masterpieces/Gallery_2003. I do admit to being somewhat critical of this art, but only in the context of examining my own shortcomings as a portraitist of migraine. I much prefer the position of Klaus Podoll, interview, June 18, 2008: "Regarding migraine art, I'm sort of like a good father. I like them all."

56 At the "Art Gallery" of the American Headache Society Committee These paintings can be found at achenet.org/gallery/view .asp?GALLERY_ID=5.

57 "She was a doctor" Oliver Sacks, "Patterns."

57 Other children make it obvious Robert A. Davidoff, Migraine, 15. Teri Robert, interview, July 9, 2008, describes this scenario.

57 One headache specialist Walter Stewart, interview, July 7, 2008.

57 Drawings like these Klaus Podoll and Derek Robinson, Migraine Art, 48, 49, 54, 55. Carl E. Stafstrom, Shira R. Goldenholz, and Douglas A Dulli, "Serial Headache Drawings by Children with Migraine: Correlation with Clinical Headache Status," 811, 812.

58 15/365 Fifth Migraine in Two Weeks Drivinginheels, flickr.com/ drivinginheels/490267853.

58 Migraine Office Fotofig Redux, flickr.com/Fotofig/1410977212.

58 On youtube: a short film apartment31film, "Migraine," youtube .com.

58 "It most likely goes without saying" zimflim, comment for "Migraine," apartment31film, youtube.com.

58 "What are you doing there" Greg Fiering, Migraine Boy: Fair Weather Friends.

59 "Hey my headache's gone" Ibid.

60 I start to stutter Robert A. Davidoff, Migraine, 55: "Aphasia is well described as an aura of a migraine attack."

60 "incoherence of ideas" Qtd. in George M. Gould, "The History and Etiology of Migraine," 30.

61 "He finds it very difficult" Oliver Sacks, Migraine, 76.

61 "The mild attacks" Qtd. in A. Karwautz et al., "Freud and Migraine: The Beginning of a Psychodynamically Oriented View of Headache a Hundred Years Ago," 22. Qtd. in Seymour Diamond and Mary A. Franklin, Headache Through the Ages, 96.

61 "when the name" Sigmund Freud, Psychopathology of Everyday Life, 52.

61 "more remote psychic motive" Ibid., 95.

Nerve-Storm

63 *"Sick headache"*   Honore de Balzac, *The Physiology of Marriage*, 308, 310.

63 *In certain cultures, Elaine Scarry observes*   Elaine Scarry, *The Body in Pain*, 38–45. The "unmaking" quote can be found on 41.

64 *"literally tortured"*   Robert A. Davidoff, *Migraine*, 106.

64 *One senses a little extra*   Ibid., vii. Russell Lane and Paul Davies, *Migraine*, x, 45: "The 'prevalence' of migraine is substantially higher among physicians than the general population and higher still among neurologists and headache specialists."

64 *And they don't want to be seen or heard*   Robert A. Davidoff, *Migraine*, 61, 62: "Withdrawal is the typical behavior for migraineurs."

65 *The list of foods*   Ibid., 60: "Eating during migraine is rarely reported."

67 *"Sick headache"*   Honore de Balzac, *The Physiology of Marriage*, 306–310.

70 *We did, oh*   Robert A. Davidoff, *Migraine*, 20: "Migraine can also significantly affect the frequency and quality of sexual relations."

70 *Light and sound*   Robert A. Davidoff, ibid., 59, writes that "66% to 88% of patients are believed to develop an amplified and usually unpleasant sensitivity to light . . . sounds of moderate intensity such as conversational speech, the noise of traffic, or the sound of a television may seem unacceptably loud." See also 106.

71 *Was it, well, real?*   Arthur Kleinman, *The Illness Narratives*, 57: "If there is a single experience shared by virtually all chronic pain patients it is that at some point those around them—chiefly practitioners, but also at times family members—come to question the authenticity of the patient's experience of pain."

76 *As the twentieth-century sociologist*   See Talcott Parsons, *The Social System*. A good summary, and the word *contract*, from Mary S. Sheridan, *Pain in America*, 5–6.

76 *I might point to another part*   See Talcott Parsons, "The Sick Role and the Role of the Physician Reconsidered," 260, 261.

Enlightenment, Part 2

78 *"The Brain—is wider than the Sky—"*   "The Brain—is wider than the Sky," *The Poems of Emily Dickinson*, ed. R.W. Franklin, 269.

80 *Visions, hallucinations?* Technically, hallucinations. See, for instance, Russell Lane and Paul Davies, *Migraine,* 93. Robert A. Davidoff, *Migraine,* 54, writes that "dreamy states, delirium, intense feelings of déjà vu or jamais vu of extended duration, and transient states of depersonalization have been noted."

81 *But everything was soon blocked* See, for instance, "Weathering Migraine Storms," Deborah-weatheringmigrainestorms.blogspot.com, Oct. 11, 2007: "The store with its ultra violet lighting; it sets off rockets red glare sound effects in my freaking ears . . . I KNOW, WHY DON'T THEY MAKE A MIGRAINE SAFE SHOPPING AREA!!!!"

83 *"'greater depth and speed'"* Oliver Sacks, *Migraine,* 84.

84 *"I saw a great star"* Hildegard of Bingen, *Scivias,* 309. See Oliver Sacks, "The Visions of Hildegard," in *The Man Who Mistook His Wife for a Hat,* 166–170. 168: "A careful consideration of these accounts and figures leaves no doubt concerning their nature; they were indisputably migrainous." See also Oliver Sacks, *Migraine,* 299–301. Fiona Maddocks, *Hildegard of Bingen,* 55. The discussion of Hildegard and migraine appears to have originated in an essay by Charles Singer, first published in 1917, revised in 1928 in his *From Magic to Science: Essays on the Scientific Twilight* (London: Ernest Benn, 1928) and since republished in 2005: Charles Singer, "The Visions of Hildegard of Bingen," *Yale Journal of Biology and Medicine* 78 (2005): 57–82. Seymour Diamond and Mary A. Franklin, *Headache Through the Ages,* 44–46. Russell Lane and Paul Davies, *Migraine,* 10.

84 *Various observers* Russell Lane and Paul Davies, ibid., 9.

84 *"a powerful internal sensation"* Siri Hustvedt, "Lifting, Lights, and Little People."

84 *"sometimes an intimation"* Richard Grossinger, *Migraine Auras: When the Visual World Fails,* 40.

84 *"idea of a presence . . . view"* Klaus Podoll and Derek Robinson, "The Idea of a Presence as Aura Symptom in Migraine," 103, 104.

85 *"like sand . . . covered over"* Virginia Woolf to V. Sackville-West, Aug. 15, 1929, Nigel Nicolson and Joanne Trautmann, eds. *The Letters of Virginia Woolf,* vol. 4 (1929–1931), 78.

85 *"a migraine almost always"* Madhuleema Chaliha, "The Beauty of Having a Migraine." Qtd. in "Migraine and Literature," migraine-aura.org.

85 *"thorn in the flesh"* H. Göbel, H. Isler, and H. P. Hasenfratz, "Headache Classification and the Bible: Was St. Paul's Thorn in the Flesh Migraine?"

Reading

87 *"Do you know what hemi crania"*   To Margaret Burne-Jones, May
3–June 24, 1886, Thomas Penney, ed., *The Letters of Rudyard Kipling, Vol. 1, 1872–89,* 132. Qtd., roughly, in Seymour Diamond and
Mary A. Franklin, *Headache Through the Ages,* 68.

88 *Get the Buddha in here first*   This passage is inspired by *The
Surangama Sutra,* in *A Buddhist Bible,* ed. Dwight Goddard, forewd.
by Robert Aitken, 108–275. References to Buddha appear only occasionally in the literature of migraine and chronic pain in America,
but they do appear. See Mary S. Sheridan, *Pain in America,* 28.

89 *In the Old Testament*   Elaine Scarry, *The Body in Pain,* 198.

89 *"God whispers to us"*   C. S. Lewis, *The Problem of Pain,* 91. Qtd.,
in variant, in Mary S. Sheridan, *Pain in America,* 35.

89 *"forceful shattering"*   Elaine Scarry, *The Body in Pain,* 203.

90 *"weapon"*   Ibid., 208, 235.

90 *It's an extraordinary transformation*   Ibid., 213: "Hence within the
Judeo-Christian tradition it is the weapon (not Jehovah) that Jesus
displaces."

90 *Christianity—like every other religion*   Ibid., 214: "God is both
omnipotent and in pain."

91 *"It is only a headache"*   Qtd. in Richard B. Sewell, *The Life of Emily
Dickinson,* 145. For Dickinson's own headaches, see 147.

91 *"I felt a Funeral"*   "I Felt a Funeral, in My Brain," *The Poems of
Emily Dickinson,* ed. R.W. Franklin, 153.

92 *But Dickinson did not*   There are a fair number of casual claims
about this poem's association with migraine. See, for instance, Nicole
Mohr, "Emily Dickinson's Poem 'I Felt a Funeral in My Brain,'"
Associatedcontent.com; "A close reading of Emily Dickinson's 'I Felt
a Funeral in My Brain,'" Capjewels.com; "I Felt a Funeral in My
Brain," Discussion, Oldpoetry.com; WAGblog, "Comments: Analysis of an Emily Dickinson Poem," Schizophrenia.com.

93 *Glossy art books*   See, for instance, Oliver Sacks, *Migraine,* 278:
"When the fragmentation is gross, patients compare the effect to that
of Cubist paintings, and if the fragmentation is very fine, to pointillist
paintings."

94 *"All at once"*   Qtd. in G. N. Fuller and M. V. Gale, "Migraine
Aura as Artistic Inspiration," 1670–1671. Qtd. in Seymour Diamond
and Mary A. Franklin, *Headache Through the Ages,* 83. There is

controversy about whether de Chirico had migraines or something different. Alan E. H. Emery, "How Neurological Disease Can Affect an Artist's Work," 367. Olaf Blanke and Theodor Landis, "The Metaphysical Art of Giorgio de Chirico," 191: "The main characteristic of migraine-recurrent headache—is strikingly absent in his writings." Nicola Ubaldo and Klaus Podoll, "The Migraine of Giorgio de Chirico," 625. Podoll, interview, June 18, 2008: "We have stuck to our migraine diagnosis."

94   *"bathing my feet"* Ulysses S. Grant, *Personal Memoirs,* vol. 2 (Charles L. Webster, 1894), 483. See also William S. McFeely, *Grant: A Biography,* 217–218; Bruce Catton, *Grant Takes Command,* 459.

94   *"those terrible headaches"* To Julia Dent Grant, July 13, 1861, in Ulysses S. Grant, *Memoirs and Selected Letters,* 970.

95   *"fearful pain"* George Meade, qtd. in William S. McFeely, *Grant: A Biography,* 217.

95   *"the instant"* Ulysses S. Grant, *Personal Memoirs,* vol. 2 (Charles L. Webster, 1894), 485. See also Seymour Diamond and Mary A. Franklin, *Headache Through the Ages,* 124; Jan R. McTavish, *Pain and Profits,* 8–9.

95   *That gorgeous slur* See, for instance, Stephen Silberstein, qtd. in "Is It a Migraine?" Part 1, Illumistream, youtube.com: "Much of the King's well-publicized drug use was actually an attempt to self-medicate his headaches as opposed to hedonistic pursuit."

95   *Those drugs swirling* "Elvis Presley's Private Struggle with Intractable Migraines Revealed." For the link between ergots and LSD, see Stewart Tepper, *Understanding Migraine and Other Headaches,* 48.

95   *"This melancholy"* Anne Olivier Bell, ed., *The Diary of Virginia Woolf,* vol. 3, 241. Qtd. in Hermione Lee, *Virginia Woolf,* 181.

95   *"60 days"* Anne Olivier Bell, ed., *The Diary of Virginia Woolf.* vol. 2, 125. Qtd. In Hermione Lee, *Virginia Woolf,* 185.

96   *"partly mystical"* Anne Olivier Bell, ed., *The Diary of Virginia Woolf,* vol. 3, 287. Qtd. in Hermione Lee, *Virginia Woolf,* 187.

96   *"odd whirr of wings"* Anne Olivier Bell, ed., *The Diary of Virginia Woolf,* vol. 3, 286. Qtd. in Hermione Lee, *Virginia Woolf,* 187.

96   *"a kind of vibration"* Anne Olivier Bell, ed., *The Diary of Virginia Woolf,* vol. 1, 298. Qtd. in Hermione Lee, *Virginia Woolf,* 187.

96   *"becomes chrysalis . . . pen"* Anne Olivier Bell, ed., *The Diary of Virginia Woolf,* vol. 3, 287. Qtd. in Hermione Lee, *Virginia Woolf,* 187.

96   *"I feel my brains"*   Nigel Nicolson, ed., *The Letters of Virginia Woolf*, vol. 1 (1888–1912), 412. Qtd. in Hermione Lee, *Virginia Woolf*, 187.

96   *"Amid the torments"*   Friedrich Nietzsche, trans. Duncan Large, *Ecce Homo*, 7.

96   *"constant headaches . . . dream"*   Qtd. in Joachim Kohler, *Zarathustra's Secret: The Interior Life of Friedrich Nietzsche*, trans. Ronald Taylor, 30.

96   *As he grew*   Arnold P. Friedman, "The Headache in History, Literature, and Legend," 666. "The Lonely Nietzsche and His Migraine," 726. Joachim Kohler, *Zarathustra's Secret: The Interior Life of Friedrich Nietzsche*, trans. Ronald Taylor, 139.

97   *"I am sitting here"*   Qtd. in Joachim Kohler, ibid.

97   *"I was made to suffer"*   Qtd. in Joachim Kohler, ibid., 207.

97   *"a profusion of fantastic flowers . . . madness"*   Qtd. in Leonard Sax, "What Was the Cause of Nietzsche's Dementia?" 49. As Sax notes, Nietzsche's migraines argue against those who believe that he suffered from syphilis and argue for something like "meningioma of the right optic nerve" (49).

97   *"He told me"*   Qtd. in Joachim Kohler, *Zarathustra's Secret: The Interior Life of Friedrich Nietzsche*, trans. Ronald Taylor, 222.

97   *"headaches had the highest"*   Qtd. in J. Haan and M. D. Ferrari, "Mahler's Migraine," 254.

97   *Karl Marx*   J. M. Jones, "Great Pains: Famous People with Headaches," 629. For a profile gallery of famous migraineurs, see Stephen D. Silberstein, "Historical Aspects of Migraine," in Stephen D. Silberstein, M. Alan Stiles, and William B. Young, eds., *Atlas of Migraine and Other Headaches*, 26–31. There are many more names here than I have included. In truth, the diagnosis of dead people with live illnesses is not reliable, and it is not difficult to find contrary diagnoses for many of these individuals, or to find, upon closer inspection, that the evidence that labels them as migraineurs is sometimes slight and even playful. In certain cases—Jefferson, for instance, or de Chirico—I have consciously sided with medical scholars who diagnose migraine, even if other medical scholars diagnose something else. In other cases, I have chosen to portray the ambiguity of diagnosis as ambiguity. In still other cases, I have disregarded cases I don't find persuasive.

97   *Julius Caesar*   J. M. Jones, "Great Pains: Famous People with Headaches," 627, citing J. Gomez, J. Kotler, and J. Long, "Did Caesar

Have a Brain Tumor?" *Journal of the Florida Medical Association* 82 (1995): 199–201.

97   *John Calvin*   Seymour Diamond and Mary A. Franklin, *Headache Through the Ages,* 55. Arnold P. Friedman, "The Headache in History, Literature, and Legend," 663–664, lists Calvin, Madame Pompadour, Karl Marx, Alfred Nobel, etc. J. M. Jones, "Great Pains: Famous People with Headaches," 629, lists many of these, including Harry Truman.

97   *Composers*   Arnold P. Friedman, "The Headache in History, Literature, and Legend," 662.

97   *"I have rolled with my eyes"*   J. Haan and M. D. Ferrari, "Mahler's Migraine," 254.

97   *"horrible hours . . . illness"*   Ibid.

98   *Migraine ran in Charles Darwin's family*   See Stephen D. Silberstein, "Historical Aspects of Migraine," in Stephen D. Silberstein, M. Alan Stiles, and William B. Young, eds., *Atlas of Migraine and Other Headaches,* 16.

98   *"My last two days"*   Qtd. in William Irvine, intro. Julian Huxley, *Apes, Angels, and Victorians: The Story of Darwin, Huxley, and Evolution,* 77. Qtd. in Seymour Diamond and Mary A. Franklin, *Headache Through the Ages,* 74. Qtd. in Arnold P. Friedman, "The Headache in History, Literature, and Legend," 668.

98   *"The children played"*   Qtd. in Seymour Diamond and Mary A. Franklin, *Headache Through the Ages,* 75. Qtd. in Arnold P. Friedman, "The Headache in History, Literature, and Legend," 668.

98   *"head whiz"*   Qtd. in Janet Browne, *Charles Darwin: The Power of Place,* 227.

98   *"partial memory loss . . . sinking fits"*   Ibid., 400.

98   *But he had headaches that helped*   See Elizabeth Loder, "What Is the Evolutionary Advantage of Migraine?" 630.

98   *"a very useful . . . religion"*   William Irvine, intro. Julian Huxley, *Apes, Angels, and Victorians: The Story of Darwin, Huxley, and Evolution,* 64.

98   *"a mind of"*   Qtd. in J. M. Jones, "Great Pains: Famous People with Headaches," 629.

99   *"involuntary transmission . . . will"*   Charles Darwin, *The Expressions of the Emotions in Man and Animals,* intro. and ed. Edward O. Wilson, 1300, 1306. A detailed application of this Darwin book to migraine can be found in Oliver Sacks, *Migraine,* 217–218, 224.

99 *Thomas Jefferson, during one*   Fawn Brodie, *Thomas Jefferson: An Intimate History,* 253.

100 *He describes the disappearance*   Eve LaPlante, *Seized,* 4.

100 *"me . . . but me gone mad"*   Qtd. In Eve LaPlante, ibid.

101 *"All fail . . . Wonderland"*   John Pudney, *Lewis Carroll and His World,* 69.

101 *"religious ecstasy . . . seizures"*   Qtd. In Eve LaPlante, *Seized,* 39.

101 *"What if it is disease?"*   Fyodor Dostoyevsky, *The Idiot,* trans. Constance Garnett, 218. Variant qtd. in Eve LaPlante, *Seized,* 39.

101 *So what if*   The use of "rabbit hole" to describe migraine is frequent. See, for instance, Roger Cady, interview, June 18, 2008, describing treatment as "looking backwards through the rabbit hole to see what was before." Or Paula Kamen, "Leaving the Rabbit Hole."

102 *Researchers have considered*   See Oliver Sacks, *Migraine,* 274–285; Oliver Sacks, "Patterns"; Klaus Podoll, e-mail interview, June 18, 2008: "It's a common notion in research on visual hallucinations."

102 *"prototype(s)"*   John F. W. Herschel, "On Sensorial Vision," 412.

102 *"hallucinatory . . . personality"*   Heinrich Kluver, *Mescal and Mechanisms of Hallucinations,* 67, 68, 73, 75.

102 *"are psychosomatically like dreams"*   Richard Grossinger, *Migraine Auras: When the Visual World Fails,* 83.

103 *She mentions migraines there*   See, for instance, Fiona Maddocks, *Hildegard of Bingen,* 63.

103 *"Then I saw as it"*   Hildegard of Bingen, *Scivias,* 73.

103 *"I saw watery air"*   Ibid., 93.

103 *"I could not see any light"*   Qtd. In Fiona Maddocks, *Hildegard of Bingen,* 91.

103 *Picasso*   John Richardson, collab. Marilyn McCully, *A Life of Pablo Picasso,* vol. 1, 115, 277, 452; vol. 2, 147, 281.

104 *"illusory vertical splitting"*   See Klaus Podoll and Derek Robinson, "Splitting of the Body Image as Somesthetic Aura Symptom in Migraine."

104 *"the face . . . great difficulties"*   M. D. Ferrari and J. Haan, "Migraine Aura, Illusory Vertical Splitting, and Picasso," 686. See also Oliver Sacks, *Migraine,* 85.

105   *We do not need to try to guess*   John Pudney, *Lewis Carroll and His World,* 7, 10.

105   *"Visual distortions"*   Richard Restak, "Alice in Migraineland," 308.

106   *"This morning, on getting up"*   Lewis Carroll, *The Diaries of Lewis Carroll,* vol. 2, ed. Roger Lancelyn Green (New York: Oxford University Press, 1954): 459. Qtd. In Richard Restak, "Alice in Migraineland," 308. Qtd. in Peter van Vugt, "CL Dodgson's Migraine and Lewis Carroll's Literary Inspiration: A Neurolinguistic Perspective." See also Seymour Diamond and Mary A. Franklin, *Headache Through the Ages,* 79–81. There are other references to headache in Carroll's letters and diaries. "I have been 'taking it easy,' now, for a good while, and my headaches are getting fewer, and my brain recovering its usual power," he writes to Edith Blakemore, April 26, 1891, in *The Letters of Lewis Carroll, Vol. 2, 1886–1898,* ed. Morton N. Cohen with Roger Lancelyn Green (New York: Oxford University Press, 1979): 837.

106   *He owned a book*   Richard Restak, "Alice in Migraineland," 308.

106   *"epileptic, no doubt"*   Qtd. In Richard Restak, ibid., 310. There remains debate between those who argue that Carroll had migraines and those who believe he had epilepsy. See, for instance, Restak, 311, quoting Sandor Burstein, "a physician and an internationally recognized authority on Carroll": "Based on my reading of the accounts of Carroll's loss of consciousness, I note that each was accompanied by a headache. I am now convinced that nothing more than migraine is needed to account for these episodes. Migraine answers all." For the other view, see Eve LaPlante, *Seized,* 69–73.

106   *"carefully executed"*   Klaus Podoll and Derek Robinson, "Lewis Carroll's Migraine Experiences," 1366. Qtd. in Richard Restak, "Alice in Migraineland," 308.

106   *Others have noted*   J. Todd, "The Syndrome of Alice In Wonderland," 704. See Seymour Diamond and Mary A. Franklin, *Headache Through the Ages,* 79–82: "first described by Lippman in 1952, although the name was not given to this phenomena until 1955 by Todd." See also Loren Rolak, "Literary Neurologic Syndromes: Alice in Wonderland." R. W. Evans, "Reversible Palinopsia and the Alice in Wonderland Syndrome Associated with Topiramate Use in Migraineurs."

107   *"hot day . . . next"*   Lewis Carroll, *Alice in Wonderland,* in *Alice in Wonderland* and *Through the Looking Glass,* 16, 17.

107   *"There seems to be a sort of hole"*   Oliver Sacks, *Migraine*, 94.

107   *"She says: 'There is nothing there'"*   Ibid., 95.

107   *"DRINK ME"*   Lewis Carroll, *Alice in Wonderland*, in *Alice in Wonderland* and *Through the Looking Glass*, 21.

107   *"EAT ME"*   Ibid., 24.

107   *"gallons of tears"*   Ibid., 27.

108   *" 'I'm sure those' "*   Ibid., 30.

108   *The abrupt crying*   Teri Robert, interview, July 9, 2008.

108   *"She waited for a few minutes"*   Lewis Carroll, *Alice in Wonderland*, in *Alice in Wonderland* and *Through the Looking Glass*, 23.

108   *"Very occasionally"*   Caro W. Lippman, "Certain Hallucinations Peculiar to Migraine," 347.

108   *"I have a very peculiar feeling"*   Ibid., 348.

108   *That last one*   Ibid., 349. See also Richard Restak, "Alice in Migraineland," 306.

108   *"When she looked down"*   Lewis Carroll, *Alice in Wonderland*, in *Alice in Wonderland* and *Through the Looking Glass*, 26.

109   *"When walking down the street"*   Caro W. Lippman, "Certain Hallucinations Peculiar to Migraine," 348.

109   *"My head would seem far"*   Ibid., 350.

109   *"It vanished quite slowly"*   Lewis Carroll, *Alice in Wonderland*, in *Alice in Wonderland* and *Through the Looking Glass*, 89.

109   *"Talking with a friend"*   Karl Lashley, "Patterns of Cerebral Integration Indicated by the Scotoma of Migraine," 338.

110   *"Who am I, then?"*   Lewis Carroll, *Alice in Wonderland*, in *Alice in Wonderland* and *Through the Looking Glass*, 31.

110   *"I wanted to run from myself"*   Caro W. Lippman, "Certain Hallucinations Peculiar to Migraine," 348.

110   *"Alice had got so much"*   Lewis Carroll, *Alice in Wonderland*, in *Alice in Wonderland* and *Through the Looking Glass*, 25.

110   *"After a few minutes of feeling large"*   Caro W. Lippman, "Certain Hallucinations Peculiar to Migraine," 350.

111   *"I felt that this summer afternoon"*   Oliver Sacks, *Migraine*, 86.

111   *"I get all tired out"*   Caro W. Lippman, "Certain Hallucinations Peculiar to Migraine," 350.

111   *"We're all mad here"*   Lewis Carroll, *Alice in Wonderland*, in *Alice in Wonderland* and *Through the Looking Glass*, 86.

111   *"off with her head"*   Ibid., 108.

111   *"who stole the tarts"*   Ibid., 145.

111   *"the twinkling of the tea"*   Ibid., 150–152.

112   *"rippling, shimmering"*   Oliver Sacks, *Migraine,* 56.

The Four Paths of the Migraineur

113   *"But I"*   Hildegard of Bingen, *Scivias,* 60. See also Fiona Maddocks, *Hildegard of Bingen,* 49.

115   *"If pain could have cured us"*   Santayana, "Pain," 27. Qtd., in variant, in Mary S. Sheridan, *Pain in America,* 31.

116   *"the spacetime continuum"*   Qtd. in Oliver Sacks, *Migraine,* 139.

117   *"I had sensed in myself"*   Hildegard of Bingen, *Scivias,* 59–60. See also Fiona Maddocks, *Hildegard of Bingen,* 15, citing Hildegard of Bingen in *Vita:* "I was only in my third year when I saw a heavenly light which made my soul tremble, but because I was a child I could not speak out."

117   *"But I"*   Hildegard of Bingen, *Scivias,* 60. See also Fiona Maddocks, *Hildegard of Bingen,* 49.

119   *"not a little putt"*   Qtd. in Sarah Hutton, *Anne Conway, A Woman Philosopher,* 49.

119   *"passe(d) through"*   Ibid., 99.

119   *"I could not have read"*   Anne Conway to Henry More, January 26, 1652/3, in Marjorie Hope Nicolson, ed., *Conway Letters,* 70. Qtd. in Sarah Hutton, *Anne Conway, A Woman Philosopher,* 29.

119   *"You write like a man"*   Lord Conway to Anne Conway, July 8, 1651, in Marjorie Hope Nicolson, ed., *Conway Letters,* 32. Qtd. in Sarah Hutton, *Anne Conway, A Woman Philosopher,* 19.

119   *"genius . . . other"*   Qtd. in Sarah Hutton, ibid., 39.

119   *"a right ffinch"*   Ibid., 29.

119   *"Sometimes"*   Thomas Willis, *Two Discourses Concerning the Souls of Brutes,* 121. Qtd. in Macdonald Critchley, "The Malady of Anne, Viscountess Conway," 44.

120   *"Remedies"*   Thomas Willis, *Two Discourses Concerning the Souls of Brutes,* 122. Qtd. in Macdonald Critchley, "The Malady of Anne, Viscountess Conway," 46.

120   She tried an *"oyntment of Quicksilver"*   Thomas Willis, *Two Discourses Concerning the Souls of Brutes,* 122. Qtd. in Sarah Hutton, *Anne Conway, A Woman Philosopher,* 120–121. Qtd. in Macdonald Critchley, "The Malady of Anne, Viscountess Conway," 46.

120 *By 1665, in her early thirties*   Sarah Hutton, *Anne Conway, A Woman Philosopher*, 122.

120 *"opening of the skull"*   Thomas Willis, *Two Discourses Concerning the Souls of Brutes*, 119. Macdonald Critchley, "The Malady of Anne, Viscountess Conway," 47.

120 *Her brother, John Finch*   Sarah Hutton, *Anne Conway, A Woman Philosopher*, 98.

120 *She devoured medical texts*   Ibid., 122–124.

121 *As the pain increased*   Ibid., 128–148.

121 *"I have attained"*   Qtd. in Sarah Hutton, ibid., 24, 147.

121 *"They haue been"*   Anne Conway to Henry More, February 4, 1675, in Marjorie Hope Nicolson, ed., *Conway Letters*, 421. Qtd. in Sarah Hutton, *Anne Conway, A Woman Philosopher*, 179.

121 *She died at the age of*   Sarah Hutton, ibid., 215.

122 *"broken Fragments"*   Qtd. in Sarah Hutton, ibid., 5.

122 *"productions"*   Anne Conway, *The Principles of the Most Ancient and Modern Philosophy*, trans. and ed. Allison P. Coudert and Taylor Corse, 39.

122 *"Spirit and body"*   Ibid., 48. This is, of course, what philosophers call the "materialist" position regarding the mind–body problem. See Jerry Fodor, "The Mind–Body Problem," 168: "The mental is not distinct from the physical."

122 *"Why does the spirit or soul"*   Qtd. in Sarah Hutton, *Anne Conway, A Woman Philosopher*, 116.

122 *Likewise, she meshed*   Sarah Hutton, ibid., 7, 107.

123 *"the particular acquaintance"*   Anne Conway to Henry More, February 4, 1675, in Marjorie Hope Nicolson, ed., *Conway Letters*, 422. Qtd. in Sarah Hutton, *Anne Conway, A Woman Philosopher*, 179.

123 *"20 individuals strong"*   Qtd. In Peter Gay, *Freud: A Life for Our Time*, 74–75.

123 *"psychoanalysis"*   See Peter Gay, ibid., 103: "Freud first used the fateful term *psychoanalysis* in 1896." For the general uncertainty of Freud's career at this stage, see 76: "Freud's scientific prospects were still hard to predict."

124 *"I was suffering from migraine"*   Qtd. in A. Karwautz et al., "Freud and Migraine: The Beginning of a Psychodynamically Oriented View of Headache a Hundred Years Ago," 22. Qtd., in variant, in Seymour Diamond and Mary A. Franklin, *Headache Through the Ages*, 94–95.

124   *"cocainiz(ing)"*   To Wilhelm Fliess, May 30, 1893, *The Complete Letters of Sigmund Freud to Wilhelm Fliess, 1887–1904,* ed. Jeffrey Moussaieff Masson, 49.

124   *By 1895*   Max Schur, *Freud: Living and Dying,* 92.

124   *By this point*   A. Karwautz et al., "Freud and Migraine: The Beginning of a Psychodynamically Oriented View of Headache a Hundred Years Ago," 23. See also Max Schur, *Freud: Living and Dying,* 414.

124   *He also befriends*   Peter Gay, *Freud: A Life for Our Time,* 55.

124   *He operates*   Qtd. in A. Karwautz et al., "Freud and Migraine: The Beginning of a Psychodynamically Oriented View of Headache a Hundred Years Ago," 23.

124   *"migraines rather frequent(ly)"*   To Wilhelm Fliess, Feb. 13, 1896, *The Complete Letters of Sigmund Freud to Wilhelm Fliess, 1887–1904,* ed. Jeffrey Moussaieff Masson, 146.

125   *But Fliess also encourages*   Peter Gay, *Freud: A Life for Our Time,* 58.

125   *"a migraine from which I thought I would die"*   To Wilhelm Fliess, June 27, 1899, *The Complete Letters of Sigmund Freud to Wilhelm Fliess, 1887–1904,* ed. Jeffrey Moussaieff Masson, 357.

125   *"One has a sort of feeling"*   "Migraine: Established Points," to Wilhelm Fliess, Oct. 5, 1895, *The Complete Letters of Sigmund Freud to Wilhelm Fliess, 1887–1904,* ed. Jeffrey Moussaieff Masson, 142.

125   *"migraine represents a toxic effect"*   Ibid., 143.

125   *"tyrant"*   To Wilhelm Fliess, Nov. 5, 1895, *The Complete Letters of Sigmund Freud to Wilhelm Fliess, 1887–1904,* ed. Jeffrey Moussaieff Masson, 150.

125   *"Well, my good spirits"*   To Wilhelm Fliess, Jan. 22, 1898, ibid., 295.

126   *"Everything fine"*   To Wilhelm Fliess, Oct. 20, 1895, ibid., 146.

126   *"the most touching"*   To Wilhelm Fliess, June 9, 1898, ibid., 316.

126   *"analogy in fantasy"*   To Wilhelm Fliess, Jan. 16, 1899, ibid., 340.

126   *"My mood, too"*   To Wilhelm Fliess, Oct. 9, 1899, ibid., 378.

126   *"splendid migraine(s)"*   To Wilhelm Fliess, Feb. 22, 1900, ibid., 400.

126   *"gorgeous migraine(s)"*   To Wilhelm Fliess, Nov. 5, 1899, ibid., 382.

126   *"My health has been excellent"*   To Wilhelm Fliess, Mar. 11, 1900, ibid., 402.

127   *"Totem work"*   Qtd. in Peter Gay, *Freud: A Life for Our Time,* 325.

127 *"intense stress"* Max Schur, *Freud: Living and Dying,* 99–100.

129 *And Jefferson, in turn* John D. Battle Jr., in "The 'Periodical Head-achs' of Thomas Jefferson," argues that "a better diagnosis" is "nervous tension or muscular contraction headaches" (531). J. M. S. Pearce, "The Headaches of Thomas Jefferson," suggests "cluster headaches or coincident migraines" (473). Jeff Unger, "Migraine Headaches: A Historical Perspective, a Glimpse into the Future, and Migraine Epidemiology," 368–369, identifies "chronic daily headache" as a possibility. Many, however, claim that Jefferson's headaches were migraine. For instance, Arnold P. Friedman, "The Headache in History, Literature, and Legend," 664. See also Robert Whyte, *Observations on the Nature, Causes, and Cure of Those Disorders Which Have Been Commonly Called Nervous, Hypochondriac, or Hysteric,* 305–308: "periodical headachs," for Whyte, include headaches that are clearly migraine.

129 *"almost a new man"* To John Page, May 17, 1776, in Julian P. Boyd, ed., *The Papers of Thomas Jefferson,* vol. 1, 293. Qtd. in Fawn Brodie, *Thomas Jefferson: An Intimate History,* 116.

129 *Migraine pushed Jefferson* See Edwin Botts and James A. Bear, ed., *The Family Letters of Thomas Jefferson* (Columbia: University of Missouri Press, 1966): 58. Qtd. in Mary McTavish, *Pain and Profits,* 15.

129 *At first, they came to him* See Fawn Brodie, *Thomas Jefferson: An Intimate History,* 43.

129 *"scheme . . . totally frustrated"* To William Fleming, March 20, 1764, in Julian P. Boyd, ed., *The Papers of Thomas Jefferson,* vol. 1, 16. Qtd. in Fawn Brodie, *Thomas Jefferson: An Intimate History,* 66.

129 *"paroxysms"* To Thomas Cooper, Oct. 27, 1808. Qtd. in Fawn Brodie, ibid., 114–115.

129 *He only got them* Fawn Brodie, ibid., 254.

129 *He had two episodes* ibid., 360, 396.

130 *"an attack of my periodical head ach"* To William Short, March 1, 1784, in Julian P. Boyd, ed., *The Papers of Thomas Jefferson,* vol. 6, 570. Qtd. in Fawn Brodie, *Thomas Jefferson: An Intimate History,* 180. Qtd., in variant, in Seymour Diamond and Mary A. Franklin, *Headache Through the Ages,* 71.

130 *"The art of life"* To Maria Cosway, Oct. 12, 1786, in Julian P. Boyd, ed., *The Papers of Thomas Jefferson,* vol. 10, 448. Qtd. in Seymour Diamond and Mary A. Franklin, *Headache Through the Ages,* 71.

130   *"inveterate head ach"*   John Randolph, qtd. in Fawn Brodie, *Thomas Jefferson: An Intimate History,* 115.

130   *They believed, instead*   Fawn Brodie, ibid., 114.

130   *"I have been so long"*   To John Page, qtd. in ibid., 116.

131   *The Continental Congress cleaned it up*   See, for instance, ibid., 117.

131   *"six-day illness"*   Ibid., 244.

131   *"the most original"*   Ibid., 244.

131   *"self-evident . . . to the living"*   To James Madison, Sept. 6, 1789, in Julian P. Boyd, ed., *The Papers of Thomas Jefferson,* vol. 15, 392. Qtd. in Fawn Brodie, *Thomas Jefferson: An Intimate History,* 244.

132   *"into the abyss . . . Heaven"*   Thomas Jefferson, ed. William Peden, *Notes on the State of Virginia,* 24–25.

132   *"a different form"*   Oliver Sacks, "Creativity, Imagination and Perception," 32.

133   *"Has / the circus"*   "The StormSpinner" (Karla Dorman), "Migraine." Qtd. in "Migraine and Literature," migraine-aura.org.

133   *"comorbid"*   Stewart J. Tepper, *Understanding Migraine and Other Headaches,* 15. A good review article: F. Radat and J. Swendsen, "Psychiatric Comorbidity in Migraine: A Review."

PART THREE

137   *"Equally for no reason"*   Anne Olivier Bell, ed., *The Diary of Virginia Woolf,* vol. 1, 298. Qtd. in Hermione Lee, *Virginia Woolf,* 187.

Opening the Case

139   *"One night as I was awakening"*   Qtd. in Klaus Podoll, "Migraine Art in the Internet: A Study of 450 Contemporary Artists," 94.

141   *In fact, I'm completely typical*   Seymour Diamond, Marcelo E. Bigal, Stephen Silberstein, Elizabeth Loder, Michael Reed, and Richard B. Lipton, "Patterns of Diagnosis and Acute and Preventive Treatment for Migraine in the United States: Results from the American Migraine Prevalence and Prevention Study," 356, 358–361. See, for instance, Stewart J. Tepper, *Understanding Migraine and Other Headaches,* 5: "In 1999 a population-based survey was done of

people with headache in Maryland . . . fifty-two percent of the participants in this survey who met IHS criteria had not received the diagnosis of migraine." Robert A. Davidoff, *Migraine,* 7–8.

142 *Medical schools* Teri Robert, interview, July 9, 2008; Stewart Tepper, interview, Aug. 15, 2008.

142 *Large grant-giving institutions* Teri Robert, interview, July 9, 2008. See Allianceforheadacheadvocacy.org, "Proposed Appropriations Report Language."

142 *or dole out much money* R. E. Shapiro and P. J. Goadsby, "The Long Drought: The Dearth of Public Funding for Headache Research," 992. R. E. Shapiro, "NIH Funding for Research on Headache Disorders: Does It Matter?" *Headache: The Journal of Head and Face Pain* (July/Aug. 2007): 993. Teri Robert, interview, July 9, 2008.

142 *Investigators* "Insurance Limits, Costs Keep Migraine Patients from Meds."

143 *"real disease"* Richard B. Lipton and Marcelo E. Bigal, "Headache as a Real Disease," 707.

144 *founded in 1981* Klaus Podoll and Derek Robinson, *Migraine Art,* 39. See also www.i-h-s.org.

144 *In 1988, led by Danish headache researcher* Rigmor Jensen and Peer Tfelt-Hansen, "Milestones in Headache Research. A Tribute to Jes Olesen," 747.

145 *Headache clinics* Robert S. Kunkel, "The American Headache Society: Looking Back," 683.

145 *Patient–physician support* Richard B. Lipton and Marcelo E. Bigal, "Headache as a Real Disease," 709.

145 *The migraine was now defined* Stewart J. Tepper, *Understanding Migraine and Other Headaches,* 10.

145 *"primary"* "The International Classification of Headache Disorders," 2nd ed., 16–17. Walter Stewart, interview, July 7, 2008. ICHD-II does not use the term "transformed migraine." Stewart J. Tepper, *Understanding Migraine and Other Headaches,* 3; Russell Lane and Paul Davies, *Migraine,* 42. The longer list of names for this headache can be found in Richard B. Lipton and Marcelo E. Bigal, "Ten Lessons on the Epidemiology of Migraine," 57.

145 *"episodic disorder"* Marcelo E. Bigal and Richard B. Lipton, "Concepts and Mechanisms of Migraine Chronification," 7.

146 *"progressive . . . progression"* Richard B. Lipton, interview, Sept. 27, 2008.

146 *Old names receded*   This comparison between Wolff and Blau is made in Robert A. Davidoff, *Migraine,* 45. See J. N. Blau, "Adult Migraine: The Patient Observed," in J. N. Blau, ed., *Migraine: Clinical, Therapeutic, Conceptual and Research Aspects,* 3. Blau makes the same comparison. Note, as well, that he used slightly different terminology in earlier work, substituting "resolution" for "headache termination." See also J. N. Blau, "Migraine Prodromes Separated from the Aura: Complete Migraine."

146 *"free interval"*   Robert A. Davidoff, *Migraine,* 55.

146 *"the familial hemiplegic"*   See, for instance, Stewart Tepper, *Understanding Migraine and Other Headaches,* 23.

146 *"typical"*   "The International Classification of Headache Disorders," 2nd ed., 28.

147 *"explicit . . . other"*   "The International Classification of Headache Disorders," 2nd ed., 12.

147 *"meet criteria"*   Marcelo E. Bigal, Daniel Serrano, Michael Reed, and Richard B. Lipton, "Chronic Migraine in the Population: Burden, Diagnosis, and Satisfaction with Treatment," 559–560. This refers to a revision of ICHD-II known as CM-R.

147 *"migraine without aura"*   Ibid., 24–27. A fine summary (from ICHD-I, not ICHD-II) can be found in Stewart J. Tepper, *Understanding Migraine and Other Headaches,* 3–4 (migraine without aura), and 7 (migraine with aura); another fine summary in Russell Lane and Paul Davies, *Migraine,* 43.

147 *"nausea"*   See, for instance, Robert A. Davidoff, *Migraine,* 59–60: "Approximately 90% of patients report that they experience nausea."

148 *"free text"*   "The International Classification of Headache Disorders," 2nd ed., 14.

148 *While acknowledging*   Robert A. Davidoff, *Migraine,* 8: "A number of investigators have concentrated on the severity of headache rather than a classification scheme."

148 *"is scored"*   Richard B. Lipton and Marcelo E. Bigal, "Ten Lessons on the Epidemiology of Migraine," 86. See also Walter F. Stewart, Richard B. Lipton, Kenneth B. Kolodner, James Sawyer, Clara Lee, and Joshua N. Liberman, "Validity of the Migraine Disability Assessment (MIDAS) Score in Comparison to a Diary-Based Measure in a Population Sample of Migraine Sufferers."

148 *"the 3 best"*   Richard B. Lipton and Marcelo E. Bigal, "Ten Lessons on the Epidemiology of Migraine," 85.

148   *"dirty little secret"*   Stewart J. Tepper, interview, Aug. 15, 2008. See also Stewart J. Tepper, *Understanding Migraine and Other Headaches*, 5.

149   *"between 475"*   Robert A. Davidoff, *Migraine*, v.

149   *"protean"*   Ibid., 3.

149   *"hardwired . . . Everyone . . . 'migraine'"*   Russell Lane and Paul Davies, 45. Lane and Davies make this the focus of *Migraine*, vii, describing it as two of their "three basic and at times controversial hypotheses": "that all primary headache is migraine; that all human brains are potentially susceptible to the migraine mechanism and its many manifestations." Robert A. Davidoff, *Migraine*, 4.

149   *"convergence hypothesis . . . nervous system"*   Roger Cady, Curtis Schreiber, Kathleen Farmer, and Fred Sheftell, "Primary Headaches: A Convergence Hypothesis," 204, 214.

150   *And what makes the switch go click*   Stewart Tepper, *Understanding Migraine and Other Headaches*, 24: "Problems exist with all theories for the causes of migraine." The "switch" metaphor is recurrent. See, for instance, Russell Lane and Paul Davies, *Migraine*, 65: "This supports the concept that failure of the migraine mechanism to 'switch off' for whatever reason, is likely to be a common cause of chronic daily headache."

150   *Here's why*   Russell Lane and Paul Davies, ibid., 52: "It is notoriously difficult to recruit and study patients who are in the throes of an acute migraine attack." D. Kernick, "Migraine: New Perspectives from Chaos Theory," 563: "Although the continual monitoring of brain electrical activity in migraineurs may present practical difficulties in the experimental setting, other systems that are more readily accessible to investigation may demonstrate associated and relevant behaviour." See also Arne May, "Headache: Lessons Learned from Functional Imaging," 223, 225. Richard B. Lipton, Sept. 27, 2008.

150   *And here's why*   See, for instance, Arne May, "Headache: Lessons Learned from Functional Imaging." F. Michael Cutrer, "Functional Imaging in Primary Headache Disorders." Russell Lane and Paul Davies, *Migraine*, 68–69, discuss the use of glyceryl trinitrate to induce migraine-like attacks. Richard B. Lipton, interview, Sept. 27, 2008, describes the financial pressure of needing to reserve time on expensive scan machines, making testing on men and women with unpredictable attacks very difficult, and also discusses the use of

patients with "regular triggers"—a woman whose migraines come at a set point in her menstrual cycle, for instance. A well-known anecdote exists about the functional imaging work of F. M. Cutrer, Mayo Clinic, Rochester, and a patient who reliably got migraines whenever he played basketball.

151   *What these studies*   See Russell Lane and Paul Davies, *Migraine*, 55.

151   *"Nobody has decided"*   Stewart Tepper, interview, Aug. 15, 2008.

151   *"silent" auras*   Russell Lane and Paul Davies, *Migraine*, 73. Stewart Tepper, interview, Aug. 15, 2008.

151   *And others still*   Ibid. Russell Lane and Paul Davies, *Migraine*, xi: "Presumably the neural activation sometimes fails to excite the pain pathways, resulting in aura symptoms without headache."

151   *"rheostat"*   Stewart J. Tepper, interview, August 15, 2008.

151   *Other researchers have mapped*   The ascendancy of neural over vascular theories in contemporary migraine theory and research is well discussed. See, for instance, Russell Lane and Paul Davies, *Migraine*, viii. It's not about blood *or* nerves anymore, although a "hierarchy" might tilt toward the role of nerves: Russell Lane and Paul Davies, *Migraine*, 30. See also Michael A. Moskowitz, "Defining a Pathway to Discovery from Bench to Bedside," 688. And it's not about something on the surface *or* something deep in the brain anymore: at least hypothetically, it's about "both peripheral and central sensitization," according to Stephen Silberstein and Avi Ashkenazi of the Jefferson Headache Center in Philadelphia, "Botulinum Toxin Type A for the Treatment of Headache," 147.

151   *"migraine generator"*   C. Weiller, A. May, V. Limmroth, M. Jüptner, H. Kaube, R. V. Schayck, H. H. Coenen, and H. C. Diener, "Brain Stem Activation in Spontaneous Human Migraine Attacks," *Nature Medicine* 7 (1995): 658–660. Michael E. Cutrer, "Functional Imaging in Primary Headache Disorders," 705. The migraine mechanism is well described for a lay reader in Stewart Tepper, *Understanding Migraine and Other Headaches*, 25–27; Russell Lane and Paul Davies, *Migraine*, 31, 57. Robert A. Davidoff, *Migraine*, 237: "The source of the pain is in a location different from the place where the pain is actually perceived."

151   *This may sound counterintuitive*   Stewart J. Tepper, *Understanding Migraine and Other Headaches*, 9. Russell Lane and Paul Davies, *Migraine*, 2–3.

151 *"pathways"* Russell Lane and Paul Davies, *Migraine,* 46.

153 *"locus . . . 15q11–13"* Ibid., 82. Robert A. Davidoff, *Migraine,* 36, 40.

154 *"polygenic"* Stewart J. Tepper, *Understanding Migraine and Other Headaches,* 14, 24. Russell Lane and Paul Davies, *Migraine,* 79.

154 *And when one cross-references* Russell Lane and Paul Davies, ibid., 82. Robert A. Davidoff, *Migraine,* 91, 93, writes that "attacks may be multifactorial."

154 *"hyperexcitable"* S. K. Aurora and E. Wilkinson, "The Brain Is Hyperexcitable in Migraine." See also Stewart Tepper, *Understanding Migraine and Other Headaches,* 21. Russell Lane and Paul Davies, *Migraine,* 77. Others prefer "vigilant," even "hypervigilant": Roger Cady, interview, July 8, 2008.

154 *Some researchers argue* S. K. Aurora and E. Wilkinson, "The Brain Is Hyperexcitable in Migraine," 1442, 1446.

154 *Others still theorize* Salynn Boyles, "Migraine Sufferers Have Different Brains."

154 *"unitary hypothesis"* Rami Burstein and Moshe Jakubowski, "Unitary Hypothesis for Multiple Triggers of the Pain and Strain of Migraine," 9.

154 *"greater sensory openness . . . imprinting"* Peter Kropp, "Learning from Headaches? Old Problems and New Insights in Migraine," 335.

155 *"aura . . . breeze"* Russell Lane and Paul Davies, *Migraine,* 8–9.

155 *"eloquent . . . noneloquent"* See Russell Lane and Paul Davies, ibid., 73.

155 *"The scintillations"* Karl Lashley, "Patterns of Cerebral Integration Indicated by the Scotoma of Migraine," 337.

157 *"subclinical brain lesions"* Mark C. Kruit, Mark A. van Buchem, Paul A. M. Hoffman, Jacobus T. N. Bakkers, Gisela M. Terwindt, Michel D. Ferrari, and Lenore J. Launer, "Migraine as a Risk Factor for Subclinical Brain Lesions." Marcel E. Bigal and Richard B. Lipton, "Concepts and Mechanisms of Migraine Chronification," discuss "recent evidence" that "suggests that migraine, particularly migraine with aura, is a risk factor for anatomical brain lesions" (7). See also 11.

157 *"types of brain lesions"* Mark C. Kruit, Mark A. van Buchem, Paul A. M. Hoffman, Jacobus T. N. Bakkers, Gisela M. Terwindt, Michel

D. Ferrari, and Lenore J. Launer, "Migraine as a Risk Factor for Subclinical Brain Lesions," 428. Richard B. Lipton, interview, Sept. 27, 2008, suggests that the lesions are caused by some auras.

157 *"To conceive"* Elaine Scarry, *The Body in Pain*, 285.

Taking the Cure

159 *"No headaches"* Anonymous comment, Askapatient.com, Oct. 5, 2006.

159 *"new daily persistent headache"* Stewart J. Tepper, interview, Aug. 15, 2008.

161 *"The word 'serendipity'"* Elizabeth Loder, "Prophylaxis: Headaches That Never Happen," 694.

161 *"about 50% reduction"* Seymour Solomon, "Major Therapeutic Advances in the Past 25 Years," 820. A good summary of the different classes of preventive drugs can be found in this source.

161 *My three drugs of choice* Marcelo E. Bigal, Daniel Serrano, Michael Reed, and Richard B. Lipton, "Chronic Migraine in the Population: Burden, Diagnosis, and Satisfaction with Treatment," 563, provide an excellent chart showing the rates of use among chronic migraineurs of different preventive drugs: Roughly 10 percent, for instance, have tried magnesium, riboflavin, and feverfew as described later in this chapter. Topimirate has been tried by almost one in three.

161 *Imitrex* Seymour Solomon, "Major Therapeutic Advances in the Past 25 Years," 820. Stephen D. Silberstein, "Historical Aspects of Migraine," in Stephen D. Silberstein, M. Alan Stiles, and William B. Young, eds., *Atlas of Migraine and Other Headaches*, 19. Jeff Unger, "Migraine Headaches: A Historical Perspective, a Glimpse into the Future, and Migraine Epidemiology," 370.

161 *"migraine truly is an organic disease"* Patrick P. A. Humphrey, "The Discovery and Development of the Triptans, a Major Therapeutic Breakthrough," 685.

162 *A triptan opens them* See Stewart Tepper, *Understanding Migraine and Other Headaches*, 51–54, 61.

162 *Atenolol* Ibid., 74–75.

163 *Topamax* Ibid., 94.

163 *Or it might be working on the ion channels* Ibid., 23.

163 *Besides anti-hypertension drugs like the beta-blockers* Ibid., 40–42.

164 *Calcium channel blockers* See, for instance, Stewart Tepper, ibid., 23, 81.

164 *"Migraines occur"* Jay S. Cohen, *The Magnesium Solution,* 9–10.

164 *The store of herbal remedies* For B$_2$, see Stewart Tepper, *Understanding Migraine and Other Headaches,* 23.

164 *"It may thus be the case"* E. B. Blanchard, M. L. Peters, C. Hermann, S. M. Turner, T. C. Buckley, K. Barton, and M. L. Dentinger, "Direction of Temperature Control in the Thermal Biofeedback Treatment of Vascular Headache," 243. Qtd. in Mark S. Schwartz and Frank Andrasik, "Headache," 327.

164 *Likewise, some studies* Enrico Facco, Aldo Liguori, Filomena Petti, Gastone Zanette, Flaminia Coluzzi, Marco De Nardin, and Consalvo Mattia, "Traditional Acupuncture in Migraine: A Controlled, Randomized Study." Other studies both support and dispute the conclusion that acupuncture helps migraine.

165 *"an invasion"* Ruth Kidson, *Acupuncture for Everyone: What It Is, Why It Works, and How It Can Help You,* 62–63.

165 *"corner of the forehead"* Ibid., 111.

165 *"rescue"* Stewart Tepper, *Understanding Migraine and Other Headaches,* 64.

165 *Stress* Ibid., 69. Russell Lane and Paul Davies, *Migraine,* 74. Robert A. Davidoff, *Migraine,* 93–94.

165 *"aggravating factor"* "The International Classification of Headache Disorders," 2nd ed., 33. Many refer to "stress" as a trigger, not an "exacerbating factor"—the difference has important rhetorical implications. Teri Robert, interview, July 9, 2008.

165 *But sometimes triggers are not obvious* John F. Rothrock, "The Truth About Triggers," 499.

165 *Because there is no clear gestation period* On food triggers, note Robert A. Davidoff, *Migraine,* 95: "50% of migraine patients believe that a percentage of all of their attacks are induced by foods; other studies indicate that the incidence may be as low as 10%." Davidoff, 98.

166 *They need to worry, too, about ambient modern triggers* Robert A. Davidoff, *Migraine,* 107.

166 *Even the sure things are not sure things* Robert A. Davidoff, ibid., 105, writes that "up to 78% of patients indicate that variations in weather patterns trigger bouts of migraine."

166   Not *the amount of stress*   Stewart Tepper, *Understanding Migraine and Other Headaches*, 19.

166   *While many physicians still cite chocolate*   Robert A. Davidoff, *Migraine*, 98.

167   *Even more remarkably, triggers seem*   This comparison is made in Robert A. Davidoff, *Migraine*, 96, 100. R. C. Peatfield, V. Glover, J. T. Littlewood, M. Sandler, and Rose F. Clifford, "The Prevalence of Diet-Induced Migraine." A. Pradalier and H. Oilat, "Migraine and Alcohol," 179: "It is interesting to note that red wine was reported in one of the last positions, while its consumption in France is much higher than that of white wine. . . . In Great Britain, for example, the predominant factor reported is red wine. The explanation for this difference is unclear: a particular 'ethnic' sensitivity to the constituents of wines; different compositions of wines; or simply a 'notoreity bias' of white wine in France due to socio-cultural or psychological differences."

167   *"confused"*   Roger Cady, Curtis Schreiber, Kathleen Farmer, and Fred Sheftell, "Primary Headaches: A Convergence Hypothesis," 214.

167   *Not sure whether*   See also Stewart Tepper, *Understanding Migraine and Other Headaches*, 35. See also 39: "The trick to making migraine medication work is to get the medication in at the earliest glimmer of the migraine, earlier than early."

168   *What "converges"*   See, for instance, Robert A. Davidoff, *Migraine*, 6, writing about this gray area: "Some patients with migraine do not meet the criteria even though they respond to anti-migraine therapy."

169   *"Educate yourself"*   Teri Robert, interview, July 9, 2008.

170   *And I would have to make peace*   Stewart Tepper, *Understanding Migraine and Other Headaches*, 68: "Tapering down or off of caffeine can be very useful in reducing the frequency of headache."

170   *Likewise, some exercise*   Robert A. Davidoff, *Migraine*, 104.

170   *But since researchers*   Ibid., 95, 102: "Elimination diets have been reported to relieve migraine headaches completely, or almost completely, in a very high proportion of migraineurs."

171   *Maybe you should give up sex*   Ibid., 105.

171   *"benign orgasm headache"*   S. Ucler, B. Karakurum, A. Akahn, H. T. Atasoy, L. E. Inan, and F. C. Tulunay, "Headache Associated

with Sexual Activity in Turkish Headache Patients," in "Session 8: Epidemiology," 363.

171   *"Maui migraine"*   Stewart Tepper, *Understanding Migraine and Other Headaches,* 69.

171   *"let-down migraine"*   Robert A. Davidoff, *Migraine,* 95.

Migraine Parties

177   *"We are all potential migraineurs"*   Paul Davies and Russell Lane, *Migraine,* ix.

181   *Many do not*   On aspartame, see Robert A. Davidoff, *Migraine,* 101.

183   *There are support groups*   S. J. Peroutka, "A Proposed Editorial Review System for 'Headache' Information on the Internet," in "Session 8: Epidemiology," 360.

184   *the American Migraine Study II*   Richard B. Lipton, Walter F. Stewart, Seymour Diamond, Merle L. Diamond, and Michael Reed, "Prevalence and Burden of Migraine in the United States: Data from the American Migraine Study II," 646. Richard B. Lipton, interview, Sept. 27, 2008.

184   *"mild or moderate disability"*   Henry X. Hu, Leona E. Markson, Richard B. Lipton, Walter F. Stewart, and Marc L. Berger, "Burden of Migraine in the United States," 815. Richard B. Lipton, Walter F. Stewart, Seymour Diamond, Merle L. Diamond, and Michael Reed, "Prevalence and Burden of Migraine in the United States: Data from the American Migraine Study II," 646.

185   *Someone with migraines*   Henry X. Hu, Leona E. Markson, Richard B. Lipton, Walter F. Stewart, and Marc L. Berger, "Burden of Migraine in the United States," 816. They suggest that this figure might be low. Robert A. Davidoff, *Migraine,* 18, cites studies that "estimated that female migraineurs required 56 bed rest days and male migraineurs, 38 days each year," for instance. Jeff Unger, "Migraine Headaches: A Historical Perspective, a Glimpse into the Future, and Migraine Epidemiology," 376, provides a good summary of other studies.

185   *Together, the migraining community*   Estimates differ, and there are numerous studies. See, for instance, Mary S. Sheridan, *Pain in America,* 9. J. T. Osterhaus, D. L. Gutterman, and J. R. Plachetka, "Healthcare Resource and the Lost Labour Costs of Migraine Head-

ache in the US." R. E. Shapiro and P. J. Goadsby, "The Long Drought: The Dearth of Public Funding for Headache Research," 991. Henry X. Hu, Leona E. Markson, Richard B. Lipton, Walter F. Stewart, and Marc L. Berger, "Burden of Migraine in the United States," 813, report "112 million bedridden days."

185 *sometimes it takes the drug* Paula Kamen, "Leaving the Rabbit Hole." Walter Stewart, interview, July 7, 2008.

185 *"a significant problem"* Walter Stewart, ibid.

185 *"the revolutionary phenomenon"* Paula Kamen, "Beyond Kittens, Beyond Angels."

185 *"migraine Barbie"* Migrainechickie.blogspot.com, "Migraine Chick: One Girl Chronicling Her Misadventures in Migraine Land."

186 *"mothership"* Paula Kamen, "Beyond Kittens, Beyond Angels."

186 *"migraine nation"* Ginny, comments, Oct. 26, 2007, in Judith Warner, "The Migraine Diet."

186 *The celebrity endorsers* Teri Robert, July 9, 2008, cites Serena Williams, Monica Seles, and Marcia Cross of *Desperate Housewives*.

186 *"Mine primarily starts"* Darla Atlas, "Aikman Learned to Play Through the Pain." Alicia Bodine, "Troy Aikman Serves as Spokesman for the Know Your Migraine Game Plan Education Initiative."

186 *"For men out there"* Darla Atlas, "Aikman Learned to Play Through the Pain."

186 *"blank(ing) out"* Chris Jenkins, "Running Against the Migraine— Denver Broncos Running Back Terrell Davis was Most Valuable Player in the 1988 Super Bowl Despite Suffering from a Migraine Headache for Part of the Game."

186 *Kareem Abdul-Jabbar* Dave Anderson, "Transferring a Headache."

187 *There are socioeconomic* See Stewart Tepper, *Understanding Migraine and Other Headaches*, 16: "The reason for this (the frequency of migraines among lower socioeconomic classes) was a 'downward spiral' caused by the recurring migraines themselves." Walter E. Stewart, Richard B. Lipton, D. D. Celentano, and M. L. Reed, "Prevalence of Migraine Headache in the United States: Relation to Age, Income, Race, and Other Sociodemographic Factors." See also Amanda Gardner, "Poorer Kids at Higher Migraine Risk": another possibility is that individuals in lower socioeconomic classes are more exposed to migraine triggers and exacerbating factors.

187   *Then there are racial breakdowns*   Walter F. Stewart, Richard B.
      Lipton, and Joshua Liberman, "Variation in Migraine Prevalence
      by Race." Walter F. Stewart, Richard B. Lipton, D. D. Celentano,
      and M. L. Reed, "Prevalence of Migraine Headache in the United
      States: Relation to Age, Income, Race, and Other Sociodemographic
      Factors." Walter F. Stewart, interview, July 7, 2008, explored the pos-
      sible reasons: perhaps "we're not seeing a constitutional difference,
      but an environmental difference."

187   *Migraine and depression*   Robert A. Davidoff, *Migraine,* 21. A good
      phrase from Walter F. Stewart, interview, July 7, 2008: depression,
      anxiety, migraine "all occupy the same brain space." F. Radat and
      J. Swendsen, "Psychiatric Comorbidity in Migraine: A Review,"
      166–169, 171.

188   *Epilepsy*   Richard B. Lipton, interview, Sept. 27, 2008.

188   *If you have high blood pressure*   B. Preza, I. Ciraku, and D. Hax-
      hihyseni, "Headache and Hypertension," in "Session 8: Epidemi-
      ology," 362–363. Robert A. Davidoff, *Migraine,* 23, suggests the
      "association between mild-to-moderate migraine and hypertension
      is probably coincidental."

188   *If you have migraine . . . asthma*   Gail Davey, Philip Sedgwick, Will
      Maier, George Visick, David P. Strachan, and H. Ross Anderson,
      "Association Between Migraine and Asthma: Matched Case-Control
      Study," 723.

188   *And if you have migraine*   See Stewart Tepper, *Understanding Mi-
      graine and Other Headaches,* 17: "All migraine patients have a slight
      increase in the risk for stroke compared to people who do not have
      migraine, although the mechanism for this risk is unknown." Robert
      A. Davidoff, *Migraine,* 23–24. Marcelo E. Bigal and Richard B. Lip-
      ton, "Concepts and Mechanisms of Migraine Chronification," 13.
      Sonja Schwaag, Darius G. Nabavi, Achim Frese, Ingo-W. Husstedt,
      and Stefan Evers, "The Association Between Migraine and Juvenile
      Stroke: A Case-Control Study." See also K. R. Merikangas, B. T. Fen-
      ton, S. H. Cheng, M. J. Stolar, and N. Risch, "Association Between
      Migraine and Stroke in a Large-Scale Epidemiological Study of the
      United States," *Archives of Neurology* 54 (April 1997). Miranda
      Hitti, "Stroke Risk Linked to Some Migraines." Richard B. Lipton,
      interview, Sept. 27, 2008.

188   *The numbers, when you see*   Richard B. Lipton, ibid.

188   *Observers reporting on conditions*   See Signsofwitness.com, Dec.

22, 2006. See also "Political Intelligence," Texasobserver.org, April 20, 2007.

189 *But the best-researched* Kathleen Doheny, "Soldiers in Iraq Have More Migraines." Brett J. Theeler, Jay C. Erickson, and Renee Mercer, "Prevalence and Impact of Migraine Among U.S. Soldiers Deployed to a Combat Theater," Research Poster Presentation, 48th Annual Scientific Meeting of the American Headache Society, Los Angeles, June 23, 2006. Cited in "Soldiers in Iraq: Migraine Up, Management Down," headaches.about.com/od/advocacyissues/a/mx_prev_iraq .htm. See also Erek K. Helseth and Jay C. Erickson, "The Prevalence and Impact of Migraine on US Military Officer Trainees," 5. See also "Migraine Strong Indicator of Comorbid Psychiatric Conditions in US Iraq Veterans," Medscape.com/viewarticle/556268. Kurt Samson, "Iraq Conflict Poses Special Problems for Deployed Neurologists." B. J. Mundell, "Migraines Can Signal Psychiatric Woes in Returning Iraq Vets."

189 *"headache"* Geoffrey Ling and Cornelius Maher, "US Neurologists in Iraq: Personal Perspective," 16.

189 *"Our data suggests"* Kathleen Doheny, "Soldiers in Iraq Have More Migraines."

191 *Walter F. Stewart* Walter F. Stewart, interview, July 7, 2008. Stewart describes that "after about 15 headaches," the traditional migraine symptoms "diminish"; the pain might be "less pronounced," but the "persistent presence of pain is the dominant feature." He speaks eloquently of "the fluidity by which migraine can change, go into a quiescent phase, and come back." See Russell Lane and Paul Davies, *Migraine,* 75: "Migraine headaches can also 'cluster' chronologically." See also Richard B. Lipton and Marcelo E. Bigal, "Ten Lessons on the Epidemiology of Migraine," 57.

192 *"marries . . . as ever"* Qtd. in Janet Browne, *Charles Darwin: Voyaging,* 429.

193 *But other researchers estimate* Laurie Edwards, *Life Disrupted,* 216.

193 *The rate of anxiety and depression* Teri Robert, interview, July 9, 2008.

193 *If you have migraine* Teri Robert, interview, July 9, 2008. For concern about children, see "Rain," comment, Diana Lee, *Somebody Heal Me,* Feb. 13, 2008, somebodyhealme.dianalee.net, and Lee: "Being in severe pain is horrible, but I have to imagine it is much worse to see your child in pain."

193 *"If my wife is mine"* Honore de Balzac, *The Physiology of Marriage*, 309.

194 *The rudeness, I think* For saying the "rude thing," see migraine page.com/dcforum/discussion/21315.html, "beth_150": "What is the meanest thing said to you about your migraines?" Brendaenglish: "She uses migraines to get out of anything she doesn't want to do." Crt: "You're just trying to get out of a task, a party, going to work." See also "Melanie," *Life in My Head,* terirobert. typepad.com/lifeinmyhead/migraines_migraine_disease/, April 23, 2006: "Tim accused me, jokingly, of wanting to sleep my life away . . . and he's right."

194 *"Getting a divorce"* Elizabeth, comments, Oct. 27, 2007, Judith Warner, "The Migraine Diet." For the reasonable divorce, see "Alison," migrainepage.com/dcforum/discussion/21036.html. For the unreasonable divorce, see "hubby_n_need," migrainepage.com/dcforum/discussion/21036.html.

195 *There is no guidebook* Many of the ideas in this section are culled from migrainepage.com discussion forums on marriage and migraine.

Weather

196 *"There is a sort of elation"* Avis Berman, "Hopper," 57.

198 *But if one was forced to choose* Probably some overstatement here, but the idea that migraine treatment requires pharmacologic and nonpharmcologic solutions is well established. See Stewart Tepper, *Understanding Migraine and Other Headaches,* 31.

201 *As likely, however, migraines are not useless* Elizabeth Loder, "What Is the Evolutionary Advantage of Migraine," 625: "It is important to consider whether the negative effects of the disorder in question are somehow counterbalanced by other advantages." See also 628: "Migraine could be a trait that natural selection has simply not yet had a chance to eliminate." This argument has been made for a long time. See, for instance, Edward Liveing, as qtd. in Russell Lane and Paul Davies, *Migraine,* 82: "Megrim" exists to "periodically resolve the accumulation of nerve-force in paroxysmal or sometimes truly explosive symptoms," and Lane and Davies themselves, 83: "Migraine is a consequence of disordered sensory control . . . one could suggest, then, that the migraine mechanism is engaged to reset a temporary

fault in the control of sensory input . . . migraine is a protective and restorative process."

201 *"vasoconstrictive emergenc(y)"* Elizabeth Loder, "What Is the Evolutionary Advantage of Migraine," 627.

201 *"exquisitely responsive"* Ibid., 626.

201 *"novel or complex environments"* Ibid. Randolph M. Nesse and George C. Williams, "Evolution and the Origins of Disease," write about "the African savanna, where the modern human design was fine-tuned."

201 *Diseases and abnormalities* Randolph M. Nesse and George C. Williams, "Evolution and the Origins of Disease." Elizabeth Loder, "What Is the Evolutionary Advantage of Migraine," 628–629.

202 *"hair triggers . . . regulation mechanisms"* Randolph M. Nesse and George C. Williams, "Evolution and the Origins of Disease." Qtd. In Elizabeth Loder, "What Is the Evolutionary Advantage of Migraine," 627.

202 *And migraine might be caused* Elizabeth Loder, ibid., 628–630.

205 *Consider, too* Erika Dyck, "Flashback: Psychiatric Experimentation with LSD in Historical Perspective," 382.

206 *"Prehistory"* Giorgio De Chirico, *Hebdomeros,* 191.

206 *"The more we learn"* Arun A. Kalra and Debra Elliott, "Acute Migraine: Current Treatment and Emerging Therapies," 449.

206 *"satisfactory monotherapy"* Seymour Solomon, "Major Therapeutic Advances in the Past 25 Years," writes that "the new agent was not quite as potent as the triptans and not as easily delivered" (821).

207 *CGRPs* Henri Doods, Kirsten Arndt, Klaus Rudolf, and Stefan Just, "CGRP Antagonists: Unravelling the Role of CGRP in Migraine." Jeff Unger, "Migraine Headaches: A Historical Perspective, a Glimpse into the Future, and Migraine Epidemiology," 371.

207 *"outside the box"* Stewart J. Tepper, interview, Aug. 15, 2008.

207 *For chronic migraineurs, for instance* See Avi Ashkenazi and Stephen Silberstein, "Botulinum Toxin Type A for the Treatment of Headache." Stewart Tepper, *Understanding Migraine and Other Headaches,* 94.

207 *"compliance issues"* Roger Cady and Curtis Schreiber, "Botulinum Toxin Type A as Migraine Preventive Treatment in Patients Previously Failing Oral Prophylactic Treatment Due to Compliance Issues," 900.

207 *"transcranial magnetic stimulation"* Kathleen Doheny, "Magnetic

Pulses May 'Zap' Migraine Pain." Richard B. Lipton, interview, Sept. 27, 2008.

208 *The music churns* See Iynelleh.blogspot.com, "The Revolution and Evolution of a Migraineur," Aug. 18, 2005: "I'm singing along to KISS and Motley Crue and Offspring . . ."

208 *And yet, during the maturing* Laurie Lisle, *Portrait of an Artist: A Biography of Georgia O'Keeffe,* 81: "One of the drawings, later labeled *Number Nine,* showed volcano-like fissures erupting with fire and steam that she visualized during one of the frequent, severe headaches with which she was afflicted at the time." 90: "He asked where one image had come from, and she replied that it came to her when she had a headache."

Bibliography

BOOKS

Aegineta, Paulus, trans. and comm. Francis Adams. *The Seven Books of Paulus Aeginata,* vol. 1. London: Sydenham Society, 1844.

American Council on Headache Education, with Lynne M. Constantine and Suzanne Scott. *Migraine: The Complete Guide.* New York: Dell, 1994.

Aretaeus, ed. and trans. Francis Adams. *The Extant Works of Aretaeus, the Cappadocian.* Birmingham, AL: Classics of Medicine Library, 1990.

Balzac, Honore de, intro. Sharon Marcus. *The Physiology of Marriage.* Baltimore: Johns Hopkins University Press, 1997.

Black, William George. *Folk-Medicine: A Chapter in the History of Culture.* Kraus Reprints, 1967 (1883).

Blau, J. N., ed. *Migraine: Clinical, Therapeutic, Conceptual and Research Aspects.* London: Chapman and Hall, 1987.

Borghouts, J. F., ed. and trans. *The Magical Texts of Papyrus Leiden I 348.* Leiden: E. J. Brill, 1971.

Brodie, Fawn M. *Thomas Jefferson: An Intimate History.* New York: W. W. Norton & Company, 1974.

Browne, Janet. *Charles Darwin: The Power of Place.* New York: Knopf, 2002.

———. *Charles Darwin: Voyaging.* New York: Knopf, 1995.

Bryan, Cyril P., trans., intro. G. Elliot Smith. *Ancient Egyptian Medicine: The Papyrus Ebers.* Chicago: Ares Publishers, 1972.

Buchholz, David, forewd. Stephen Reich. *Heal Your Headache: The 1-2-3 Program for Taking Charge of Your Pain.* New York: Workman Publishing, 2002.

Carroll, Lewis, intro. Camille Paglia. *Alice in Wonderland* and *Through the Looking Glass.* New York: Quality Paperback, 1994.

——, ed. Roger Lancelyn Green. *The Diaries of Lewis Carroll.* New York: Oxford University Press, 1954.

——, eds. Morten N. Cohen and Roger Lancelyn Green. *The Letters of Lewis Carroll,* 2 vols. London: Oxford University Press, 1979.

Catton, Bruce. *Grant Takes Command.* Boston: Little, Brown, 1969.

Cervantes, Miguel de, trans. Edith Grossman, intro. Harold Bloom. *Don Quixote.* New York: HarperCollins, 2003.

Chesnut, Mary Boykin, ed. C. Vann Woodward. *Mary Chesnut's Civil War.* New Haven: Yale University Press, 1981.

Cohen, Jay S. *The Magnesium Solution for Migraine Headaches: How to Use Magnesium to Prevent and Relieve Migraine and Cluster Headaches Naturally.* Garden City Park, NY: Square One, 2004.

Conway, Anne, trans. and ed. Allison P. Coudert and Taylor Corse. *The Principles of the Most Ancient and Modern Philosophy.* Cambridge: Cambridge University Press, 1996.

Darwin, Charles, ed. Frederick Burkhardt. *The Correspondence of Charles Darwin,* vol. 13. New York: Cambridge University Press, 2003.

——, intro. and ed. Edward O. Wilson. *The Expressions of the Emotions in Man and Animals,* in *From So Simple a Beginning: The Four Great Books of Charles Darwin.* New York: Norton, 2006, 1255–1477.

——, intro. and ed. Edward O. Wilson. *The Voyage of the Beagle,* in *From So Simple a Beginning: The Four Great Books of Charles Darwin.* New York: Norton, 2006, 21–432.

Darwin, Emma, ed. Henrietta E. Litchfield. *Emma Darwin: A Century of Family Letters, 1792–1896,* vol. 2. Cook Press, 2007. See also: http://darwin-online.org.uk/content/frameset?viewtype=side&itemID -F1553.2&pageseq=79. (Scanned by John Van Wyhe, transcribed by AEL Data, corrections by Van Wyhe.)

Davidoff, Robert A. *Migraine: Manifestations, Pathogenesis, and Management,* 2nd ed. New York: Oxford University Press, 2002.

Davies, Paul, and Russell Lane. *Migraine.* New York: Taylor and Francis Group, 2006.

De Chirico, Giorgio, intro. John Ashbery, trans. John Ashbery, Louise Bourgeois, Robert Goldwater, Damon Krukowski, and Mark Polizzotti. *Hebdomeros, With Monsieur Dudron's Adventure and Other Metaphysical Writings*. Cambridge: Exact Change, 1992.

——, trans. and intro. Margaret Grosland. *The Memoirs of Giorgio de Chirico*. Cambridge: Da Capo Press, 1994.

Diamond, Seymour, and Mary Franklin. *Headache Through the Ages*. West Islip, NY: Professional Communications, Inc., 2005.

Dickinson, Emily. *The Poems of Emily Dickinson,* ed. R.W. Franklin. Cambridge, MA: Belknap Press, 1998.

Dostoyevsky, Fyodor, trans. Constance Garnett. *The Idiot*. New York: Bantam, 1981.

Edwards, Laurie. *Life Disrupted: Getting Real About Chronic Illness in Your Twenties and Thirties*. New York: Walker and Company, 2008.

Fiering, Greg, intro. Michael Stipe. *Migraine Boy: Fair Weather Friends*. New York: St. Martin's Griffin, 1996.

Foster, Benjamin R. *Before the Muses: An Anthology of Akkadian Literature,* 2 vols. Bethesda, MD: CDL Press, 1993.

Fox, Barry, and Alexander Mauskop. *What Your Doctor May Not Tell You About Migraines: The Breakthrough Program That Can Help End Your Pain*. New York: Warner Wellness (Warner Books), 2001.

Freud, Sigmund, trans. James Strachey. *The Interpretation of Dreams*. New York: Bard (Avon Books), 1998.

——, intro. and trans. A. A. Brill. *Psychopathology of Everyday Life*. New York: Macmillan, 1954.

Gay, Peter. *Freud: A Life for Our Time*. New York: W. W. Norton Company, 2006 (1998).

Goddard, Dwight, forewd. Robert Aitken. *A Buddhist Bible*. Boston: Beacon Press, 1994 (1970).

Grant, U. S. *Memoirs and Selected Letters: Personal Memoirs of U. S. Grant, Selected Letters 1839–1865*. New York: Library of America, 1990.

Griffith, Francis Llewellyn, and Edward Herbert Thompson. *The Leyden Papyrus: Egyptian Magic*. Forgotten Books, 2008 (1904).

Grossinger, Richard, pref. Klaus Podoll and Markus Dahlem. *Migraine Auras: When the Visual World Fails*. Berkeley: North Atlantic Books, 2006.

Haskell, E. F., ed. R. L. Shep. *Civil War Cooking: The Housekeeper's Encyclopedia*. Mendocino, CA: R. L. Shep, 1992 (1861).

Hayman, Ronald. *Nietzsche: A Critical Life*. New York: Penguin, 1982.

Hildegard of Bingen, trans. Manfred Pawlik and Patrick Madigan, eds. Mary Palmquist and John Kulas. *Holistic Healing*. Collegeville, MN: Order of St. Benedict, Inc., 1994.

————, trans. Mother Columba Hart and Jane Bishop, intro. Barbara J. Newman, pref. Caroline Walker Bynum. *Scivias.* New York: Paulist Press, 1990.

Hutton, Sarah. *Anne Conway: A Woman Philosopher.* Cambridge: Cambridge University Press, 2004.

Irvine, William, intro. Julian Huxley. *Apes, Angels, and Victorians: The Story of Darwin, Huxley, and Evolution.* New York: Time Inc., 1955.

James, William. *Varieties of Religious Experience: A Study in Human Nature.* Charleston: Bibliobazaar, 2007.

Jefferson, Thomas, ed. William Peden. *Notes on the State of Virginia.* New York: Norton, 1982.

————, ed. Julian P. Boyd. *The Papers of Thomas Jefferson,* vol. 1 (1760–1776), vol. 6 (May 1781 to March 1784), vol. 10 (22 June to December 1786), vol. 15 (March 1789 to November 1798), vol. 16 (November 1789 to July 1790). Princeton University Press: 1950, 1952, 1958, 1961, 1964.

Kamen, Paula. *All in My Head: An Epic Quest to Cure an Unrelenting, Totally Unreasonable, and Only Slightly Enlightening Headache.* Cambridge: Da Capo Press, 2005.

Kidson, Ruth. *Acupuncture for Everyone: What It Is, Why It Works, and How It Can Help You.* Rochester, VT: Healing Arts Press, 2000.

Kipling, Rudyard, ed. Thomas Pinney. *The Letters of Rudyard Kipling, Vol. 1, 1872–89.* Iowa City: University of Iowa Press, 1990.

Kleinman, Arthur. *The Illness Narratives: Suffering, Healing, and the Human Condition.* New York: Basic Books, 1988.

Kluver, Heinrich. *Mescal and Mechanisms of Hallucinations.* Chicago: University of Chicago Press, 1966 (1930).

Kohler, Joachim, trans. Ronald Taylor. *Zarathustra's Secret: The Interior Life of Friedrich Nietzsche.* New Haven: Yale University Press, 2002.

Kramer, Samuel N., trans. *Enki and Ninhursag: A Sumerian "Paradise" Myth.* New Haven: American Schools of Oriental Research, 1945.

Lance, James W., and Peter Goadsby. *Mechanism and Management of Headache,* 7th ed. Philadelphia: Elsevier Butterworth Heinemann, 2005.

LaPlante, Eve. *Seized: Temporal Lobe Epilepsy as a Medical, Historical, and Artistic Phenomenon.* New York: HarperCollins, 1993.

Lee, Hermione. *Virginia Woolf.* New York: Knopf, 1997.

Lewis, C. S. *The Problem of Pain*. New York: HarperCollins, 2001 (1944).

Lisle, Laurie. *Portrait of an Artist: A Biography of Georgia O'Keeffe*. New York: Washington Square Press, 1986.

Liveing, Edward. *On Megrim, Sick Headache, and Some Allied Disorders: A Contribution to the Pathology of Nerve-storms*. Birmingham, AL: The Classics of Neurology and Neurosurgery Library, 1986 (1873).

Loder, Elizabeth, and Dawn A. Marcus. *Migraine in Women*. Hamilton: B. C. Decker Inc., 2004.

Maddocks, Fiona. *Hildegard of Bingen: The Woman of Her Age*. New York: Doubleday, 2001.

Manguso, Sarah. *The Two Kinds of Decay*. New York: Farrar Straus and Giroux, 2008.

Masson, Jeffrey Moussaieff, trans. and ed. *The Complete Letters of Sigmund Freud to Wilhelm Fliess, 1887–1904*. Cambridge, MA: The Belknap Press of Harvard University Press, 1985.

McFeely, W. S. *Grant—A Biography*. New York: Norton, 1982.

McHenry, Lawrence C., rev. ed., forewd. Derek E. Denny-Brown. *Garrison's History of Neurology*. Springfield, IL: Charles C. Thomas, 1969.

McTavish, Jan. R. *Pain & Profits: The History of the Headache and Its Remedies in America*. New Brunswick: Rutgers University Press, 2004.

Melville, Herman, note James D. Hart, design Andrew Hoyen, illus. Barry Moser. *Moby-Dick or, The Whale*. Berkeley: Arion, 1979.

Nicolson, Marjorie Hope. *Conway Letters: The Correspondence of Anne, Viscountess Conway, Henry More, and Their Friends, 1642–1684*. New Haven: Yale University Press, 1930.

Nietzsche, Friedrich, trans. Duncan Large. *Ecce Homo*. New York: Oxford University Press, 2007.

Olesen, Jes, Peer Tfelt-Hansen, K. Michael, and A. Welch. *The Headaches*, 2nd ed. New York: Lippincott Williams and Wilkins, 2000.

Parsons, Talcott. *The Social System*. New York: Free Press, 1951.

Peters, John. *A Complete Treatise on Headaches and Diseases of the Head*. New York: William Radde, 1859.

Plato, trans. Thomas G. West and Grace Starry West. *Charmides*. Indianapolis: Hackett Publishing, 1986.

Podoll, Klaus, and Derek Robinson. *Migraine Art: The Migraine Experience from Within*. Berkeley: North Atlantic Books, 2008.

Pope, Alexander, ed. Cynthia Wall. *The Rape of the Lock*. Boston: Bedford, 1998.

Pudney, John. *Lewis Carroll and His World*. New York: Scribner's, 1976.

Richardson, John, collab. Marilyn McCully. *A Life of Pablo Picasso*, vol. 1 (1881–1906), vol. 2 (1907–1917). New York: Random House, 1991, 1996.

Robert, Teri. *Living Well with Migraine Disease and Headaches: What Your Doctor Doesn't Tell You . . . That You Need to Know*. New York: HarperCollins, 2005.

Rose, Clifford F., ed. *The Neurobiology of Painting*. San Diego: Academic Press, 2006.

————, ed. *Neuroscience Across the Centuries*. London: Smith-Gordon and Company, 1989.

Sacks, Oliver. *A Leg to Stand On*. New York: Touchstone, 1998 (1984).

————. *The Man Who Mistook His Wife for a Hat and Other Clinical Tales*. New York: Touchstone, 1998 (1985).

————. *Migraine*, rev. ed. New York: Vintage, 1999.

Scarry, Elaine. *The Body in Pain: The Making and Unmaking of the World*. New York: Oxford University Press, 1985.

Schur, Max. *Freud: Living and Dying*. New York: International Universities Press, 1972.

Schwartz, Mark S., and Frank Andrasik, eds. *Biofeedback: A Practitioner's Guide*, 3rd ed. New York: Guilford Press, 2003.

Scurlock, JoAnn, and Burton R. Andersen, trans. and comm. *Diagnoses in Assyrian and Babylonian Medicine: Ancient Sources, Translations, and Modern Medical Analyses*. Urbana: University of Illinois Press, 2005.

Sewell, Richard B. *The Life of Emily Dickinson*. Cambridge: Harvard University Press, 1980.

Sheridan, Mary S. *Pain in America*. Tuscaloosa, AL: University of Alabama Press, 1992.

Silberstein, Stephen D., M. Alan Stiles, and William B. Young, eds. *Atlas of Migraine and Other Headaches*, 2nd ed. New York: Informa, 2005.

Stein, Michael. *The Lonely Patient: How We Experience Illness*. New York: Harper, 2007.

Tepper, Stewart J. *Understanding Migraine and Other Headaches*. Jackson: University of Mississippi Press, 2004.

Thompson, Campbell R. *The Devils and Spirits of Babylonia*, vols. 1 and 2. London: Luzac and Co., 1904.

Twain, Mark, forewd. Shelley Fisher Fishkin, intro. Gore Vidal, after. Fred

Kaplan. *Following the Equator and Anti-Imperialist Essays*. New York: Oxford University Press, 1996.

Whyte, Robert. *Observations on the Nature, Causes, and Cure of Those Disorders Which Have Been Commonly Called Nervous, Hypochondriac, or Hysteric*. Edinburgh, 1765.

Willis, Thomas. *Two Discourses Concerning the Souls of Brutes*. London, 1683.

Wolff, Harold G. *Headache and Other Head Pain*, 2nd ed. New York: Oxford University Press, 1948, 1950 (1934).

Woolf, Virginia, ed. Anne Olivier Bell. *The Diary of Virginia Woolf*, vols. 1, 2, and 3. New York: Harcourt Brace Jovanovich, 1977–1980.

———, ed. Nigel Nicolson. *The Letters of Virginia Woolf*, vol. 1 (1888–1912). New York: Harcourt Brace Jovanovich, 1975.

———, eds. Nigel Nicolson and Joanne Trautmann. *The Letters of Virginia Woolf*, vol. 4 (1929–1931). New York: Harcourt Brace Jovanovich, 1979.

ARTICLES

Adler, Jerry, and Adam Rogers. "The New War Against Migraines," *Newsweek* (Jan. 11, 1999).

Airy, Hubert. "On a Distinct Form of Transient Hemiopsia," *Philosophical Transactions of the Royal Society of London* 160 (1870): 247–264.

Alvarez, W. C. "Some Characteristics of the Migrainous Woman," *New York State Journal of Medicine* 59 (1959): 2176.

———. "Was There Sick Headache in 3000 BC?" *Gastroenterology* 5 (1945): 524.

Anderson, Dave. "Transferring a Headache," *New York Times* (May 28, 1984).

Ashkenazi, Avi, and Stephen Silberstein. "Botulinum Toxin Type A for the Treatment of Headache," *Archives of Neurology* 65 (Jan. 2008): 146–149.

Atlas, Darla. "Aikman Learned to Play Through the Pain," interview with Troy Aikman, *Dallas Morning News* (June 5, 2007).

Aurora, S. K., and F. Wilkinson. "The Brain Is Hyperexcitable in Migraine," *Cephalalgia* 27 (2007): 1442–1453.

Battle, John D. "The 'Periodical Head-achs' of Thomas Jefferson," *Cleveland Clinic Quarterly* 51 (1984): 531–539.

Berman, Avis. "Hopper," *Smithsonian* 38 (July 2007): 56–65.

Bigal, Marcelo E., and Richard B. Lipton. "Concepts and Mechanisms of Migraine Chronification," *Headache: The Journal of Head and Face Pain* 48 (2008): 7–15.

Bigal, Marcelo E., Daniel Serrano, Michael Reed, and Richard B. Lipton. "Chronic Migraine in the Population: Burden, Diagnosis, and Satisfaction with Treatment," *Neurology* 71 (2008): 559–566.

Blanchard, E. B., M. L. Peters, C. Hermann, S. M. Turner, T. C. Buckley, K. Barton, and M. L. Dentinger. "Direction of Temperature Control in the Thermal Biofeedback Treatment of Vascular Headache," *Applied Psychophysiology and Biofeedback* 22 (4): 227–245.

Blanke, Olaf, and Theodor Landis. "The Metaphysical Art of Giorgio de Chirico," *European Neurology* 50 (2003): 191–194.

Blau, J. N. "Adult Migraine: The Patient Observed," in *Migraine: Clinical, Therapeutic, Conceptual and Research Aspects,* ed. J. N. Blau. London: Chapman and Hall, 1987, 3–30.

———. "Migraine Prodromes Separated from the Aura: Complete Migraine," *British Medical Journal* 281 (1980): 658–660.

———. "Towards a Definition of Migraine Headache," *The Lancet* (Feb. 25, 1984): 444–445.

Bodine, Alicia. "Troy Aikman Serves as Spokesman for the Know Your Migraine Game Plan Education Initiative," associatedcontent.com.

Boyles, Salynn. "Migraine Sufferers Have Different Brains," MedicineNet. com, Nov. 19, 2007.

"Bronco Running Back Terrell Davis Launches New Migraine Foundation; Super Bowl MVP Unveils Foundation to Educate People About Overcoming Migraine," *PR Newswire,* July 28, 1998.

Bruyn, G. W. "Migraine Phylakteria: Magic Treatment of Migraine," in *Neuroscience Across the Centuries,* ed. Frank Clifford Rose. London: Smith-Gordon and Company, 1989, 31–40.

Buchanan, W. W. "Illness in Literature: An Example in Middle Scots," *Journal of Royal College of Physicians Edinburgh* 35 (2005): 371–373.

Burstein, Rami, and Moshe Jakubowski. "Unitary Hypothesis for Multiple Triggers of the Pain and Strain of Migraine," *Journal of Comparative Neurology* 497 (2005): 9–14.

Cady, Roger, and Curtis Schreiber. "Botulinum Toxin Type A as Migraine Preventive Treatment in Patients Previously Failing Oral Prophylactic Treatment Due to Compliance Issues," *Headache: The Journal of Head and Face Pain* 48 (2008): 900–913.

Cady, Roger, Curtis Schreiber, Kathleen Farmer, and Fred Sheftell. "Primary Headaches: A Convergence Hypothesis," *Headache: The Journal of Head and Face Pain* 42 (2002): 204–216.

Chaliha, Madhuleema. "The Beauty of Having a Migraine," e-mail, http://www.mail-archive.com/assam@pikespeak.uccs.edu/msg04629.html.

Critchley, Macdonald. "Bygone Remedies for Migraine," *Headache Quarterly* 2 (1991): 171–176.

———. "Discarded Theories of the Past Fifty Years," in *Migraine: Clinical, Therapeutic, Conceptual and Research Aspects,* ed. J. N. Blau. London: Chapman and Hall, 1987, 241–246.

———. "The Malady of Anne, Viscountess Conway," *King's College Hospital Gazette* 16 (1937): 44–49.

———. "Migraine from Cappadocia to Queen Square," in *Background to Migraine,* vol. 1, ed. R. Smith. London: Heinemann, 1967, 28–39.

Cutrer, F. Michael. "Functional Imaging in Primary Headache Disorders," *Headache: The Journal of Head and Face Pain* 48 (May 2008): 704–706.

Davey, Gail, Philip Sedgwick, Will Maier, George Visick, David P. Strachan, and H. Ross Anderson. "Association Between Migraine and Asthma: Matched Case-Control Study," *British Journal of General Practice* 52 (Sept. 2002): 723–727.

Diamond, Seymour, Marcelo E. Bigal, Stephen Silberstein, Elizabeth Loder, Michael Reed, and Richard B. Lipton. "Patterns of Diagnosis and Acute and Preventive Treatment for Migraine in the United States: Results from the American Migraine Prevalence and Prevention Study," *Headache: The Journal of Head and Face Pain* 47 (2007): 355–363.

Didion, Joan. "In Bed," in *The White Album.* New York: Simon and Schuster, 1979, 168–172.

Dodick, David W., and J. Jay Gargus. "Why Migraines Strike: Biologists Finally Are Unraveling the Medical Mysteries of Migraine, from Aura to Pain," *Scientific American* (July 21, 2008).

Doheny, Kathleen. "Magnetic Pulses May 'Zap' Migraine Pain," *WebMD Health News,* June 27, 2008. www.medscape.com/migraines-headaches/news/20080627/magnetic-pulses-may-zap-migraine-pain.

———. "Soldiers in Iraq Have More Migraines," *WebMD Health News,* http://www.medscape.com/viewarticles/537289.

Doods, Henri, Kirsten Arndt, Klaus Rudolf, and Stefan Just. "CGRP Antagonists: Unravelling the Role of CGRP in Migraine," *Trends in Pharmacological Science* 28 (2007): 580–587.

Dyck, Erika. "Flashback: Psychiatric Experimentation with LSD in Historical Perspective," *Canadian Journal of Psychiatry* 50 (June 2005): 381–388.

Edmeads, J. "The Treatment of Headache: A Historical Perspective," in *Therapy for Headache,* ed. R. M. Gallagher. New York: Marcel Dekker, 1990.

Eisenbud, Jule. "The Psychology of Headache: A Case Studied Experimentally," *Psychiatric Quarterly* 11 (1937): 592–619.

"Elvis Presley's Private Struggle with Intractable Migraines Revealed," National Migraine Association, April 19, 1999, http://www.migraines .org/new/news9904.htm.

Emery, Alan E. H. "How Neurological Disease Can Affect an Artist's Work," *Practical Neurology* 4 (2004): 366–371.

Evans, R. W. "Reversible Palinopsia and the Alice in Wonderland Syndrome Associated with Topiramate Use in Migraineurs," *Headache: The Journal of Head and Face Pain* 46 (May 2006): 815–818.

Facco, Enrico, Aldo Liguori, Filomena Petti, Gastone Zanette, Flaminia Coluzzi, Marco De Nardin, and Consalvo Mattia. "Traditional Acupuncture in Migraine: A Controlled, Randomized Study," *Headache: The Journal of Head and Face Pain* (2008): 398–407.

Ferrari, M. D., and J. Haan. "Migraine Aura, Illusory Vertical Splitting, and Picasso," *Cephalalgia* 20 (Oct. 2000): 686.

Fodor, Jerry. "The Mind–Body Problem," in *Philosophy of Mind: A Guide and Anthology,* ed. John Heil. New York: Oxford University Press, 2004, 168–182.

Fothergill, J. "Remarks on That Complaint, Commonly Known Under the Name of Sick Head-ach," in *Medical Observations and Enquiries by a Society of Physicians in London,* vol. 6. London: T. Cadell, 1784, 103–137.

Freud, Sigmund. "Migraine: Established Points," to Wilhelm Fliess, Oct. 5, 1895, in *The Complete Letters of Sigmund Freud to Wilhelm Fliess, 1887–1904,* ed. Jeffrey Moussaieff Masson. Cambridge, MA: Harvard University Press, 1985, 142–144.

Friedman, Arnold P. "The Headache in History, Literature, and Legend," *Bulletin of the New York Academy of Medicine* 48 (1972): 661–681.

Fuller, G. N., and M. V. Gale. "Migraine Aura as Artistic Inspiration," *British Medical Journal* 297 (1988): 1670–1672.

Gardner, Amanda. "Poorer Kids at Higher Migraine Risk," MedicineNet .com, July 3, 2007.

Glasgow, William. "On Certain Measures for the Relief of Congestive Headaches," *New York Medical Journal* 46 (1887): 260–262.

Göbel, H., H. Isler, and H. Hasenfratz. "Headache Classification and the Bible: Was St. Paul's Thorn in the Flesh Migraine?" *Cephalalgia* 15 (1995): 180–181.

Gould, George M. "The History and Etiology of Migraine," *Journal of the American Medical Association* 42 (1904): 168–172, 239–244.

Graham, J. R., and H. G. Wolff. "Mechanisms of Migraine Headache and Action of Ergotamine Tartrate," *Archives of Neurology and Psychiatry* 39 (1938): 737–763.

Haan, J., and M. D. Ferrari. Letter to the Editor, "Mahler's Migraine," *Cephalalgia* 20 (2000): 254.

Hadjikhani, Nouchine. "Brain Scans Show Migraines Are More Than Bad Headaches," *New Scientist* 196 (Nov. 24, 2007): 19.

"The Headaches of Thomas Jefferson," *Cephalalgia* 23 (July 2003): 472–473.

Helseth, Erek K., and Jay C. Erickson. "The Prevalence and Impact of Migraine on US Military Officer Trainees," *Headache: The Journal of Head and Face Pain* 10 (2007): 1–7.

Herschel, John F. W. "On Sensorial Vision," in *Familiar Lectures on Scientific Subjects.* Scholarly Publishing Office, University of Michigan Library, 2005 (1866), 400–418.

Hirschhorn, Norbert, and Polly Longsworth. "'Medical Posthumous': A New Look at Emily Dickinson's Medical Conditions," *New England Quarterly* 69 (June 1996): 299–316.

Hitti, Miranda. "Stroke Risk Linked to Some Migraines," MedicineNet .com, Aug. 9, 2007.

Hu, X. Henry, Leona E. Markson, Richard B. Lipton, Walter F. Stewart, and Marc L. Berger. "Burden of Migraine in the United States," *Archives of Internal Medicine* 159 (1999): 813–818.

Humphrey, Patrick P. A. "The Discovery and Development of the Triptans, a Major Therapeutic Breakthrough," *Headache: The Journal of Head and Face Pain* 48 (2008): 685–687.

"Insurance Limits, Costs Keep Migraine Patients from Meds," Medi cineNet.com, June 7, 2007.

"The International Classification of Headache Disorders," 2nd ed. *Cephalalgia* 24 (2004): supplement 1.

Isler, H. "Prospect," in *Migraine: Clinical, Therapeutic, Conceptual and Research Aspects,* ed. J. N. Blau. London: Chapman and Hall, 1987, 659–674.

———. "Thomas Willis' Two Chapters on Headache of 1672: A First

Attempt to Apply the 'New Science' to this Topic," *Headache: The Journal of Head and Face Pain* 26 (1986): 95–98.

Isler, H., and Rose F. Clifford. "Historical Background," in *The Headaches,* ed. J. Oleson, P. Tfelt-Hansen, and K. M. A. Welch. Philadelphia: Lippincott, Williams and Wilkins, 2000.

Isler, H., H. Hasenfratz, and T. A. O'Neill. "A Sixth Century Irish Headache Cure and Its Use in a South German Monastery," *Cephalalgia* 16 (1996): 536–640.

Jenkins, Chris. "Running Against the Migraine—Denver Broncos Running Back Terrell Davis Was Most Valuable Player in the 1988 Super Bowl Despite Suffering from a Migraine Headache for Part of the Game," *Sporting News* (Feb. 2, 1998).

Jensen, Rigmor, and Peer Tfelt-Hansen. "Milestones in Headache Research. A Tribute to Jes Olesen," *Cephalalgia* 21 (2001): 747.

Johnston, W. W. "The Ill Health of Charles Darwin," *American Anthropologist* 3 (1901): 139–158.

Jones, J. M. "Great Pains: Famous People with Headaches," *Cephalalgia* 19 (1999): 627–630.

Kalian, Moshe, Vladimir Lerner, and Eliezer Witztum. "Creativity and Affective Illness," letter to the editor, *American Journal of Psychiatry* 159 (2002): 675–676.

Kalra, Arun A., and Debra Elliott. "Acute Migraine: Current Treatment and Emerging Therapies," *Therapeutics and Clinical Risk Management* 3 (2007): 449–459.

Karwautz, A., C. Wober-Bingol, and C. Wober. "Freud and Migraine: The Beginning of a Psychodynamically Oriented View of Headache a Hundred Years Ago," *Cephalalgia* 16 (1996): 22–26.

Kenney, Susan M. "Two Endings: Virginia Woolf's Suicide and *Between the Acts,*" *University of Toronto Quarterly* 44 (Summer 1975): 265–289.

Kernick, D. "Migraine: New Perspectives from Chaos Theory," *Cephalalgia* 25 (2005): 561–566.

Kew, John Alexa Wright, and Peter W. Halligan. "Somesthetic Aura: The Experience of Alice in Wonderland," *Lancet* 351 (June 27, 1998).

Kropp, P. "Learning from Headaches? Old Problems and New Insights in Migraine," *Expert Review of Neurotherapeutics* 4 (2004): 333.

Kruit, Mark C., Mark A. van Buchem, Paul A. M. Hoffman, Jacobus T. N. Bakkers, Gisela M. Terwindt, Michel D. Ferrari, and Lenore J. Launer. "Migraine as a Risk Factor for Subclinical Brain Lesions," *Journal of the American Medical Association* 291 (2004): 427–434.

Kunkel, Robert S. "The American Headache Society: Looking Back," *Headache: The Journal of Head and Face Pain* 48 (2008): 680–684.

Lashley, Karl. "Patterns of Cerebral Integration Indicated by the Scotoma of Migraine," *Archives of Neurology and Psychiatry* 46 (1941): 331–339.

Lauritzen, Martin. "Pathophysiology of the Migraine Aura: The Spreading Depression Theory," *Brain* 117 (1994): 199–210.

Leao, A. A. P. "Spreading Depression of Cortical Activity in the Cerebral Cortex," *Journal of Neurophysiology* 7 (1944): 359–390.

Leao, A. P. P., and R. S. Morrison. "Propagation of Spreading Cortical Depression," *Journal of Neurophysiology* 8 (1945): 33–45.

Lillie, Malcolm C. "Cranial Surgery Dates Back to Mesolithic," *Nature* 391 (Feb. 1998): 854.

Ling, Geoffrey, and Cornelius Maher. "US Neurologists in Iraq: Personal Perspective," *Neurology* 67 (2006): 14–17.

Lippman, Caro W. "Certain Hallucinations Peculiar to Migraine," *Journal of Nervous and Mental Disease* 116 (1952): 346–351.

Lipton, Richard B., and Marcelo E. Bigal. "Headache as a Real Disease," *Headache: The Journal of Head and Face Pain* 48 (2008): 707–710.

———. "Ten Lessons on the Epidemiology of Migraine," *Headache: The Journal of Head and Face Pain* 47 (2007): Supp. 1, S2–S9.

Lipton, Richard B., S. W. Hamelsky, K. B. Kolodner, T. J. Steiner, and Walter F. Stewart. "Migraine, Quality of Life, and Depression: A Population-Based Case-Control Study," *Neurology* 55 (2000): 629–635.

Lipton, Richard B., Walter F. Stewart, Seymour Diamond, Merle L. Diamond, and Michael Reed. "Prevalence and Burden of Migraine in the United States: Data from the American Migraine Study II," *Headache: The Journal of Head and Face Pain* 41 (July/Aug. 2001): 646–657.

Liveing, Edward. "Observations on Megrim or Sick Headache," *British Medical Journal* 1 (1872): 364–366. Reprinted from the *British Medical Journal* 1 (April 12, 1919): 469.

Loder, Elizabeth. "Prophylaxis: Headaches That Never Happen," *Headache: The Journal of Head and Face Pain* 48 (2008): 694–696.

———. "What Is the Evolutionary Advantage of Migraine?" *Cephalalgia* 22 (Oct. 2002): 624–632.

"The Lonely Nietzsche and His Migraine." *Minnesota Medicine* 53 (1970): 726.

Major, Ralph H. "The Papyrus Ebers," *Annual of Medical History* (New Series) 2 (1930): 547–555.

Marcussen, Robert, and Harold G. Wolff. "A Formulation of the Dynamics of the Migraine Attack," *Psychosomatic Medicine* 11 (1949): 251–256.

May, A. "Headache: Lessons Learned from Functional Imaging," *British Medical Bulletin* 65 (March 1, 2003): 223–234.

McKim, A. Elizabeth. "Making Poetry of Pain: The Headache Poems of Jane Cave Winscom," *Literature and Medicine* 24 (Spring 2005): 93–108.

"Migraine Strong Indicator of Comorbid Psychiatric Conditions in US Iraq Veterans," *Medscape Medical News*, http://www.medscape.com/viewarticle/556268.

"Migraines Often Triggered by Change in the Weather," about.com, Aug. 10, 2006.

Mohr, Nicole. "Emily Dickinson's Poem 'I Felt a Funeral In My Brain,'" Associatedcontent.com, 2007.

Moskowitz, Michael A. "Defining a Pathway to Discovery from Bench to Bedside," *Headache: The Journal of Head and Face Pain* 48 (2008): 688–690.

Mundell, E. J. "Migraines Can Signal Psychiatric Woes in Returning Iraq Vets," MedicineNet.com.

Nesse, Randolph M., and George C. Williams. "Evolution and the Origins of Disease," *Scientific American* 279 (Nov. 1998).

Olesen, Jes. "The International Classification of Headache Disorders," *Headache: The Journal of Head and Face Pain* 48 (2008): 691–693.

Osterhaus, J. T., D. L. Gutterman, and J. R. Plachetka. "Healthcare Resource and the Lost Labour Costs of Migraine Headache in the US," *Pharmaeconomics* 2 (July 1992): 67–76.

Owen, G. R. "The Famous Case of Lady Conway," *Annals of Medical History* 9 (1937): 567–571.

Parsons, Talcott. "The Sick Role and the Role of the Physician Reconsidered," *Milbank Memorial Fund Quarterly: Health and Society* 53 (Summer 1975): 257–278.

Patterson, Stephanie, and Stephen D. Silberstein. "Sometimes Jello Helps: Perceptions of Headache Etiology, Triggers and Treatment in Literature," *Headache: The Journal of Head and Face Pain* 33 (1993): 76–81.

Pearce, J. M. S. "The Headaches of Thomas Jefferson," *Cephalalgia* 23 (2003): 472–473.

Peatfield, E. C., V. Glover, J. T. Littlewood, M. Sandler, and Clifford Rose. "The Prevalence of Diet-Induced Migraine," *Cephalalgia* 4 (1984): 179–183.

Podoll, Klaus. "Migraine Art in the Internet: A Study of 450 Contemporary Artists," in *The Neurobiology of Painting,* ed. F. Clifford Rose. San Diego: Elsevier, 2006, 89–107.

Podoll, Klaus, and Derek Robinson. "The Idea of a Presence as Aura Symptom in Migraine," *Neurology, Psychiatry and Brain Research* 9 (2001): 71–74.

———. "Lewis Carroll's Migraine Experiences," *Lancet* 353 (April 17, 1999): 1366.

———. "Splitting of the Body image as Somesthetic Aura Symptom in Migraine," *Cephalalgia* 22 (2002): 62–65.

Podoll, Klaus, Derek Robinson, and U. Nicola. "The Theosophists's Aura Vision and the Visual Migraine Aura: A Phenomenological Comparison," *Neurology, Psychiatry and Brain Research* 11 (2004): 171–178.

Pradalier, A., and H. Oilat. "Migraine and Alcohol," *Headache Quarterly* 2 (1991): 177–186.

Radat, F., and J. Swendsen. "Psychiatric Comorbidity In Migraine: A Review," *Cephalalgia* 25 (2005): 165–178.

Rapoport, Alan, and John Edmeads. "Migraine: The Evolution of Our Knowledge," *Archives of Neurology* 57 (2000): 1221–1223.

"Remarkable Case of a Young Gardener," *Gentleman's Magazine* 41 (1771): 152.

Restak, Richard M. "Alice in Migraineland," *Headache: The Journal of Head and Face Pain* 46 (Feb. 2006): 306–311.

Rolak, Loren. "Literary Neurologic Syndromes: Alice in Wonderland," *Archives of Neurology* 48 (1991): 649–651.

Rosner, Fred. "Headache in the Writings of Moses Maimonides and Other Hebrew Sages," *Headache* 33 (1993): 315–319.

Rothrock, John F. "The Truth About Triggers," *Headache: The Journal of Head and Face Pain* (March 2008): 499–500.

Sacks, Oliver. "Creativity, Imagination, and Perception," in *The Bloomsbury Book of the Mind,* ed. Stephen Wilson. London: Bloomsbury, 2003, 29–32.

Samson, Kurt. "Iraq Conflict Poses Special Problems for Deployed Neurologists," *Neurology Today* 4 (Sept. 2004): 1–16.

Santayana, George. "Pain," in *Little Essays Drawn from the Writings of George Santayana,* ed. Logan Pearsall Smith (with the collaboration of the author). Freeport, NY: Books for Libraries Press, 1967 (1920), 27.

Sax, Leonard. "What Was the Cause of Nietzsche's Dementia?" *Journal of Medical Biography* 11 (2003): 47–54.

Schrock, Karen. "Looking at the Sun Can Trigger a Sneeze," *Scientific American,* Jan. 10, 2008.

Schulman, Elliott A. "Breath-Holding, Head Pressure, and Hot Water: An Effective Treatment for Migraine Headache," *Headache: The Journal of Head and Face Pain* 42: 1048–1050.

Schwaag, Sonja, Darius G. Nabavi, Achim Frese, Ingo-W. Husstedt, and Stefan Evers. "The Association Between Migraine and Juvenile Stroke: A Case-Control Study," *Headache: The Journal of Head and Face Pain* 43 (Feb. 2003): 90–95.

Schwartz, Mark S., and Frank Andrasik, "Headache," in *Biofeedback: A Practitioner's Guide,* 3rd ed., ed. Mark S. Schwartz and Frank Andrasik. New York: Guilford Press, 2003, 275–348.

"Session 8: Epidemiology," Poster Presentations, *Cephalalgia* 20 (2000): 360–370.

Shapiro, R. E. "NIH Funding for Research on Headache Disorders: Does It Matter?" *Headache: The Journal of Head and Face Pain* (July/Aug. 2007): 993–995.

Shapiro, R. E., and P. J. Goadsby. "The Long Drought: The Dearth of Public Funding for Headache Research," *Cephalalgia* 27 (2007): 991–994.

Silberstein, Stephen D. "Historical Aspects of Headache," in *Atlas of Migraine and Other Headaches,* 2nd ed., ed. S. D. Silberstein, M. Alan Stiles, and William B. Young. New York: Informa, 2005.

Silberstein, Stephen D., Richard B. Lipton, and N. Breslau. "Migraine: Association with Personality Characteristics and Psychopathology," *Cephalalgia* 15 (Oct. 1995): 358–369.

Smith, Robert. "Impact of Migraine on the Family," *Headache: The Journal of Head and Face Pain* 38 (1998): 1526–1546.

Solomon, Seymour. "Major Therapeutic Advances in the Past 25 Years," *Headache: The Journal of Head and Face Pain* 47 (2007): Suppl. 1, S20–S22.

Sontag, Susan. "Illness as Metaphor," in *Illness as Metaphor and AIDS and Its Metaphors.* New York: Picador, 1990 (1978): 3–87.

Stafstrom, Carl E., Shira R. Goldenholz, and Douglas A. Dulli. "Serial Headache Drawings by Children with Migraine: Correlation with Clinical Headache Status," *Journal of Child Neurology* 20 (2005): 809–813.

Stafstrom, Carl E., Kevin Rostasy, and Anna Minster. "The Usefulness of Children's Drawings in the Diagnosis of Headache," *Pediatrics* 109 (2002): 460–472.

Stewart, Walter F., Richard B. Lipton, D. D. Celentano, and M. L. Reed.

"Prevalence of Migraine Headache in the United States: Relation to Age, Income, Race, and Other Sociodemographic Factors," *Journal of the American Medical Association* 267 (Jan. 1, 1992).

Stewart, Walter E., Richard B. Lipton, Kenneth B. Kolodner, James Sawyer, Clara Lee, and Joshua N. Liberman. "Validity of the Migraine Disability Assessment (MIDAS) Score in Comparison to a Diary-Based Measure in a Population Sample of Migraine Sufferers," *Pain* 88 (2000): 41–52.

Stewart, Walter F., R. B. Lipton, K. Kolodner, J. Liberman, and J. Sawyer. "Reliability of the Migraine Disability Assessment Score in a Population-Based Sample of Headache Sufferers," *Cephalalgia* 19 (1999): 107–114.

Stewart, Walter F., Richard B. Lipton, and Joshua Liberman. "Variation in Migraine Prevalence by Race," *Neurology* 47 (1996): 52–59.

Sundquist, J. "The Influence of Exile and Repatriation on Mental and Physical Health: A Population-Based Study," *Social Psychiatry and Psychiatric Epidemiology* 31 (1): 21–28.

Teive, H. A. G., Pa Kowacs, P. M. Filho, E. J. Plovesan, and L. C. Wenreck. "Leao's Cortical Spreading Depression: From Experimental Artifact to Physiological Principle," *Neurology* 65 (Nov. 8, 2005): 1455–1459.

Terwindt, G. M., M. D. Ferrari, M. Tijhuis, S. M. A. Groenen, H. S. J. Picavet, and L. J. Launer. "The Impact of Migraine on Quality of Life in the General Population: The GEM Study," *Neurology* 55 (2000): 624–629.

Todd, J. "The Syndrome of Alice in Wonderland," *Canadian Medical Association Journal* 73 (1955): 701–704.

Trompoukis, Constantinos, and Konstantinos Vadikolias. "The 'Byzantine Classification' of Headache Disorders," *Headache: The Journal of Head and Face Pain* 47 (2007): 1063–1068.

Ubaldo, Nicola, and Klaus Podoll. "The Migraine of Giorgio de Chirico," *Cephalalgia* 23 (2003): 625.

Unger, Jeff. "Migraine Headaches: A Historical Perspective, a Glimpse into the Future, and Migraine Epidemiology," *Disease-A-Month* 52 (10): 367–384.

Van den Bergh, V., W. K. Amery, and J. Waelkens. "Trigger Factors in Migraine: A Study Conducted by the Belgian Migraine Society," *Headache: The Journal of Head and Face Pain* 27 (1987): 191–196.

Van Vugt, Peter. "C. L. Dodgson's Migraine and Lewis Carroll's Literary Inspiration: A Neurolinguistic Perspective," *Humanising Language Teaching* 6 (Nov. 2004): 3–4.

Varga, Laszlo. "Creativity and Affective Illness," *American Journal of Psychiatry* 159 (April 2002): 676–677.

Wand, Martin, and Richard B. Sewall. "'Eyes Be Blind, Heart Be Still': A New Perspective on Emily Dickinson's Eye Problem," *New England Quarterly* 52 (Sept. 1979): 400–406.

Werner, David. "Healing in the Sierra Madre," *Natural History* 79 (1970): 61–66.

Wilkinson, Marcia, and Derek Robinson. "Migraine Art," *Cephalalgia* 5 (Sept. 1985): 151–157.

Wilson, Marie. "From Obsession to Betrayal: The Life and Art of Pablo Picasso," *Sexual Addiction and Compulsivity* 11 (2004): 163–182.

Wilson, Sheena K. "The Brain Is Hyperexcitable in Migraine," *Cephalalgia* 27 (Dec. 2007): 1442–1453.

Wojaczynska-Stanek, Katarzyna, Robert Koprowski, Zygmunt Wrobel, and Malgorzata Gola. "Headache in Children's Drawings," *Journal of Child Neurology* 23 (2008): 184–191.

Wolff, Harold G. "Personality Features and Reactions of Subjects with Migraines," *Archives of Neurology and Psychiatry* 37 (1937): 895–921.

Wollaston, William Hyde. "On Semi-decussation of the Optic Nerves," *Philosophical Transactions of the Royal Society of London* 114 (1824): 222–231.

Woolf, Virginia. "On Being Ill," in *Collected Essays,* vol 4. New York: Harcourt, Brace & World, 1967, 193–203.

INTERVIEWS

Roger Cady, June 18, 2008, phone interview.
Andrew George, Sept. 26–Oct. 3, 2008, e-mail correspondence.
Richard B. Lipton, Sept. 27, 2008, phone interview.
Klaus Podoll, June 18, 2008, e-mail correspondence.
Teri Robert, July 9, 2008, phone interview.
Walter Stewart, July 7, 2008, phone interview.
Stewart Tepper, Aug. 15, 2008, phone interview.

SONGS CITED

"Fell in Love with a Girl," The White Stripes, *Elephant* (2001).
"Jagged," Old 97s, *Fight Songs* (1999).

ELECTRONIC SOURCES
CITED/CONSULTED

Achenet.org, American Headache Society Committee for Headache Education, source for Migraine Art Competition.

Achronicdose.blogspot.com, Laurie Edwards blog.

Allianceforheadacheadvocacy.org.

Alt.support.headaches.migraines.

Americanheadachesociety.org, American Headache Society Web site.

Askapatient.com.

Asking—One of the Four Pillars of Evaluation.mht, "Sacred Lotus Arts Traditional Chinese Medicine."

AuthorsDen.com, "Migraine," poem by "The StormSpinner" (Karla Dorman).

Capjewels.com, "A Close Reading of Emily Dickinson's 'I Felt a Funeral in My Brain.'"

Chronicbabe.com.

Claytonpc.com/node.295, "God the Promise Keeper: Abraham by Monte Johnston," on the Clayton Presbyterian Church Web site, Clayton, NC.

Dailyheadache.com.

Darwin-online.org.uk.EmmaDiaries.html, diaries of Emma Darwin.

Deborah-weatheringmigrainestorms.blogspot.com.

Dizziness-and-balance.com/culture/aura.html, great Web address, "Depictions of Migraine Aura, Timothy Hain, MD. "Sandoz Pharmaceuticals publishes a book of artist depictions of migraine aura."

Dziewczeta.net, "Migraine Headaches: Some Interesting Facts."

Flickr.com, search on "migraine."

Headache-Remedy.blogspot.com, discussion of "Famous Migraine Sufferers."

Headaches.org, National Headache Foundation, source for Migraine Art Competition.

Headachetest.com.

I-h-s.org, International Headache Society.

Ihs-classification.org, International Headache Society classifications.

Marriageconfessions/wordpress.com/2008/04/03/migraines-meditation-marriage/: Confessions of a Young Married Couple, "Migraines, Meditation, and Marriage."

Migraine.org, the Web site of the National Migraine Association.

Migraine.org.uk, Migraine Action Association, source for Migraine Art Competition.

Migraine-Aura.org, Web site of the Migraine Aura Association, "The Migraine Art Concept," Klaus Podoll.

Migraineblog.com.

Migraine.blogs.nytimes.com, following entries: Paula Kamen, "Beyond Kittens, Beyond Angels," Mar. 10, 2008; Jeff Tweedy, "Shaking It Off," Mar. 5, 2008; Siri Hustvedt, "Curiouser and Curiouser," Feb. 24, 2008; Oliver Sacks, "Patterns," Feb. 13, 2008; Paula Kamen, "Leaving the Rabbit Hole," Feb. 19, 2008; Siri Hustvedt, "Arms at Rest," Feb. 7, 2008; Siri Hustvedt, "Lifting, Lights, Little People," Feb. 17, 2008.

Migrainechickie.blogspot.com, "Migraine Chick: One Girl Chronicling Her Misadventures in Migraine Land."

Migrainedaily.com.

Migrainepage.com, "Ronda's Migraine Page."

Migrainepage.com, Discussion Forums: Migrainepage.com/dcforum/discussion/8220.html, Migrainepage.com/dcforum/discussion/21036.html, Migrainepage.com/dcforum/discussion/21139.html, Migrainepage.com/cforum/discussion/21315.html.

Migraineresearchfoundation.org.

Mymigraineconnection.com. A weekly podcast.

Nyheadache.com, the Web site of the New York Research Center.

Oldpoetry.com, discussion of "I Felt a Funeral in My Brain."

Photos.peloriadesign.com, "Blinding Migraine," photos.peloriadesign.com, Heather Powers is the photographer.

Relieve-migraine-headache.com.

Schizophrenia.com, WAGblog, "Comments: Analysis of an Emily Dickinson Poem."

Sfhac.com, headache test from the San Francisco Headache Center.

Signsofwitness.com, discussion of T. Don Hutto Residential Center, Taylor, Texas.

Somebodyhealme.net, "Somebody Heal Me, The Musings of a Chronic Migraineur."

Themigrainegirl.blogspot.com, "The Migraine Girl."

Warner.blogs.nytimes.com/2007/10/25/the-migraine-diet/. "The Migraine Diet," Judith Warner, New York Times, Oct. 27, 2007.

Youtube.com: "What Triggers Your Migraine," Illumistream Health.

Acknowledgments

In writing this book, I relied on several migraine textbooks, by Robert A. Davidoff, Stewart J. Tepper, Russell Lane and Paul Davies in particular, and I am grateful for the many insights their works rewarded me. I relied, too, on the work of others in the history of migraine, appearing, largely, in the introductions to medical books about migraine, in review articles in medical journals: these are all cited. I am also grateful to the physicians, epidemiologists, and patient advocates who allowed me to interview them, and who read parts of the manuscript and helped scour out errors of fact and judgment. Special thanks to Stewart J. Tepper, Director of Research, Center For Headache and Pain, Cleveland Clinic Foundation, to Walter F. Stewart, Associate Chief Research Officer and Director, Hood Center for Health Research, Geisinger Health System, to Roger Cady, Director of the Headache Care Center in Springfield, Missouri, to Richard B. Lipton, Professor of Neurology, Epidemiology and Population Health, Albert Einstein College of Medicine, Bronx, NY, Director, Montefiore Medical Center. A special thanks to Klaus Podoll, to Teri Robert for her responsiveness and for her heroic patient advocacy work, to Robert E. Shapiro, and to Kate Edgar.

I am grateful to Wendy Byers and Internal Medicine of Carmel, and Beth Hutchinson and Heartland Neurology, for helping bring my migraines under control.

I would also like to thank Butler University for providing me time to write this manuscript, and in particular, thank the Office of Dean of Liberal Arts and Sciences, and Michael Zimmerman, and the Head of my Department, Hilene Flanzbaum, for their support and their generosity.

I am grateful, as always, to Butler's Office of Interlibrary Loan, and Susan Berger, for responding promptly and with imagination and patience to my many requests. I absolutely could not have done this book without their help.

People who read the manuscript, and gave me wonderful advice: Fred Leebron, Ann Cummins, Anne Kornblatt, Dan Barden, and Philip Baruth. Thank you all. Thanks to my brother, Elliott, for vetting the book from both professional and familial perspectives. Thanks to my family for their sympathetic readings and accounts: to Joe, to my mother, to my father. Thanks to Stuart Glennan, Susan and Michael Sutherlin, Jason Goldsmith, Patrick Klauss, Kate McGinn, Philip Goff, for your perspectives. Thanks to Chad Bauman for help with the Buddha, and Andrew George of the School of Oriental and Asian Studies, University of London, for help with the Sumerians, Assyrians, and Babylonians. And the friends and acquaintances who appear in these pages, anonymously, of course: yes, I used our conversations. You were all gracious, and thoughtful, and I thank you again for talking to me.

The talented folks at Simon & Schuster who put together this book: Loretta Denner, Mary Dorian, Kyoko Watanabe, and Jackie Seow.

As always, thanks to my brilliant agent, Lydia Wills. I handed her something unpublishable, and she found its heart, like she always does. And Sarah Hochman of Simon & Schuster, who edited wonderfully and calmly, and made me want to write wonderfully and calmly. Hope it worked.

Lastly, I would like to thank my wife, Siobhán, and my son, Aedan, for putting up with me through my headaches, and through the writing of this book—both of which required and require me to disappear for too long. You are the stars in my kaleidoscope. No doubt about it.

Index

About the Author

Andrew Levy is Edna Cooper Chair in English and director of the Writer's Studio at Butler University in Indianapolis. He is author of *The Culture and Commerce of the American Short Story*, coauthor of *Creating Fiction: A Writer's Companion*, and coeditor of *Postmodern American Fiction: A Norton Anthology*. His most recent book, *The First Emancipator*, was cited as a "Best of 2005" by the *Chicago Tribune*, Amazon, and *Booklist*, and received the Slatten Award from the Virginia Historical Society. His essays and reviews have appeared in *Harper's*, *The American Scholar*, *Dissent*, *The Best American Essays*, *The Philadelphia Inquirer*, *Chicago Tribune*, and elsewhere. He currently lives in Indianapolis with his wife, Siobhán, and son, Aedan.